BYZANTINE ART

Nicosia, Cyprus, Church of Agios Cassionos
Panel Painting: The Ascension (*c.* 1440)

BYZANTINE ART

By

D. TALBOT RICE

Watson Gordon Professor of Fine Art
University of Edinburgh

OXFORD
AT THE CLARENDON PRESS
1935

IN COLLABORATION WITH THE COURTAULD INSTITUTE OF ART UNIVERSITY OF LONDON

ROMANESQUE ARCHITECTURE IN WESTERN EUROPE. By A. W. CLAPHAM. 1935.

BYZANTINE ART. By D. TALBOT RICE. 1935.

PREFACE

THIS small volume aims at giving a general outline of Byzantine art, of all that it stood for, of all that it led to, and of what it was derived from. It is intended for the general reader and the student, and it makes no attempt to supplant the various manuals which have appeared in English or in other languages. Detailed references have hence in most cases been omitted; the student who needs them must turn to the larger works mentioned in the bibliography at the end of the book, or in the special bibliographies at the end of each chapter. An attempt has, however, been made to include here the results of all the more important recent research, and notes and references to objects, monographs, or articles that have appeared since the publication of Dalton's *East Christian Art* or the second edition of Diehl's *Manuel de l'Art byzantin* have been included. In some cases these recent discoveries or publications may perhaps be of less importance than older ones, which receive no mention in text or footnotes. They have been included in order to provide an easy and ready access to the latest research. In choosing the illustrations a similar attempt has been made to use new or less familiar photographs, but a number of well-known reproductions have also been included on account of the very great bearing which they have on the history of the subject as a whole.

Some explanation of the author's attitude should perhaps be given, for this book deals with Byzantine art, and an attempt has been made throughout to treat it as art. The approach is that of the art-historian, not that of the archaeologist. And it is moreover that of an art-historian who is interested in the modern movement, of one who sees in Byzantine art something which links it, as far as its aims and methods are concerned, with the art of to-day. More than one instance of similarity in aim and content has been alluded to in the text. The similarities are due to kindred feeling and to the abstract quality at the back of both, and it is the author's belief that a study of the one may well help towards an understanding of the other. Critical suppositions and comments have been included, but the author has in every case attempted to keep these clearly distinct from statements of fact.

The author takes this opportunity of expressing his most sincere thanks to Professor W. G. Constable, Director of the Courtauld Institute, without whose encouragement the book could hardly have been undertaken; to Mr. Deane Jones, of Merton College, Oxford, for reading the manuscript and for giving most valuable advice at a time when he was already more than fully occupied with other work; to Mr. S. Casson, of New College, Oxford, for reading the proofs; to Mr. Patrick Roberts, of the Foreign Office, for assistance in the transliteration of Serbian names; to M. Theodore Macridy of the Benaki Museum, Athens, and to M. Xyngopoulos, Ephor of Byzantine Antiquities in Greece, for the loan of photographs, and finally to the officials of the Clarendon Press for assistance throughout.

D. T. R.

COLN ROGERS, 1934.

CONTENTS

PART III

(*For special bibliographies see section at the end of each chapter.*)

LIST OF ILLUSTRATIONS

TEXT FIGURES

PLATES (*at end*)

The photographs of Plates 2, 7, 15 *b*, 16, 17, 18 *a*, and 37 *b* are by the author.

MAPS (*at end*)

PART I

Chapter I

BYZANTIUM—THE HISTORICAL BACKGROUND

THIS small volume on Byzantine art aims at approaching the subject from an aesthetic rather than from an archaeological or historical standpoint. Yet it would be absurd, if not completely useless, to disregard entirely the historical background, and the greater part of the first chapter is therefore devoted to a short sketch of Byzantine history. Before embarking on the history, however, it is essential to define the meaning which will be laid upon the word Byzantine, since hitherto it has been employed in various senses by different authorities, some using it laxly as a general term, others restricting it to describe some special and definite aspect of Christian art in the Nearer East.

Byzantium, strictly speaking, is in reality only the name of the ancient Greek city-state which was founded at the junction of the Golden Horn and the sea of Marmora in the eighth century B.C., and which stood until Constantine transferred the capital of the civilized world thither from Rome in A.D. 330. The new city was called after him, but the old name has been retained by scholars to describe the new imperial civilization and culture. For some archaeologists and art historians 'Byzantine' serves therefore as a general term by which to designate every object produced within or under the influence of the Empire between the foundation of Constantinople in 330 and its fall in 1453. Others limit the term, in any case so far as it can be used in complimentary spirit, to the earlier manifestations of the art, and regard the first few centuries as the most purely and most essentially Byzantine. This interpretation was put upon the word by Peirce and Tyler in their small book *Byzantine Art*, and they retain it in their larger work, *L'Art byzantin*, which is now in course of publication. A third group of writers prefers to call the whole of the pre-iconoclast age the 'Early Christian', believing that Byzantine art in the true sense of the word only appears in the ninth century, though its manifestations continue at least until the seventeenth century. Such an employment of the word is in general use in Greece to-day,[1] and to a great extent also in the Balkan countries which are the more or less direct inheritors of Byzantine culture. By others again the term is used to describe East Christian art in general, whether it be Syrian, Anatolian, or Constantinopolitan. As we shall hope to show in the course of this book, a definite distinction must be made between the Syrian and the Constantinopolitan elements, and the characteristics of each will be described as we proceed. This use of the word is thus unsatisfactory for the specialist, though it may sometimes be convenient as a general portmanteau term.

Of the first three interpretations it is the second that seems to us to be most definitely at fault, for the art of the first centuries only shows faint glimmerings of that spirit which seems to us distinctively characteristic of Byzantine art. This early art is, rather, Roman or Hellenistic art, changed to some extent by the influence of environment or of Christianity. By the sixth century, however, Byzantine art as distinct from Hellenistic, from Roman, or from eastern art has taken its established place in the world, and the characteristic Byzantine style has been evolved at the capital. From now on this art reigns in the Christian Near East. As long as Byzantine rule lasts it flourishes and sees a number of revivals. After the fall of the Empire the style persists, and survives in the Balkans and in Greece almost to the present day.

The term Byzantine is thus for us definite. All that it

[1] See, for instance, Soteriou, *Guide du Musée byzantin d'Athènes*, 1932, p. 19.

stands for can only be fully realized when we are intimately acquainted with the art, but in general it may be understood to include all the work produced in the Byzantine sphere, and more especially at Constantinople, after the synthesis of East and West—of Greek, of Roman, of Syrian and of Persian elements—had been brought about as the outcome of the adoption of Christianity as the State religion. The fusion was gradual, and we see it achieved in occasional instances only in the fifth century. By the sixth it had progressed farther, and in that century appeared the first really great manifestation of Byzantine art, the Cathedral of St. Sophia at Constantinople (537). This church was to be the centre of Christianity, the very nucleus of the cultured universe. It has survived to this day, although it was converted to the worship of Islam when the Turks conquered Constantinople (1453), and it is still not only the greatest monument of Byzantine art, but also the greatest monument of all Christian art. Justinian, when he entered St. Sophia on its completion, exclaimed in awe, 'Glory be to God, who has found me worthy to finish so great a work, and to excel thee, O Solomon'. Solomon's temple has not survived; but no other faith, no other benefactor, has ever been responsible for a structure that can in beauty, in space, or in its religious atmosphere surpass the church of the Holy Wisdom at Constantinople.

With the use of the word defined, we may, before passing on to a summary of the history, draw some attention to the character of Byzantine art as compared to that of the other arts of the world that flourished before or that have flourished since. Speaking broadly, we may say that classical art in Greece, in Rome, and at a later date in Renaissance Italy, is a naturalistic or representational art, which is in the main concerned with the depiction of living forms, and which uses as its principal model in painting and in sculpture the human form. The subjects are idealized and there is, in the resulting work of art, a great deal more than a photographic reproduction of nature, however exquisite the natural object may have been in itself. It is with the art of this family that we have till recently been most familiar. But modern research, most notably that of Strzygowski, has shown us that there existed, as a contemporary of the classical arts of Greece or Rome, another type which centred as far as we know at present in the East, and which was characterized by a formalistic or a completely non-representational style. Such art sought, not to portray things as they appear in nature, but rather to produce by means of balance of line, by means of what Clive Bell and Roger Fry call significant form, something which can awake in the spectator an emotional response just as genuine and just as great as that which the classicist experiences when he admires the finest piece of ancient sculpture, or the lover of the Italian Renaissance when he looks at a canvas which is a masterpiece of the period. This eastern art used as its media plant, animal, or imaginary forms, but adapted them to suit its own purposes, so that it is often very difficult to discover the origin of developed motives without the aid of intermediary links in the chain that connect such motives to their prototypes. It is not our aim in this book, as it is of certain enthusiasts, to champion this art by decrying that of the West; but at the outset there must be taken for granted not only its existence, but also the fact that it could produce results of exquisite beauty, as fine in their own way as anything that we know elsewhere or in another manner.

Just as the art of Greece penetrated the East at the time of Alexander, so did the art of the East come westwards, and we see its influence already marked in the architecture, sculpture, and decoration of the Hellenistic period from about 280 B.C. onwards. This influence appears in sculpture and ornament of the age in Syria, and we see it more strongly accentuated in the mausoleum of Diocletian at Spalato, which was built shortly after A.D. 300. This is, in fact, the first mighty example of the blending of the arts of East and West that we have in the Mediterranean area. But in the three centuries that follow more and more intermixture and development takes place, until the first climax of the hybrid style is reached with the construction of St. Sophia in the sixth century.

We have long known to what mournful results Greek art could sometimes be reduced by an uninspired mimicking, and until recent years it has been generally held that a decline which set in at Rome was only carried farther during the Byzantine period. The critics of the last century sought in Byzantine art something similar to that which they found in classical art, and when they failed to find it, except in a few early manifestations, they condemned the art as decadent. They should rather have blamed the inadequacy of their own standards of judgement. Just as work which is produced by modern artists, whether in painting, in architecture, or in sculpture, demands a rather different attitude in the spectator from that demanded by the art most admired in the last century, so must we adopt a rather different standpoint when we come to criticize Byzantine or East Christian art. Our standards need not be in any way more lenient: instead must a new language be learnt. To appreciate French poetry one must first learn French; and so, to appreciate Byzantine art to the full, one must first become familiar with its own particular idiom. And to do this it is necessary to approach it with an open mind, and to remember that the classical was not the only mould which could serve for the casting of a new form.

In 330 Constantine transferred the seat of the imperial court and government from Rome to Constantinople and adopted Christianity as the State religion, in much the same way as the Turks of to-day have transferred their capital to Angora and adopted an entirely new policy of nationalism and judicious westernization in place of the old procrastination. And just as Angora, a typically Turkish hill-town in the middle of Anatolia, is an ideal centre for the development of a national policy, so was Constantinople in the fourth century the ideal capital for an empire which comprised within its bounds most of the civilized Nearer East and which took as its faith a religion which was at that date more firmly entrenched in Syria and Asia Minor than it was in Italy or the West.

Together with the imperial court and all the paraphernalia of government, the imperial art of Rome was brought to the new capital, and during the next two hundred years this art was developed and transformed to suit the demands of changing conditions and of a refounded State. This age, from the death of Constantine in 337 to that of Anastasius I in 518, is best termed the Eastern- or Early-Christian, and during its course Byzantine culture was born. The idea at one time held by the majority of authorities that Byzantine culture was entirely evolved from that of imperial Rome is now superseded, and it is generally believed that other elements, eastern as well as western, religious as well as imperial, all played their part. The idea of a triple fusion of three essentials, Christianity, Hellenism, and the East, is in fact welcomed by historians as well as by archaeologists. But inviting though the hypothesis is, it would seem to throw the contribution of Rome somewhat too much into the background as far as the fourth and fifth centuries are concerned. Latin was still retained as the language of officialdom, though Greek was the more natural tongue. Roman forms were introduced wholesale in art as well as in statecraft and in everyday life, while the city of Rome remained secondary only to Constantinople.[1] On the other hand, Athens, though still a centre

[1] She had her own separate emperors who ruled conjointly with those of the East till 480.

of literature and philosophy, exercised no direct influence on the new capital.

The most important personality of this period was probably Theodosius I, the Great (379–95), an administrator of ability and a builder who did much to improve the capital. It was during his reign, in 393, that the Olympic games were held for the last time at Constantinople, a number of antique monuments being brought to adorn the capital for the occasion. Under his successor Arcadius there was, on the other hand, a renewal of friendly relations with Sasanian Persia, for the emperor appointed the Sasanian king Yesdigird I as guardian of his successor Theodosius II.[1] The rule of this emperor was energetic and enlightened; a university was established at Constantinople in 425, teaching being given in both Latin and Greek; new walls were built around the city;[2] other important buildings were founded. Slightly later, under Zeno (474–91), we meet the first traces of the separation of the churches of Rome and Constantinople—a dispute which was to rack Christendom for centuries to come—and it was during the reign of the same emperor that the Bulgars, who in later days played so important a role in Byzantine history, first established themselves in the Balkans.

This period is brought to a close with the death of Anastasius I in 518. In the sphere of art it is best known for its mosaics and major sculpture, and, though its style is in the main Roman, enough change is to be observed to warrant its designation as the age of formation of Byzantine culture.

The second main period in Byzantine history and the first of pure Byzantine art opens with the accession of Justin I, the founder of a new dynasty, in 518. The first period had been in Constantinople one of formation, but in Italy one of decline,

[1] Vasiliev, *Histoire de l'Empire byzantin*, i, p. 122.

[2] Rome fell in 410, and this warning of the growing power of the barbarians was taken at Constantinople.

the Goths having harried the country and looted the towns. Now we see a return of prosperity in the West, as a result of the development of Byzantine culture at Constantinople. Some two hundred years earlier Byzantium had been no more than the child of Italy. Now Constantinople is the supreme centre of civilization, and from Constantinople emanated the power which could set her tottering parent on a sure footing. The role of Italy as a creator in art and culture had come to an end almost with the age of Constantine, and in the fourth and fifth centuries she did little even as a conserver. It was in reality not so much the old heritage of Rome as the inspiration of Constantinople which was responsible for the superb buildings and mosaics constructed in Rome and Ravenna in the fifth and sixth centuries.

In the military sphere the age of Justinian (527–65) was a remarkably prosperous one. Italy, Dalmatia, and Sicily, taken by the Goths in the first age, were reabsorbed in the Empire by 554; in 550 Justinian made conquests in Spain and founded a province in what is now Andalusia, which remained under the rule of Constantinople for the next seventy years.[1] In the East the Persians were driven out of Asia Minor and the bounds of the Empire were established as widely as in the grandest days of Imperial Rome (see map I). In the cultural sphere success was even more marked: the code of Justinian took its place as one of the world's most famous legal systems; St. Sophia, one of the world's most glorious buildings, was erected; an essentially Byzantine architectural style was established, and buildings of the first importance both religious and secular arose not only in the capital but also over the whole Byzantine area. Trade flourished and embraced an amazingly wide field, and long journeys of exploration were undertaken; an account of one

[1] Gaul and the North were already under Frankish control, and it is from this period that their independent power and culture begins to grow to importance.

of them, that of Cosmas Indicopleustes, has since come to be recognized as one of the most important literary products of the age.[1] All the resources of a seemingly limitless treasury were expended on the expansion, development, and adornment of the Empire and of its capital.

The brilliance and vast expenditure of Justinian's day left a hard task for his successors; it was a task beyond the abilities of most of them, and it was made even more difficult by the rising power and energy of the Lombards and Franks in the West and of the Persians and later of the Arabs in the East. In 570 the Lombards invaded Italy; shortly afterwards Slavs began to penetrate Greece, and the physical type of many of the inhabitants to-day serves as proof of the depth to which this penetration reached. In 611 the Persians conquered Syria and took the True Cross away with them to Ctesiphon. These losses were soon afterwards made good to a greater or lesser extent, and Heraclius, founder of the Heraclian dynasty (610–717), not only defeated the Goths in 626, but also reconquered all the territories that had been lost in the East. A more serious foe, however, soon nullified his victories, and the Arabs, spurred on by the militant faith of Islam, conquered first the Persians and then the Byzantine provinces of Syria, Palestine, and Egypt. The first Islamic capital was established at Damascus in 634.[2]

About a century later the dynasty which had supported such reverses bravely, if not gloriously, came to an end, and with the death of Theodosius III in 717 an age which was one of the most eventful of all Byzantine history was brought to a close. It is an age which we know best through its wars;

[1] It was at this date that the cultivation of silk was introduced from the East; see p. 177.

[2] The first Islamic dynasty was the Omayyad, which ruled at Damascus till 749, when a new house, the Abbasid, established the capital at Baghdad. Omayyad art and culture centred in Syria, and was in the main derived from the Byzantine and from the local Hellenistic, whereas that of the Abbasids was more purely Persian in character.

in the sphere of art it is less clearly distinguished from that of Justinian. Yet craftsmen and artists of the very first rank were still to be found, and the superb mosaics of the Dome of the Rock at Jerusalem and the Great Mosque at Damascus, though executed for Islamic patrons, must be classed as Byzantine monuments.

For the next century and a half the Empire was under the control first of the Isaurian, then of the Amorian dynasties. It is a period which is known as the iconoclast (image-breaking), and is one of great importance in the development of later Byzantine art, for during it eastern influence penetrated to a considerable degree.[1] Between 717 and 843 no representation of the Divine, even of the saintly form, was permitted in religious art. Numerous earlier monuments, more especially mosaics, which depicted Christ, the Virgin, or important saints were actually destroyed, while any new church decoration was strictly confined to non-representational subjects, such as the cross, or some form of decorative floral or geometrical motive. In secular art, on the other hand, representation of the human form was permitted, and it has been suggested that a considerable amount of work of a secular character was produced at this period which served to keep alive Hellenic feeling and talent at the capital. But little of it has survived, and the importance which certain authorities attach to such secular work is probably somewhat exaggerated. A striking result of iconoclasm was the fact that numerous artists were forced to fly the State and to seek employment in the West. As research makes us more familiar with Carolingian art, we shall come to realize more and more how considerable was the role that these artists played in its development.[2]

[1] The iconoclast doctrine supported by the court and army was most strictly enforced at Constantinople. On the coasts of Asia Minor and Greece, more especially in monastic circles, it was never generally accepted.

[2] Though already hinted at by Kondakov, *Iconography of the Virgin*,

The ideas directly underlying the iconoclast movement have been differently interpreted by various writers. Some regard the movement as directed primarily against the growing power of the monasteries, an attempt at a general dissolution of monasteries being screened by a popular cry of artistic impropriety. Others, most notably Bréhier, distinguish two main aspects, the question of actual image worship, and the problem of the legitimacy of religious art—of how far any human being had the right to represent the supernatural.[1] But the most striking feature of the movement from the artistic point of view is its eastern character, the iconoclast emperors all being of eastern origin, and the army—on which they depended for support—being principally drawn from the eastern provinces. When we remember the purely non-representational character which Islamic religious art assumed at much the same period, the strength of the movement in Byzantine lands need hardly surprise us, and there seems every reason to attribute it to an underlying feeling which was both powerful and universal all over Hither Asia at the time.

In the political sphere the early days of Isaurian rule were marked by wars with the Arabs. In 718 Leo III succeeded in driving them out of Asia Minor—even from the very walls of Constantinople—and, though frontier skirmishes continued, the Moslems were left powerless to undertake any serious attack for a century or more. Soon after the commencement of Amorian rule (820), however, these skirmishes assumed a more imposing character, and the attacks of the Arabs met with definite success, especially at sea. In the reign of Michael II (820–9) the Byzantines lost Crete, and Sicily fell soon after. Nearer home the Slavs threatened to be almost as

Petrograd, 1915, ii, p. 5 (in Russian), and by other authorities, this important question has as yet received no detailed analysis.

[1] According to an old eastern legend, adopted by Islam, though doubtless conceived at an earlier date, the artist would be required to give life at the day of judgement to all the figures painted by him on earth.

dangerous as the Arabs, for in 813 the Bulgar king, Krum, penetrated as far as the defences of Constantinople. His successor concluded a thirty years' peace, however, and in 864 Boris, king of the Bulgars, was baptized and Christianity became the official Bulgar religion. More formidable than the Bulgars were the Slavs of Russia, who made a first advance in 860. Yet here again Christianity triumphed, and slightly more than a hundred years later the orthodox faith was adopted as the State religion by Vladimir, and Kiev became the most powerful outpost and successor of Byzantium in the artistic as in the religious sphere. Until the revolution of 1917 the art of Russia remained faithful to the Byzantine tradition, and even to-day, in spite of the absence of religious stimulus, the Byzantine heritage still lives. In the West the main event of the age was the coronation of Charlemagne at Rome as Emperor of the West, in 800. Though in later times this event proved to mark a breaking-point, a final separation of the Roman and Byzantine worlds, it probably had at the time no very far-reaching influence, and the trend of life and culture at Constantinople was unaffected. The arts in fact already showed promise of the golden period to come, and the Empire itself was set on a sure footing by the Isaurian rulers.

The period from the end of iconoclasm (843) until the Latin conquest of Constantinople in 1204 may from the artistic point of view be regarded as a single unit, for though there was naturally a vast deal of change and evolution in these three hundred and sixty years, the period was marked by no sudden variation. It is usually known as the second Golden Age, though some authorities prefer to restrict this term to the ninth, tenth, and eleventh centuries only. Historically the age may be subdivided into two main periods, that of the Macedonian dynasty (867–1056), and that of the Comnene dynasty (1081–1185). The whole age was one of great internal prosperity; vast riches were at the disposal of the rulers; life reached to the height of luxury; palaces were built and decorated with the finest materials; churches were endowed with the richest of treasures. The most superb textiles, the most wonderfully carved ivories, the finest enamels, the most delicate metal-work, the brightest and most exquisite mosaics both on a large and on a minute scale, were produced, and it is to this age that we owe nearly all the more sumptuous objects and decorations which survive and which provide us with our most typical specimens of Byzantine art.

The Macedonian rulers were, however, not only great art patrons. During their rule the Empire's bounds were spread over the whole Near East. In the reign of Romanus II (959–63) Crete and Cyprus were recaptured; in 969 Antioch was taken from the Moslems. Under Basil II (976–1025) Armenia and parts of the Caucasus were conquered, thus bringing the Byzantine Empire into closer touch with Persia and the East. But the main activities of this remarkable emperor were concentrated on suppressing the growing power of the Bulgarians, a task which he accomplished with such energy that he was given the nickname of Bulgaroctonos, or Bulgar-slayer. The first Bulgarian empire, founded about 800, was terminated by Basil's victories in 1018. A Christian power since 864, Bulgaria had naturally learnt a great deal from Byzantium, and her culture was essentially an offshoot of that of Constantinople. After Basil's victories this link was made even more secure, for the land became a province and Byzantine culture penetrated with renewed vigour. Bulgarian art was in fact more closely affected by Constantinople than was the art of certain regions which never enjoyed independence, such as Anatolia.

With the death of Basil II the period of territorial expansion came to an end and reverses were suffered in the East owing to the arrival on the field of a new power, the Seljuk Turks. The Seljuks, a tribe of central Asian origin, established their rule in Persia in the eleventh century and conquered Armenia about the same time. In 1071 their leader, Alp Arslan, secured a decisive victory over the Byzantines at Manzikert and from then on their power increased in western Asia; by the twelfth century Asia Minor was partitioned between them and the Byzantines. In the West again, in spite of an increase of Byzantine influence in south Italy,[1] a number of reverses marked the eleventh century. The republic of St. Mark had by now established its independence at Venice, and the Normans, who had adopted the local Byzantine culture of Calabria and Sicily, had already become so powerful that the Byzantine emperor had to seek the aid of Venice against them in return for commercial privileges. In 1130 the Norman Roger II was crowned at Palermo as king of Sicily and southern Italy. He shortly afterwards seized an opportunity to attack Greece, an event of some importance in the history of art, for he took back silk weavers and established that industry in Sicily on a large scale. The products of their looms remained, however, definitely Byzantine; and the superb mosaics which were executed for Norman patrons at Monreale, Palermo, and Cefalù must also take their place as Byzantine monuments. More important than the loss of territory was the final separation of the churches of Rome and Constantinople in 1054, a schism which divided Christianity into the Orthodox and Roman Catholic faiths, and which has remained unbridged to this day.

With France and Germany there was apparently little actual contact in the Macedonian period, though embassies were exchanged from time to time. Under the Comnenes, on the other hand, relations were much closer, and westerners visited the East in small numbers as pilgrims or travellers, and in larger bodies as members of crusading expeditions. From the Byzantine point of view the Crusaders were almost

[1] A number of Greek churches were founded in the region of Bari in the tenth century.

as much of a menace as the Islamic enemy on the eastern frontier. Alexius I (1081–1118), however, dealt with the menace of the first crusade with considerable diplomatic skill, and he took advantage of crusading advances to increase his own dominions without subjecting the Byzantine troops to any risks. But the Crusaders regarded him as little less than an open enemy, and it was with difficulty that friendly relations were maintained. The most serious bone of contention was without doubt the city of Antioch, a prize sought by Moslems, Crusaders, and Byzantines alike.

This hostile attitude towards Byzantium was not forgotten, and with the second crusade the cupidity of the Greeks was worked up as a war-cry to mask the cupidity of the French. The failure of the Crusade was ascribed to the treachery of the Emperor Manuel, and Roger II, the Norman king of Sicily, attempted to use western exasperation for his own designs on Greece and the Balkans. He planned a European coalition headed by France and the Papacy at a time when both Hungary and Serbia were at war with Byzantium. Fortunately for Manuel the Emperor Conrad III of Germany remained aloof. Had he too thrown in his support, it is possible that the Latin conquest of Constantinople would have taken place half a century earlier than it did. Roger's great design, however, came to nothing, and Byzantium, though suspect, was reprieved for a time, since failure had a discouraging effect on crusading enthusiasm.

Encouraged perhaps by the absence of western armies Manuel I (1143–80) thought himself strong enough to attempt expansion on his own; he took Antioch in 1159. But in 1176 his army was routed by the Seljuks at Myriocephalum, and in the opinion of Vasiliev Manuel's failures set the train of decline into a final motion, which could not be checked by the reforms of his successor Andronicos I. In the West Frederick Barbarossa, a more serious rival of Byzantine power even than Charlemagne, checked Manuel's attempts to regain influence in Italy, and shortly after Manuel's death the Bulgarians affronted Byzantine dignity by establishing in 1185 the second independent Bulgarian empire with its capital at Tirnovo. In the same year Salonica was looted by the Normans of Sicily.

Two years later Saladin defeated the army of the Latin kingdom in Palestine and retook Jerusalem, thus occasioning a popular outcry in the West which was responsible for the launching of the third crusade. There was little to show in the Holy Land for the fierce struggles and heavy losses of three years, but Richard I of England seized the Byzantine province of Cyprus, and the Lusignan kingdom was founded there in 1192. If the failure to retake Jerusalem incited the religious to further effort, Richard's conquest of Cyprus served to encourage more material aims. It showed in fact that the Byzantines constituted a far more desirable prey than the Moslems, and the fourth crusade, leaving the sacred cities of Palestine to the protection of fate, turned all its energies and resources to the capture of Constantinople. In 1204 the blow fell and the richest city of the world was subjected to what was probably the greatest sack of history. A Latin dynasty set up its rule in the city; Salonica became a second but minor Latin kingdom, and the members of the Greek ruling house established themselves as best they could in Epirus, at Trebizond, and at Nicaea.

Of the three minor Greek empires which were founded as a result of the Latin conquest of Constantinople that of Epirus was short lived; that of Trebizond survived without interruption till 1461, though it was of purely local significance; that of Nicaea showed in the most striking manner those remarkable powers of recovery so characteristic of the Greeks. Theodore Lascaris, the first emperor of Nicaea, was a man of the strongest character, and he established his empire on a sure and sound footing. His work was carried on by his successor John III Vatatzes, who was able to reconquer much of Macedonia, including Salonica, which fell to him in 1246. In 1254 Michael Palaeologos assumed control, and was crowned in 1259. Entering into a treaty with the Genoese, who had by now challenged the Venetians as the principal trading power of the Mediterranean, he captured Constantinople in 1261 and brought back with him the traditions of art, literature, and general culture which had been zealously maintained at Nicaea throughout the period of exile. This Nicaean age is, in fact, important in the history of art. Few of the finer traditions of the great middle period were lost, whereas certain new elements were introduced which served to revivify and resuscitate culture. The visual arts will be dealt with as we proceed; we may note in literature the creation of such new types as fiction and lyric poetry.

The history of the Palaeologue period at Constantinople (1258–1453) is sad, but extremely romantic. The Empire was now reduced to Constantinople, Salonica, the lands immediately bordering the Marmora, and some islands in the Aegean; after a few years the proud capital was ruling little more territory than could be seen from its own walls. The days of the great Emperors had passed; the imperial palaces were now less richly furnished than the houses of the past. The lavish imperial patrons of the Church were no more; religious edifices were now the property of the people as much as of the court or the nobles, and the finest of them were to be found in remote towns or villages as much as, if not more than, in the capital. The sumptuous treasuries of Macedonian and Comnene times had mostly been carried off as loot by the Latins, and the State was now too much impoverished to replace them. Works of art had to depend on their aesthetic merits alone, not on any enhancement afforded by the fine quality of their material. Yet the old ceremony, the old grandeur survived, and records exist which show that the vast proportions of the court were partially retained. The emperor, though forced to use the cheapest materials, was quite unable to live an economical and simple life, and the ceremonial pomp of the past was preserved, as in some noble houses of to-day, whose impoverished owners are incapable through tradition and sentiment of reducing a staff or expenditure which they are no longer in a position to support.

Historically the most important feature of the age was the gradual advance of the Turks from the East. This advance had been in progress for the last two or three hundred years, but it was now accelerated, firstly by the westward pressure exerted on the Turks themselves by the Mongols, who were advancing from central Asia (Hulagu sacked Baghdad in 1258), and secondly by the rise to power of a young and energetic tribe, the Ottoman, which superseded the older Seljuk group in Asia Minor. And the advance of the Turks was assisted by the state of affairs in the Balkans. Under the leadership of Stephen Nemanja (1169–96), the Serbians had succeeded in establishing an independent state which reached the height of its prosperity under Stephen Dushan (1331–55). Dushan, after conquering all the western parts of the Balkans, even set out to try to capture Constantinople, but he died before reaching the city, and with his death the Serbian empire crumbled. One of the chief bulwarks against Moslem conquest in the Balkans was thus removed. The Ottoman sultan Murad established his capital at Adrianople, and in 1389 he and his son Bayazid utterly routed what remained of Serbian power at Kossovo and the country fell under Turkish rule. In 1393 the Turks took Tirnovo and conquered Bulgaria, defeating a Franco-Hungarian crusade at Nicopolis in 1396. In 1422 they laid siege to Constantinople.

Serbia, Bulgaria, and other states had fallen before these great conquerors of the East, but the Byzantine capital was a sterner foe and the first attack was repulsed. In 1430, however, Salonica was captured and a Christian league of defence, with Hungary as the leading power, was utterly routed at Varna in 1444. Practically all the Balkans with the exception of Constantinople were now in Turkish hands, and Mohammed II concentrated all his energies on this last remaining enemy. For nearly ten years the preparations went forward, till the city fell after a defence which is one of the epics of history. In 1453 the end of the Byzantine Empire was accomplished. Trebizond fell in 1461, Athens in 1456, and all Greece shortly afterwards; only in Roumania and in the powerful Slavonic state of Russia was Orthodox Christianity retained as an official religion and Byzantine art revered as a national heritage. Yet as we proceed we shall find that the faith of the Christian minority in Turkish lands was a definite and important factor which upheld Byzantine culture wellnigh down to the present day.

So ends the history. Yet in art the last age is no inglorious one, and remarks such as that of Peirce and Tyler (*Byzantine Art*, p. 15) that 'the story of Byzantine art really ends with the sack of Constantinople by the Franks in 1204' are entirely misleading. The 'Byzantine renaissance' of the fourteenth and fifteenth centuries is a fact which can no longer be disputed, and modern research shows us that the revival which is to be seen in painting is also to be observed in literature and philosophy, and though the Greek world of this age never produced a Dante, it seems that the writers might have progressed wellnigh as far, had not the Moslem invasion set a term to their activities.[1] The importance of the revival in painting can hardly be exaggerated, and it is with the wall paintings of the fourteenth century and the panels of the fifteenth and sixteenth that the studies of the historians of Byzantine art have of late years been principally occupied. Yet the role that these paintings played is still little known; its importance will only be generally realized by future generations.

[1] For the importance of later Byzantine literature see Vasiliev, op cit. ii, p. 422. He gives a full bibliography of writings which bear upon the subject.

BIBLIOGRAPHY

The best and most recent complete history is that of Vasiliev, *Histoire de l'Empire byzantin*, 2 vols., Paris, 1932. The American edition, published two years earlier, is not as complete. References and detailed bibliographies of the various periods are given. On a smaller scale Runciman's *Byzantine Civilization*, London, 1933, gives a useful outline, whilst R. Byron's *The Byzantine Achievement*, London, 1929, is suggestive. The most satisfactory small book is Norman Baynes's *The Byzantine Empire*, in the Home University Library Series. An outline is given in the *Cambridge Mediaeval History*, vol. iv. See any of these works, and especially Vasiliev, for a fuller bibliography of historical works.

Chapter II

THE GEOGRAPHICAL BASIS OF BYZANTINE CULTURE

WHEN once the Byzantine character had been definitely established the importance of Constantinople as the main centre of Byzantine culture cannot be exaggerated; and this importance is to be attributed, not only to the fact that it was the capital, but also to the geographical situation of the city. A glance at the map will serve to throw this into the limelight. The city stands on a promontory, at the very eastern extremity of Europe, and on the only direct sea route between Russia and the Black Sea coast to the north, and Greece, Syria, Italy, Egypt, and all the rich and powerful area of the Mediterranean to the south. To the west stretches a broad peninsula of low hills, which present no very considerable barrier until the high mountains of Bulgaria are reached; and even here the valley of the Maritza offers a clear route inland from the Mediterranean for some two hundred miles. Nowadays this is a somewhat desolate region, owing partly to its climate and partly to the modern political situation; in Byzantine times, though never really prosperous, it was a good deal more important than its present rather barren state suggests. To the south-west of Constantinople again there is a fairly easy land route, which is now followed by the railway linking the city with Salonica and northern Greece.

Northwards there is a rather less satisfactory coastal route to the region of Burgas, the centre of Bulgaria's maritime province. With both these areas there is equally ready and more practicable connexion by sea. They are in fact more closely linked to Constantinople than almost any other region in the Byzantine sphere, and owing to the ease of communication we see both at Salonica and on that part of the Black Sea coast which is now Bulgaria an art, or at least an architecture, which was more nearly allied to that of the capital than was the art of almost any other area. The similarities will be discussed in further detail as they arise; here we may note that Salonica was throughout the Byzantine period the second city of the Empire, whose art was wellnigh identical with that of the capital, while in Bulgaria, both in the centre and on the coast, we find a series of very important monuments, not only in architecture and painting, but also in such minor arts as ceramics and incrustation (see p. 195), which are closely linked with Constantinople. As more excavations come to be undertaken, we shall probably find further proof of the closeness of this relationship. On the other hand, in the mountains of Bulgaria, in Macedonia, and in what is to-day Serbia, we find the Constantinopolitan style much less firmly established, not only because communications were less simple, but also because the mountain fastnesses always harboured old conventions and offered sanctuary for those elements of the population which were forced from more prosperous areas by more powerful new-comers.

To the east Constantinople is closely linked with the coastal fringe of Asia Minor, the city being as much a part of Asia as of Europe. But the link is close with the coastal fringe only; the main area of Asia Minor is a vast highland which rises gradually eastward till Armenia is reached. And this is the highest and most severe region of western Asia, the passes to the north and west being under snow for a good eight months of the year, while even those to the south are not easily practicable in winter. Trade between Constantinople and Syria-Mesopotamia was thus more easily carried on by sea, the greatest entrepôt to the south of Asia Minor being Antioch. Yet the direct land route across Asia Minor was far quicker, and this route, which has been employed from time immemorial, is to-day closely followed by the so-called Baghdad railway. In addition there were routes along the sea coast, most of which were more important for short than for long distances. The northern sea route (by way of the southern Black Sea coast) afforded connexion with all the cities of the Pontus and ultimately with Trebizond, a region which was thoroughly Greek and which was cut off from the interior by a high mountain barrier. The southern route along the Marmora and Aegean linked up the capital and the Greek cities of the coast-lands. These cities were also separated from the highland of Anatolia by a mountain barrier. Here again we find that geography dictated the course and spread of Byzantine art and culture, for the Pontic towns in the one direction and coast cities like Nicomedia, Nicaea, and Ephesus, or even such a minor town as Adalia, in the other, were thoroughly Byzantine. In the uplands of Anatolia, on the other hand, though there were numerous towns and villages which were essentially Christian and Byzantine in the wider sense of the word, there were not more than a few which showed traces of a direct Constantinopolitan influence. The surviving churches are usually distinct in their architecture, while the wall paintings that decorate them are definitely to be classed in a separate 'Eastern' group.

A further glance at the map will show that any impulses, whether cultural or physical, which had reached this highland region from the east or south would finally converge on the western extremity of the peninsula, and, if pressure were exerted from behind, would be forced to cross the minor barrier presented by the Dardanelles or the Bosphorus, and to continue their journey westwards into Europe. And this process is exactly what took place, and it took place repeatedly. In the classical and pre-classical periods we see continual waves of migration or invasion coming to Macedonia and Thrace from the east, and in the Christian period we see a similar migration not of peoples, but of art and architecture. The earlier migrations of peoples principally influenced Macedonia; the crossing was effected at the Dardanelles. The later artistic movement from the east is naturally to be perceived principally in the greater cities, but it is to be traced both in Bulgaria, crossing by the Dardanelles, and in Constantinople, crossing by the Bosphorus. Asia Minor constitutes as it were a bottle-neck, with its top at the Bosphorus and its base fronting on to northern Mesopotamia and Persia. The sides are formed by the Greek coast-lands; the centre is Anatolia, an area which adopted Greek culture, first Hellenistic and then Byzantine, though it was never purely Greek or purely Byzantine in spirit. Like a bottle-neck it provided a sure but a slow means of passage, and, though there was a continual westward filtration of culture and sometimes of peoples through it, we find more rapid routes being used for trade purposes, both to the north and to the south.

Of these great trade routes from the east the one has as its main junction the city of Trebizond, whence Constantinople is easily reached by sea and Persia rather less easily by land. In spite of its difficulties it was much used in ancient times, and it continues in use even to-day, in competition with the Russian railway slightly to the north, running from Tabriz to Batoum. The other route, leading by way of Mesopotamia and Syria, presented at its western land extremity several alternative lines of communication, all of which were important. Syria, Egypt, Greece, Constantinople, and the coastal and island cities could thus all be reached. Eastward its course is easily defined by the Euphrates valley; it commanded the whole of Mesopotamia and southern Persia in this direction, and it offered at the same time an alternative though more difficult route along the foot-hills of the Taurus to northern Mesopotamia, Armenia, and western Persia.

As on the northern route at Trebizond, there was also here a great half-way junction—Antioch. It was one of the most important cities of the ancient world, with a long-established culture behind it. It was easily reached from Greece or from Constantinople by sea; it was in Hellenistic times linked by sea, as well as by a coastal road, with the other great Hellenistic cities to the north-west, Ephesus, Priene, Miletus, or Pergamon; and it was linked as well by sea and by a whole series of easy land routes with the flourishing and cultured land of Syria, beyond which opened up the vast resources and the great civilization of Egypt. Antioch occupied in fact what was probably the most important position of ancient times. It stood at the meeting-point of the Mesopotamian, the Egyptian, and the Aegean civilizations. At Antioch was concentrated every possible type of merchandise, every possible object which luxurious and cultivated society could demand, and it was there that traders of every nation and every race intermingled and bargained as they do to-day in Cairo or Baghdad. But in spite of this Antioch remained a provincial city; her chance of being a capital was marred partly by this heterogeneous character, and partly by the dangerous nature of her situation, which was open to attack from every side.

In the age that concerns us the focus of culture was moving westwards and northwards. Greece had supplanted Mesopotamia, Persia, and Egypt; Rome had supplanted Greece, and a new and more clement continent, Europe, had been discovered. This new love could not be easily cast aside. The bright suns, the dry soil, the long summers of the semi-tropical areas were no longer suitable places for the capital of a world Empire. Palm trees and tropical growths were forsaken for the deciduous forests and temperate clime of Europe. Yet at the same time a convenient centre for trading and strategic purposes had to be established, and where was there a more suitable site than Constantinople, with its rains, its fertility, its refreshing breezes, its rich hinterland, and, above all, its superb position? When Constantine transferred his capital to the Golden Horn he chose a site which had all the advantages of such a trading city as Antioch without any of its disadvantages. His new capital could make herself mistress of the East without losing touch with the West; she could stand aloof, yet at the same time not fail to maintain contact; she could open wide her gates to the East and at the same time retain her European character. If Constantinople was preferable to Antioch, she was still more preferable to any other site; and in this lay her supremacy. Add to this her admirable position on a promontory, surrounded by water on two of her three sides, so that only one-quarter of the length of her walls had to be manned against an attacker by land, and the mightiness of the role which she played as the bulwark of the West and the apex of the East for so many centuries is readily explained.

Other areas of the Empire are less vital; but its essentially maritime character is shown by their distribution. In the south there was Egypt, lost to the Moslem conqueror in the seventh century, though until then of considerable importance. It could be reached by land from Antioch by way of Syria, though the more direct and simpler route was by sea. In the north were the Chersonese colonies on the north coast of the Black Sea, and here again the line of communication was essentially maritime. In the west the greater part of Italy in early times and southern Italy and Sicily in later times constituted important parts of the Empire. Of the role played by Ravenna we shall have much to say; southern Italy concerns us in medieval times, though it never loses its provincial character; Sicily's part in the history of art, though short in duration, is considerable. The Islands of the Aegean were essentially dependent on Greece in medieval times; Crete was, however, more closely linked with the East in her architecture, and Millet notes a similar eastern element in Greece. In the eighth century or thereabouts a contact which is exemplified in sculpture was established between Greece and Persia directly, apparently without touching Constantinople.

It is impossible to speak individually of every Byzantine city in this survey. All the more important sites are shown on the map, and the reader will be able, it is hoped, to gather from their situations some idea of the roles that they played. The ambidextrous character of the Empire must, however, be borne in mind throughout, for it was not only the focus of East and West: it was throughout also just as much of a maritime as of a land power, and, when hampered in the one direction, could exercise its energies in the other unimpaired.

A few additional geographical factors which had some influence on art may be noted. In the chapter on architecture we shall call attention to two main materials of construction, brick and stone. Stone is in general procurable in the highlands, though it is not always of the same quality, and we often find that brick is employed in preference to it, either because the stone is too rough to give the smooth, neat appearance sought by the architect, or owing to a conservatism of the builder, who comes as an immigrant and prefers to use the material to which he is accustomed. The most important stone-building areas are in the east; in Anatolia the stone is of fair quality, but it is usually used together with brick owing to Constantinopolitan influence; in Syria it is excellent and provides a good material for decoration, and there is moreover a long and powerful tradition in stone construction, which is never lost. In Armenia we find some of the best masonry of all, done in a hard black stone, which permits of a very firm and severe outline and of a profuse, delicately carved, though not undercut, ornament. Constantinople was in the main a brick area, though local limestone was used for binding purposes and the superb marble from the neighbouring island of the Proconnesos for sculpture. The quality of this marble, bright, hard, yet somewhat soapy in texture, doubtless had a considerable effect on the nature of Byzantine sculpture, just as did the soft limestone of the Nile valley on that of Coptic Egypt. The one tended to formalism, and sought silhouette effects, often by means of vertical undercutting, which would hardly have been possible in any other material; the other tended to impressionistic, somewhat coarse figure subjects, the fineness of line or delicacy of content which was impossible being replaced by a virile force which served to overcome the unpleasantness of the material.

This influence of material and hence of environment is an important factor in the study of any particular art, which is all too often neglected, and though it is most apparent in architecture or sculpture, where the material is a fundamental element, a similar influence is doubtless brought to bear in the other arts, though it is to be discerned only in a much more subtle manner. It seems to the author that the arid deserts of Arabia and the severity of life which they occasioned constituted an essential in the development of that trend in art which we have termed the Syrian or Semitic, and that the beauty of the surroundings and the ease of life in the coast-lands of the Mediterranean were similarly responsible for the development of the pleasant, delicate lines of the idealistic trend which we term Hellenistic. But these are problems of aesthetics which cannot be entered upon here; the reader may inquire into them for himself if he will. Let it be stressed, however, that an understanding of the build and form of a land, a knowledge of the routes of communication, and an idea of the natural resources which any area offers are factors which should be considered at the outset by every historian of art in the course of his examination of any particular region or of any particular civilization.

BIBLIOGRAPHY

The best and fullest work on the build of the land, its character and climate, is D. G. Hogarth's *The Nearer East*, London, 1902. For routes of communication see W. M. Ramsay, *The Historical Geography of Asia Minor*. An 'art-geography' of the Nearer East remains to be written. For the topography of Constantinople see Diehl, *Constantinople*, Paris, 1921 (Villes d'Art célèbres Series), where a full bibliography is given. A more popular, but excellent account, is that of George Young, *Constantinople*, London, 1926.

Chapter III

THE ORIGINS OF BYZANTINE ART

NO civilization dies without leaving some heritage behind it; no civilizations of any advanced degree are born without antecedents. To consider in turn each of the predecessors of Byzantine culture which did or could affect it, and to give a general outline of their nature and condition, is the aim of this chapter. The reader will thus conceive some idea of the nature of the various sources which exercised an effect on Byzantine art, both in the earliest days, and later, when the distinguishing character of Byzantine art had already been arrived at. Yet however important these elements may be—and of recent years authorities have been much concerned with stressing the role of one at the cost of that of another—it must always be borne in mind that the chief glory of creating a style or producing an object must be assigned to the culture to which it actually belongs. Thus a Byzantine ivory may be Hellenistic or it may be Eastern in character; it may exemplify the idealistic spirit of Greek art; it may be conceived purely in a formalist or realist eastern manner; but there is beyond this a definite quality which makes it essentially Byzantine. It is this quality which is of chief importance to the student of the history of art, but his appreciation must remain incomplete and his understanding limited unless he have some knowledge of what has gone before.

The cultures that concern us in this respect may best be considered in turn, according to region. They fall into seven principal groups: Greece and the Hellenistic world; Asia Minor; Rome and Italy; Syria and the Semitic East; northern Mesopotamia; southern Persia (Iran) and lower Mesopotamia (Iraq), and finally northern Persia, called by Strzygowski the Altai-Iran region.[1]

[1] The role of Christianity as an essential formative influence will be

I. *Greece and the Hellenistic World.* We shall discuss the dissemination of Greek culture in the East by the conquests of Alexander in a later section. Here we are concerned with the large Greek cities of the Mediterranean coast-lands in Asia Minor, in northern Syria, and in Egypt, such as Ephesus, Pergamon, Priene, Miletus, Antioch, and Alexandria. In these cities Greek culture had been long established, and it was with many of them that the more popular Greek myths and legends were concerned. Troy and Pergamon may be mentioned as examples. These cities were, as we have attempted to show in the chapter on geography, linked more closely with Greece by means of the sea than with their own hinterlands, from which they were separated by mountain barriers or political antipathies. Here, during the centuries immediately preceding the birth of Christ, the pure Greek culture of the city-states of the mainland was maintained, and as Greece itself declined and gradually assumed the role of a conserver rather than a creator, so these cities progressed, keeping up a more or less vital culture of their own. As time went on this culture tended to become somewhat less pure, being closely affected by eastern elements, but the Greek ideal was definitely maintained till a late date. From about the end of the third century B.C. these cities formed a part of the Roman Empire, but they were never more than superficially affected by Roman culture and Roman art.[1] From them, and more especially from Antioch and Alexandria, the

considered later. It may here be noted that in his recent and most penetrating examination of the origins of Byzantine art Guyer regards the Christian religion and the character of Byzantine thought as far more important than either the 'Orient' or 'Rome' of Strzygowski. See Guyer, *Am Wesen der Byzantinischen Kunst*, Münchner Jahrbuch der bildenden Kunst, N.F. viii, 1931, Heft 2, p. 99. He distinguishes two trends in thought, which affect decoration, the exterior or Hellenistic and the interior, the mystic or eastern.

[2] The influence was in fact rather in the converse direction, and we see in Rome and at Pompeii much that is unquestionably to be attributed to Alexandria or Hellenistic Syria.

Hellenic tradition was conveyed to Byzantine civilization, though the old Greek town of Byzantium, whose site was chosen for Constantinople, had also some contribution to make.

II. *Asia Minor*. We have already noted that the coasts and the highlands of Anatolia form two distinct regions. But in art it seems that we must go farther and distinguish between the Hellenistic culture of the great cities and a local culture akin to that of the highlands, which existed also in the country regions of the coast-land. This native culture was founded upon long antecedents, established in the land as far as we can tell even before the days of the Hittites.[1] We know little of this early Anatolian art, and for our purposes it suffices to realize that certain particular animal motives, more especially the lion and the eagle, were popular in the region from Hittite times onwards, and that in the Hellenistic period we find their reproduction continuing in a manner which is not to be reconciled with Hellenistic culture.[2] We can trace these motives and this manner in Byzantine art, more especially in sculpture, both in Constantinople and in Greece, and we see these very same animals prominent again in the Seljuk art of Anatolia of the twelfth century. This sudden reappearance of old motives is by no means fortuitous: it represents rather the revival of an age-old tradition in Asia Minor, and there can be little doubt but that this tradition also had its influence on the Byzantine art of the intervening

[1] These invaders must have found something in the nature of a fairly developed culture when they arrived between 2000 and 1500 B.C., if we are to judge by the differences in character between the monuments for which they were responsible in Asia Minor, such as Boghazkeuy and Euyuk, and those which they erected in northern Syria, most notably at Senjirli and Karkhemish.

[2] The most characteristic monuments of the art are some tombstones in the Brusa Museum, known as the Altyn-Tash stelae. See G. Mendel, *Catalogue du Musée de Brousse*, Athens, 1908, p. 35, and more especially an extremely suggestive article by Crowfoot, *Ann. Brit. School at Athens*, iv, 1897–8, p. 79.

periods. How much this influence was exerted, how important its role actually was, will only be disclosed when further research makes us more familiar with the Anatolian element in art from the twelfth century B.C. to the twelfth century A.D.

III. *Rome and Italy.* Rome, like the Hellenistic cities, founded her culture to a great extent on that of Greece, but by the beginning of the Christian era it had taken on a definitely individual form owing to local influence. Yet, though Rome was the capital of the world, she did not during her prosperity impose her art on any but her more immediate dependencies and creations, such as Pompeii. When Constantine transferred his capital to the shores of the Marmora in 330, he took with him all the panoply of an imperial court. Buildings were constructed in the Roman manner, to answer Roman demands; statues which were purely Roman in appearance were erected; Roman law, the Latin language, and indeed every aspect of Roman culture was imposed. The city was the new Rome in all its superficial aspects. Two strong forces, however, opposed this imposition of Roman culture on Constantinople, namely geography and race. Thus by the sixth century we find that the Greek tongue had replaced Latin in general usage, and by the ninth century the latter had been entirely forgotten. In art a similar change took place and purely Roman forms, such as the imperial portrait bust or the conception of Christ as a youthful beardless figure, were abandoned in the developed Byzantine manner.

IV. *Syria and the Semitic East.* The term Syrian is apt to be a confusing one to the student of Byzantine art, for it is often used without distinction in one of three ways. First, it may apply to the culture of the large Hellenistic cities of Syria, most important of which was Antioch. Secondly, it may refer to that of the slightly more orientalized caravan cities inland, the most typical of which is Dura.[1] Thirdly, it is used to describe a decided but less definitely localized

[1] For these see Rostovtzeff's *Caravan Cities*, Oxford, 1932.

trend in art, the Semitic or realist, as opposed to the Hellenic or idealist. We have already dealt with the first of these aspects under the heading of Hellenistic influence; the second we will deal with under the heading of northern Mesopotamian; the third influence is the one that concerns us most in the development of Byzantine art, and throughout the book it is this element that we mean when we speak of Syrian or Semitic. We see it exercised principally in painting and mosaic, the influence being characterized by a desire to stress not the superficial beauty, but the inner meaning of a figure or object. The art may be described as one which aims at significance; it is not concerned with pleasing, but with conveying an idea, and this aim must be achieved if necessary by the most forceful means. Certain features are characteristic of it, such as the adoption of the frontal pose; the enlargement of the head in a statue (the head being regarded as the centre of meaning); the enlargement of an individual figure to denote its importance; or the deep undercutting of a relief to convey a striking impression. The gradual intrusion of this element in Hellenistic art is to be traced as Greece declines, but the first mighty example on western soil is offered by the mausoleum of Diocletian at Spalato (early fourth century A.D.), where eastern ornament has to a great extent conquered the purely classical.

At the back of this trend are all the forces of the ancient Semitic civilization of Mesopotamia, though it can never be described as a direct Mesopotamian influence. At the back of it again is in all probability a geographical factor of the greatest importance, which has been disclosed by recent research. It is the gradual desiccation of Arabia. As the country grew drier, life became more and more difficult, and its difficulties were revealed in a search for reality and a hatred of the superficial in art. Just as the severe conditions of industrialism have produced in the art of to-day a love of the forceful, so did the troubles of life in Arabia produce similar results. Where exactly the first monuments of the art were conceived it is impossible to say—the art was rather the result of a long drawn out development—but we see its influence in the tomb paintings of Palmyra, or in the superb work of A.D. 85, discovered by Breasted at Dura in 1918.[1] At a later date Semitic or Syrian influence is of the greatest importance; we see it in mosaics and in sculpture from the fourth to the sixth century, and it is this influence which changes the style of Alexandrine ivory carving so suddenly in the fifth century. We see it perpetuated from the ninth century onward in the wall paintings of Cappadocia and Armenia, and we see it again cropping up in the paintings and miniatures of the Christian East as late as the eighteenth century. This and the Hellenistic were in fact two of the main stems from which Byzantine art sprang.

Before passing on to the next group we must call attention to Egypt, for though a pure Hellenistic style was retained at Alexandria until the fifth or sixth century, the Nile basin developed at an early date a Christian art of its own of a distinct character which we know as Coptic. Much that is Coptic is to be attributed to ancient Egypt; much is Hellenistic; but the arts of these two cultures could never have produced the Coptic without the Syrian or Semitic element. The influence penetrated by way of the Red Sea or the Isthmus of Suez, along the trade routes which had been used for so many thousands of years. It was an influence conveyed from and by way of the arid deserts, and it avoided at first the more clement shores of the Mediterranean. The degree to which it affected the hinterland can be appreciated by comparing a piece of Coptic sculpture with an Egyptian or Greek statue.

[1] It is the Semitic factor which makes these paintings so different from contemporary work in the purely Hellenistic vein, where idealism and naturalism were still supreme. In the interesting paintings of A.D. 245 in the synagogue at Dura we see a purer retention of the Hellenistic style.

V. *Northern Mesopotamia.* Mesopotamia must for the purpose of this survey fall into two divisions: a northern, wherein stone is the usual building material and where small hills are scattered over the countryside, and a southern, where brick is universal and where nothing but a dead flat landscape confronts the eye. In earlier times northern Mesopotamia had been the home of a Semitic civilization, the Assyrian. At the age when we first take up our story it was somewhat divided, the region of the Euphrates to the west being more or less hellenized, that of the Tigris to the east being more purely oriental in character. The western region, with its semi-Hellenistic cities like Dura, has already been alluded to. Its culture was half-way between that of the larger Hellenistic cities (group 1), and the Syrian Semitic (group 4), and any influence that it had on the Byzantine may be classed under those heads.[1]

The Tigris basin was rather less affected by this Hellenistic culture, though it was for a time under the control of the Seleucid empire. At the beginning of the Christian era it was the home of a civilization of strongly orientalized feeling, the Parthian; it stood in fact for a revival of old oriental ideals.[2] The important city of Hatra, south of Mosul, whose massive, stone-built vaults and arches can still be inspected

[1] In later times the Christian art of Mesopotamia, more especially architecture, preserved a Hellenistic tradition quite foreign to the Byzantine: see Guyer, 'Le Rôle de la Syrie et de la Mésopotamie', *Syria*, 1933, vol. xiv, fasc. i, p. 60, for a distinction of Syrian and Byzantine art from the third to the sixth centuries.

[2] Stelae recently discovered at Tell Halaf, which must be dated before 1800 B.C., suggest that we see revivified in Parthian art not only elements which were culled from Achaemenid Persia, but also some which were popular in the region of Parthian domination some two thousand years earlier. Bas-reliefs from Tell Halaf show a number of motives, such as the hippogryph, the winged dragon, or the human-headed bird, which are popular in Sasanian and other eastern art. They are assigned by their excavator, von Oppenheim, and by Professor Herzfeld to about 3000 B.C., but other authorities dispute this early dating. See Max von Oppenheim, *Tell Halaf*, Engl. transl., 1933.

to-day, was the principal Parthian centre, and we see here not only one of the earliest instances of stone vaulted chambers, which must have had some effect on Byzantine architecture, but also sculptures and decorative motives which are paralleled in later Byzantine sculpture. How far the similarity is to be attributed to direct Parthian influence on the Byzantine, and how far to a like adoption of earlier oriental motives in both, it is impossible to affirm until more excavations have been undertaken. But the possibility of a definite Parthian connexion must be considered.

VI. *Southern Mesopotamia and Southern Persia.* We have already noted that Mesopotamia must fall into two main divisions, and the same is true of Persia, the southern portion of that country being closely linked with southern Mesopotamia throughout the period that concerns us. In southern Mesopotamia, or Iraq, the land of the two rivers, was situated the city of Seleucia, capital of the Seleucid kings, who inherited Alexander's eastern empire. These kings were responsible for introducing an Hellenistic element into the art and culture of the whole region, which affected motives and subjects though it never completely overcame the old oriental spirit. With the gradual weakening of Seleucid power, the oriental spirit came by degrees more and more to the fore, till in A.D. 226 a final effort on the part of the Persian chieftain Ardashir was responsible for the establishment of a new and essentially eastern dynasty, the Sasanian. The rulers of this dynasty lived in southern Mesopotamia, at Ctesiphon, close to old Seleucia, in the winter, and in the highlands of southern Persia, at such cities as Shapur or Persepolis in the summer, and there arose all over their empire a number of cities wherein flourished a new and essentially Sasanian art. Recent excavations at Kish and Hira in Iraq, and at Damgan in Persia, show the marked individuality of their art and prove that Sasanian culture was at this time far more widely spread than has heretofore been realized. The influence of Sasanian art abroad was from now on considerable. It is an essential element in all Moslem art, and it has a far-reaching effect on the development, though not on the formation, of Byzantine art. We see this influence most clearly in textiles, and it is often impossible to determine whether some of the superb silks of the Middle Ages are to be assigned to a Persian or to a Byzantine factory. We see it again in ceramics,[1] in sculpture, and in metal-work in the middle period, and it can be seen, though more faintly, in Byzantine art as early as the fifth or sixth century.

VII. *The Altai-Iran.* The Sacian area to the north of Persia is in some ways easier to deal with than the Sasanian in the south, for Strzygowski associates with it a very distinct and definite type of art, and the importance of the region as far as we are concerned must stand or fall with his theories. His main thesis may be briefly summarized. From the nomads of Turkish race living in the Altai-Iran region there sprang a formalistic and non-representational art which was later to spread westwards and be developed as the medieval. It is characterized in architecture by the dome over the square plan, at first made of wood in this area, and then in more lasting material in the neighbouring lands. In decoration it favours low relief carving, which covers every available space with floral or geometric forms, executed in a black and white, silhouette-like manner where modelling is avoided. This manner belongs more properly to painting than to sculpture, and at a later date it is probably responsible for the great popularity of enamel. As regards technique a special slanting cut (*kerbschnitt*) is characteristic. These features spread westwards from the north-east corner of Persia at an early date, and are developed and changed as they go. Their first effect is to be noticed in the Hellenistic age; but a

[1] The relationship between Byzantine and the Sasanian and post-Sasanian ceramics of Persia will be traced by the author in the forthcoming *Survey of Persian Art*.

continuation of it is to be traced until the Renaissance, when the influence of the non-representational stream was entirely blotted out. During the first millennium B.C. two main routes to the West may be distinguished. One, the northern, leads from Iran to the Caucasus and thence via the northern shores of the Black Sea to Hungary and Scandinavia. Connexion was established by such tribes as the Sarmatians in early times and later the more violent Goths. The second or southern route affects the trans-Oxus country and Iran, and from there Arabia and Egypt. The principal carriers are the Sacians, the Parthians, and the Bactrian Greeks.[1]

The character of this art and the ideas underlying it are entirely opposed to the classical, though as it travels westward it becomes inextricably mixed with the classical, which was itself travelling eastward. Its role in the formation of Byzantine art is very considerable, ranking only after the Greek or idealist and the Syrian or realist tendencies. But by the beginning of the Christian era elements are so confused that it is difficult to extricate them, and more importance must, for our purposes, be attributed to Syria than to north Persia, since it was in general by way of northern Syria and Anatolia that non-representational art came to the Byzantine world.[2] Yet the existence of non-representational art cannot be disputed, and though some critics tend to deride its merits,

[1] It is not as yet generally accepted that Strzygowski is right in assigning the origin of the non-representational style to the Altai-Iran region, his assumption being based on theory rather than on fact, and it may be noted that Frankfort has traced two distinct systems, the representational and the non-representational, in the earliest potteries of Mesopotamia and Egypt. For Strzygowski's work see especially *Altai Iran und Volkerwanderungen*, and to some extent *Die Baukunst der Armenier und Europa*. His theories are also summarized in the *Eastern Origin of Christian Art* and in *Early Church Art in Northern Europe*.

[2] It seems that the two types of art are always distinct. A division which penetrated to the very depth of primitive thought, to the distinction between religion and magic, is more likely to be the real explanation of the two trends, and like results may well have been arrived at simultaneously in more than one area as a result of like conditions.

there can be no doubt as to the very remarkable manifestations for which it was responsible. That it was important in the West, and that it came to Byzantium from the East is certain. Let this, for the moment, be sufficient.

A further and rather different influence which is to be assigned to central Asia must also be considered, though as far as Byzantine art is concerned it is not of the first importance. It is that of the 'animal style'. In the last few centuries of the pre-Christian period a particular art which Rostovtzeff conveniently catalogues under this heading was brought into wide popularity by the culture known as Scythian. It was a highly formalized art and in this respect owed much to the element we have considered at the beginning of this section, the non-representational, but its essential motive was above everything else founded on the living animal. This Scythian culture, it is held, travelled westwards by way of the northern shores of the Black Sea and what is to-day Roumania, and some of its finest manifestations have been unearthed in Hungary.[1] The Far East has been suggested as its place of origin, and it has also been proposed that it had some influence in Bulgaria, where the 'animal style' nomads were established for a time, and Filow thinks that the great popularity of animals in ninth-century Bulgarian sculpture is due to a great extent to this ancestry. This may be so; but we find very similar animals in Byzantine sculpture, especially in Greece, which are to be attributed to a late Sasanian influence. And as there is a marked Sasanian influence in Bulgaria, to be seen in the plans of palaces at Aboba Pliska and in the ninth-century rock reliefs at Madara,[2]

[1] The stag from Zöldhalompuszta, now in the Budapest Museum, is probably the finest example of the art; see N. Fettich, *La Trouvaille Scythe*, Budapest, 1928. For a general survey see G. Borovka, *Scythian Art*, London, 1928. An important exhibition at Stockholm in 1933 was catalogued for the International Art Congress.

[2] See M. G. Kacarov, 'Notes sur la sculpture rupestre de Madara', in *L'Art byzantin chez les Slaves*, pt. i, vol. i, p. 87.

the animals which appear there in the sculpture of this and the following centuries are more probably to be accounted for in this manner. The theory of migration as the means by which this art was conveyed has also been criticized, and the researches of certain authorities in Soviet Russia are aimed at proving that archaeological ethnology as we know it is a science which can in no way be relied on. They maintain that certain types of art arise as a result of certain types of culture, without any necessary connexion between the two.[1] This question of independent invention is a very vexed one, but there can be no doubt that in many cases like results are produced independently by like effects; we have thus already suggested that non-representational art may have been born in several places independently and that it was a natural outcome of primitive thought rather than a system originating in a somewhat hypothetical corner of Asia. But how far these theories can be relied upon when some very definite motive such as the Scythian stag is concerned is a rather different matter, and when we have to deal with such arts as the Byzantine or the Sasanian the fact of an influence is not to be disputed. Though primitive nomad tribes in different areas would naturally tend to represent the same animal, provided they both knew it, or primitive settled tribes to conceive the same type of building, the probability of a more or less civilized community inventing exactly the same details in the portrayal of a stag or the construction of a building seems much less conceivable.

To disentangle the eventual interplay of all these elements is far beyond the scope of this volume. The existence of practically every possible contributor has, however, been

[1] See an extremely interesting article by I. Mestchaninoff, *The Value of Linguistic Material in a Study of Ancient Monuments*, G.A.I.M.K., Nos. 1 and 2, Moscow, 1932 (in Russian). Its scientific value is, however, marred by a futile use of the word 'bourgeois', where it is in no sense applicable.

noted, so that the student of Byzantine art who knows little of the Nearer East may be in some degree prepared to understand manifestations which are in no way related to the classical world. For at its basis Byzantine art was the result of a fusion, the fusion between East and West. The two elements that concern us primarily are thus the Hellenic or Greek and the Semitic or eastern, the one responsible for delicacy and idealism, and the other for strength and force of meaning. The portraiture of Rome, the formalistic, all-embracing ornament of the East, the fantastic animals of the Sasanian world, the rigidity of Anatolian sculpture, the love of non-representational ornament, all are present in the background. Yet the main role is always divided between Greece and Syria, and as we proceed we shall see that not only did these lands exercise their influence on art, but on thought also. Periods when Greek philosophical writings control the thought of the day recur, and one great age, the iconoclast, sees the supremacy of a Semitic belief, when the age-old creed of no representation in religious art sways the empire.

Yet there was something more which made Byzantine culture and Byzantine art markedly distinctive, and that was the Christian religion. Until the sixth century the religious basis was perhaps subservient to a great extent to Imperialism; but with the age of Justinian the triumph of the Church was secured and we see the energies of this emperor extended in building a number of churches and a vast cathedral, while the royal palace remains little more than a conglomeration of detached halls and apartments. The everyday life of the population was equally affected by religion, and an historian records that in the bazaar discourses upon theological matters were indulged in by the tradesmen who could hardly even sell a loaf of bread without entering into some controversy. By the following century this religious character is completely dominant in the whole civilization, and a purely religious quarrel racks the State for some two hundred years. From the ninth till the twelfth centuries all the more important art is of a religious character, and all the more important writings are theological. The Palaeologue age is remembered primarily because of its churches and monastic foundations, and the religious paintings that decorate them. Christianity was in fact not only one of the principal factors in the development of Byzantine art; it was also one of the most important in its creation. It moulded and influenced the art as a sculptor moulds the clay; it set certain bounds upon it which could never be transgressed; it dictated its form and limitations. Like the services and liturgies of the Church, the art was little affected by external and political events, and in a study of it such events must be considered as landmarks to aid our work rather than as factors which exercised any very considerable effect upon the development of the art itself.

PART II

Chapter I

THE ARCHITECTURAL BACKGROUND

TO unravel all the problems that beset the field of Byzantine architectural history, or to provide sufficient data to enable the student to date at a glance any building on stylistic grounds, is not the purpose of this chapter. Our aim is rather that of an appreciation, and we shall attempt to point out the main features of the developed Byzantine style, to show how the buildings served as a background for the other arts, and to summarize the history of the various architectural elements which go to make up the buildings. But owing to the new forms and types of building which came into vogue with the triumph of Christianity, and owing to the diversity of influences which were at play, the subject is extremely controversial, and the principal theories which have been put forward with regard to the origin of these forms must receive certain consideration.

It may further be stated at the very outset that we shall be concerned primarily with churches; few secular Byzantine buildings have survived, and from what we know of the finest of them, the Great Palace at Constantinople, it seems well-nigh certain that they presented no very important architectural features of their own. No palace in the western sense was ever built; like the Turkish sultans of the sixteenth century, the emperors preferred a series of semi-connected pavilions to a single vast edifice, and these pavilions were either of simple plan, where no particular architectural problem arose, or were closely related to the churches and thus do not demand consideration apart. Private houses and monasteries again cannot be dealt with here, though many of them, more especially those of

Athos, are amazingly spectacular. The walls and cisterns of Constantinople, though they are among the most important remains of that city, are similarly beyond the scope of this book.[1]

Four main kinds of building and two main types of material must be considered here, and the wide area with which we have to deal can be roughly divided according to the material employed, both geographically and architecturally, since a rather different class of edifice is developed as a result of the employment of brick to that which results from the use of stone.[2] In the central and lowland regions, Constantinople, Greece, the Balkans, south-western Russia, southern Mesopotamia (Iraq), Persia, and Egypt, bricks were principally used, though stones also appear to form binding courses. In the uplands, Armenia, the Caucasus, parts of Asia Minor, Syria, Crete, and Cyprus, where good quarries were at hand, stone was more or less universally employed. In the later periods the use of the one material or the other had considerable effect on the decorative details of the edifice, even if the plans were the same in main outline; and at an early date it seems that certain major features were equally affected by the material. Thus in Hellenistic Syria, where stone was universally employed, the hemispherical dome was the rule, while in Sasanian Persia, where large bricks were used, the domes were of an ovoid form. The Syrian domes were built with the aid of centring; the Persian, like Sasanian vaults, could be erected course by course without any support, the large

[1] For the cisterns and walls see Diehl, *Manuel*, i, p. 197. For the walls see Van Millingen, *Constantinople; the Walls of the City and adjoining Historical Sites*, London, 1899. For the most recent information regarding the cisterns and water-supply see Dalman, *Der Valens-Aquädukt in Konstantinopel*, Bamberg, 1933.

[2] Material also helps us to determine the place of origin of a certain style, for we sometimes see the intrusion of brick or rubble building in an area where cut stone of fine quality is available. In this case conservatism has retained a less suitable material together with an imported plan or design.

flat bricks being tilted backwards, so that each successive layer rested on that below.[1]

The four main types of building with which we have to deal are the basilica, the centralized building, the domed basilica, and the cruciform building. Each of them is in early times to be associated with a particular region, though at a later date we see a very considerable diffusion of the more popular developments of these prototypes. It will be well, however, to begin by examining each of them in its simplest form, for the subtle combination of the various prototypes is the distinctive mark of the Byzantine contribution to architecture.

THE BASILICA

The basilica was in origin essentially a classical building; it was developed in the Hellenistic region and in Rome for judicial purposes, the praetor sitting in the apse, with the judices around him. This plan was taken over direct by the Christian Church, and we see a throne for the bishop behind the altar in the apse, with seats for the clergy in a half circle on either side. Such a disposition is still in existence at Torcello, near Venice, and in many another early church. In early times these buildings faced towards the west, with entrance at the east, but by the fourth or fifth century the western entrance had become universal. Rivoira maintains that the earliest instance of the eastern apse was the basilica of Ursiana at Ravenna (370–84), and in Constantine's day in any case the western apse was usual, his church at Baalbek having three apses facing west, while his church of the Holy Sepulchre at Jerusalem had the main doors at the east.[2] The idea of first directing the church towards the east is attributed by Strzygowski to Armenia, where he thinks it was universal

[1] When further researches come to be made, the arrangement of the courses and the size and shape of the actual bricks will doubtless prove of considerable importance in tracing out lines of connexion between the various regions where brick is universal.

[2] Rivoira, *Lombardic Architecture*, ii, p. 13.

owing to the influence of the Mazdaean sun cult, which was from about 500 B.C. till the Islamic conquest the official religion. That it is due to a survival of pagan religious ideas in the Christian religion is certain, but in the absence of early buildings on Armenian soil it seems unsafe to attribute it to that country rather than to that natural unification of new and old religious ideas which certainly took place in Rome and indeed all over the Hellenistic world, and which might well have occasioned the adoption of eastern orientation by local architects, without the influence of actual eastern plans or buildings coming into play.

Basilicas, with the characteristic three aisles divided by columns, were much in favour during the first two or three centuries of the Byzantine age, for they were economical and simple to build. Marble columns could easily be looted from pagan buildings, while the roofs, which were usually composed of wood in the Hellenistic area, and of stone vaults in Syria, presented no very considerable problems. The nature of the roofs, however, had an effect on the columns, for with a wooden roof these could be tall and slender—an example is offered in the church of St. John of Studion at Constantinople (463)—whereas where the roof was of masonry they had to be stout and strong. A natural outcome of the masonry vault is the built pier, which takes the place of or alternates with the columns, as for instance in the church of St. Demetrius at Salonica, of the fifth century, now, alas! partly destroyed.

A further development which was entirely due to Christian architecture was the arcade, which took the place of the classical architrave and resulted in the use of a new kind of capital. The marble slab of the architrave could rest without difficulty on a small surface; the brick foundation of an arch necessitated a much larger support, and this was arrived at by the use of an impost or second and larger capital above the first one, shaped like a truncated pyramid placed upside down.

By the fifth or sixth century the impost block above the capital was in universal employment in buildings of every type; slightly later an impost capital was evolved, which combined the functions of the two in a wide-spreading capital, the ornament of which could not be undercut in the classical manner since all the strength of the stone was necessary to support the burden above. The demands set upon sculpture by architecture here coincided with the natural turn which sculpture and ornament were taking in the course of the development of the new art.

We see certain variations in the plans of these basilicas. Thus three or five aisles occur, and the apses are either semicircular—a feature of Syrian origin—or polygonal, as at Ravenna. But the type permitted of little further elaboration; it was not thoroughly suited to Byzantine religious demands, nor did it satisfy the ambitions of Byzantine architects; it presented, in fact, a dead end, and after the sixth century it fell into disfavour. Quite a large number of basilicas were built before this date all over the Byzantine area, but more especially in Italy; others were erected in Bulgaria, for instance at Mesembria. A few are found in Greece, more especially at Salonica, and an important later example survives at Kalabaka.

A primitive Mesopotamian type of basilica with transverse nave is of purely local importance, for the transverse narthex or outer chamber which we see for instance running along the west end of St. Sophia at Constantinople (Fig. 5) or again in so many later churches on Athos, is hardly to be derived from it. It is rather the natural result of building a passage-like porch in front of the west doors, which later took on the function of a definite part of the edifice.

THE CENTRALIZED BUILDING

The essential element of this group is the dome, but there are two main divisions in early times—that where the building is of round, and that where it is of square plan. These will best be considered in turn, though the second class is by far the more important.

A. *Dome over round plan.* Round buildings were in fairly common use as pagan mausoleums. Hitherto their origin has usually been assigned to Rome, and it is true that the earliest dated examples are to be found there. But recent discoveries in the East, most notably at Pergamon and at Constantinople, suggest that these edifices on a large scale may be a creation of the Hellenistic rather than of the Roman mind.[1] The most important instance in Rome is the Pantheon, founded by Agrippa in 27 B.C., but reconstructed by Hadrian in A.D. 120–4; the most important though not the earliest in the east is the mausoleum of Diocletian at Spalato (early IVth cent.). Wherever it originated, the circular building underwent a considerable elaboration both in the Hellenistic area and in Rome in the early Christian period, and Creswell, in his recent monumental work on the origins of Moslem architecture, has traced the line of development through a series of elaborations which were, he thinks, determined by mathematical formulae.[2] The first stage is the circular building, with dome supported on the side walls; it is elaborated as in the church of Santa Constanza at Rome (324–6) to an inner rotunda of columns, on which stands the dome, and an outer circular enclosure. In the next stage the inner circle on columns is surrounded by an octagon (Constantine's church of the Anastasis at Jerusalem, 327-335). In the next the circle surrounded by an octagon is further surrounded by a circle

[1] The Pergamon building is of the second century A.D. See Th. Wiegand, 'Zweiter Bericht über die Ausgrabungen von Pergamon, 1928–32', *Das Asklepieion*, Berlin, 1932. The Constantinople example is probably of much the same date. See D. Talbot Rice, 'Excavations at Bodrum Camii', *Byzantion*, viii, 1933, fasc. i, p. 162.

[2] See his *Early Muslim Architecture*, p. 72. This theory was first propounded in a paper *The Origin of the Plan of the Dome of the Rock*, British School of Archaeology in Jerusalem, Supp. Papers, No. 2, 1924.

in a square (the cathedral at Bosra, 512–13); in a final one we see a circle surrounded by an octagon, surrounded again by a second octagon (the Dome of the Rock at Jerusalem, 691). These Syrian elaborations are important, for not only do we find parallels in the Constantinopolitan region, but also must we remember that the Dome of the Rock, the culmination of the evolution, though built as a Moslem monument, was erected at an age when Moslem art was not as yet formed, in a country which had until a few years before been an important part of the Byzantine Empire.[1]

A few circular buildings of the simplest form survive in the central Byzantine area; the most important is the church of St. George at Salonica, a pagan edifice with eight interior niches like the Pantheon, transformed into a church in the fifth century by the addition of a choir-like presbytery at the east end. Of more elaborate type are the churches of SS. Sergius and Bacchus at Constantinople (526–37), and of San Vitale at Ravenna (526–47), where we see an octagon in a square. The church of Zwarthnotz in Armenia (641), a quatrefoil in a circle in an octagon, doubtless owes its main plan to the development traced by Creswell. Though Strzygowski assigns the quatrefoil to the East it may also well be Syrian, and Zwarthnotz would seem to be an instance of Byzantine and Syrian influence in Armenia rather than the reverse, for the decoration is of a distinctly Byzantine character and the capitals bear monograms in Greek lettering.

B. *Dome over square.* In order to make it possible to place the circular base of a dome over a building of square plan and so to combine a more convenient plan with a more elaborate and more satisfactory roof than a pointed or flat one, some

[1] Syria always retained a certain distinctive manner of her own in building, and the double dome of wood which roofs the Dome of the Rock is apparently a definitely Syrian feature. It is probably descended from the double domes of Hellenistic temples, such as the tholoi (rotundas) of Epidaurus or Olympia, and it became very popular in the region, though it was never adopted in Byzantium.

means of transition, which could transform the square into a circle, had to be devised. It is with regard to the method by which this difficulty was first solved and the region in which the solution was arrived at that some of the severest controversy of all archaeology or art history has raged. Certain authorities, most notably Rivoira, assign the honour to Italy, and suggest that the pendentive—a triangular-shaped section of a dome which fills up the corner of the square and so transforms it into a circle (Fig. 1)—was first invented in Rome. But no early examples exist there, and there is little evidence to support this theory.[1] Others, most notable of whom is Strzygowski, assign the honour to the Middle East. The idea, he thinks, was first suggested by corbelling in wood, that is to say by placing beams across the corners of a square, and then over the corners of the octagon so formed, until something approaching a circle was arrived at. Wooden domes of this type were used in the Altai-Iran region, he thinks, at an early date; the idea once conceived, execution in burnt brick was soon arrived at, and the squinch or arch across the corner was developed as a result in northern Persia in brick and in Armenia in stone.[2] From here it reached Byzantium and the West.

The squinch consists in its simplest form of a small arch spanning the corner of the square; it was elaborated to some extent in the Sasanian period and still further by Mohammedan builders, and there is every probability that it was conceived and first used in the East. Sasanian Persia seems, however, a more likely area than the rather uncertain Altai-Iran region to the north, for not only are there no surviving monuments in the latter region, whereas in the former we see an early example in the Sasanian palace of Sarvistan, but

[1] Rivoira cites the Domus Augustana (A.D. 85), but Creswell shows that we here have to do with a vault and not with a dome.

[2] For the names and dates of Armenian churches see Diehl, *Manuel*, i, pp. 338 and 471.

also Altai-Iran was as far as we know inhabited only by nomads with little culture, whereas the Sasanian region of Persia was one of the most civilized areas in the world from the fifth century B.C. until the fifth century A.D., the very period at which this evolution was taking place. And it may further be argued, why should we go to the unknown Altai-Iran when we find the dome on a small scale as a house unit both in Syria and in Assyria from the earliest times?[1]

Strzygowski's theory is attractive; but though the dome is perhaps elaborated further in the stone buildings of Armenia than anywhere else after the seventh century, there are no early examples there, and we lack concrete proof that these Armenian domes were actually introduced from the East or that they influenced Byzantine architecture to any great degree at an early date. And though Armenian domes often stand upon pendentives as do the Byzantine, it would be the squinch and not the pendentive that would be evolved from the wooden corbelling. In the study of Byzantine architecture again the squinch is of minor importance, for though it appears in a few buildings, such as S. Giovanni in Fonte at Naples (fifth century) or the monastery of St. Luke in Phocis (eleventh century) it was never generally adopted, the pendentive being far better suited to Byzantine demands (see Mosaics, p. 63).

A third school assigns the evolution of the dome to the Hellenistic area, where it was first erected upon pendentives, and the recent exhaustive examination given to the subject by Creswell has shown that, unless some very surprising finds are made in the East, the honour of first employing the pendentive on a large scale must unquestionably go to Syria.[2] It was

[1] Such a dome appears in a relief at Nineveh. C. Tchubinashvili in *Monatsheft für Kunstwissenschaft*, xv, 1922, p. 226, notes that the same is true of Georgian peasant houses.

[2] Early corbelling on a small scale occurs in Egypt about 1500 B.C., in Etruria in the seventh century B.C., and at Kertch in the Crimea in the fifth century B.C. The first true pendentives are at Amman, at Jerash,

from there that the idea in all probability reached Byzantium; and it seems likely again in view of the fact that Syrian examples date from the first or second century A.D., whereas Armenian pendentives are only of the sixth or seventh century, that it was from Syria that the Armenian architects first learnt a system which they afterwards elaborated so successfully.

In later architecture domed buildings of simple square plan are rare, for the Christian religion demanded a large meeting-hall, not only a small shrine, and when once the initial problem of supporting the dome had been overcome, elaboration and enlargement were at once embarked upon. In Armenia, however, we see a number of buildings where elaboration hardly affects the essential square plan. Thus a domed square with projecting apses on all four sides—Strzygowski calls them apse buttresses—appears at Mastara (650) and at Artik (seventh or eight century) (Fig. 2), or a domed square with apse buttresses and angle chambers at Etchmiadzin in A.D. 618 (Fig. 3). Further development in this line, however, soon produces a building of cruciform plan, as will be seen from a glance at the figures. It was thus, according to Strzygowski, that the cruciform plan was first arrived at, and he thinks that the Byzantines owe it to Armenia. But with the cross as a universal religious symbol and with a knowledge of the dome already founded, the evolution seems so natural that it may well have been arrived at in more than one area, and the early buildings of Syria seem to show that a kindred development took place there also and produced a cruciform plan long before the apse buttresses of Armenia were conceived.

THE DOMED BASILICA

This form of building, wherein the long assembly hall and the square, domed shrine are combined for the service of the

and at Samaria, all of the second or early third century A.D. Creswell, *Muslim Architecture*, ch. 7.

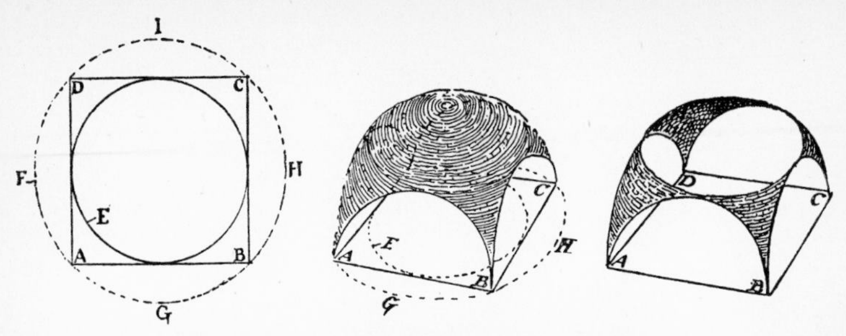

FIG. 1. The spherical triangle pendentine

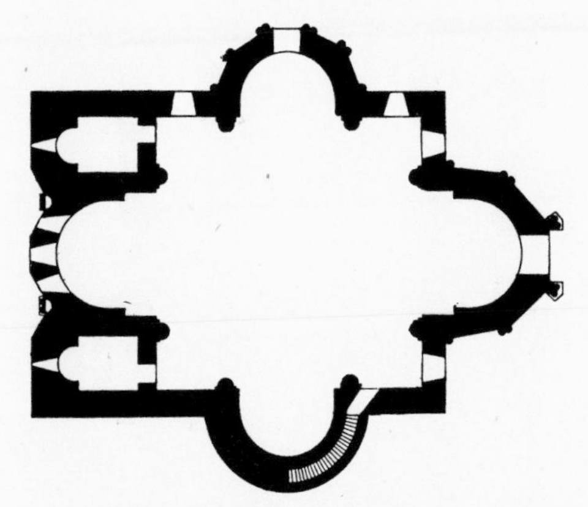

FIG. 2. Armenia, Artik Cathedral. Plan (VIIth or VIIIth century)

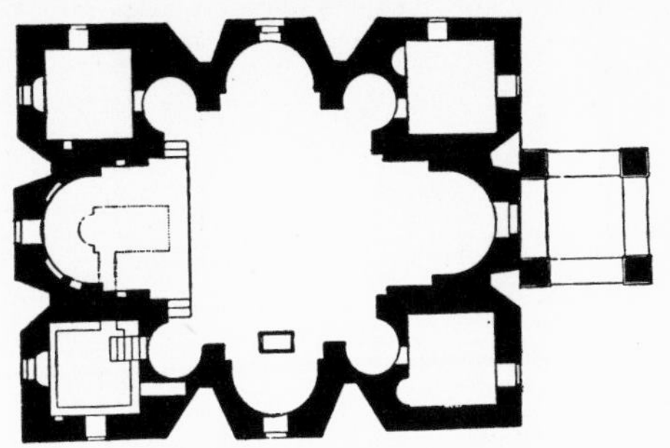

FIG. 3. Etchmiadzin, S. Hripsimeh. Plan (A.D. 618)

Fig. 4. Constantinople, S. Irene. Plan (A.D. 532)

Christian religion, is above any other typical of Byzantine architecture. It was at Constantinople that its elaboration took place, and there the principal type-buildings, St. Irene (532) and the cathedral of St. Sophia (532–7) survive to this day as the most impressive monuments of Byzantine architecture. St. Irene (Fig. 4) is fairly simple; it is a basilica, with domes set on crossing arches as a roof instead of a vault. St. Sophia (Fig. 5 and Pl. 1) presents more problems, for the dome is not only supported on arches, but also by semi-domes, which serve to counterbalance its thrust. Strzygowski regards the semi-domes as an elaboration of the niche buttresses which we have already noted in Armenia; the supporters of the Hellenistic theory regard them as developments of the niches which appear in the walls of round buildings like Diocletian's mausoleum at Spalato or many of the Hellenistic structures of Syria. Diehl and others, again, think that the semi-domes of St. Sophia were arrived at by bisecting, as it were, a domed building of centralized plan such as SS. Sergius and Bacchus, and enlarging it upwards and lengthways by pushing out the ends, filling the intermediary area with columns and imposing another and larger dome above the bisected ends. Millet, taking a less complicated and more common-sense view, believes that St. Sophia was the result of a synthesis of the various types known at the time, which would naturally arise in the mind of any architect of genius who had seen buildings of each class. But only a genius could produce from such diverse elements a building which was to be in itself so definite a unity as St. Sophia, and which was not only to mark a stage in the history of architecture, but was to survive also for some fourteen hundred years as the most glorious representation of its class. Nothing exactly similar, as large or quite as fine as St. Sophia of Constantinople was ever built again, but we can trace the influence of the great cathedral throughout, and we see it being used in the sixteenth and seventeenth centuries as a model for most of the large mosques which the conquering Turks erected in their new capital.

Millet's is the most plausible explanation of the evolution of the plan, for the elements belonging to the square building topped by a dome, the columned basilica, and the free-cross type can easily be distinguished by a glance at the interior of St. Sophia (Pl. 1). The cruciform plan which we see in embryo here would naturally be arrived at and elaborated not only for religious, but also for constructional reasons, the arms serving as buttresses for the support of the dome. Various stages of development and elaboration are to be seen in different buildings, though the most fully evolved are not of course in every case the latest in date. Thus such buildings as St. Sophia at Salonica (Vth or VIth cent.) and the church of the Assumption at Nicaea are transitional in development between the domed basilica and the Greek cross group. Bréhier thinks that they belong to a type which first appeared in Asia Minor early in the fifth century, St. Sophia being the first example in Europe. The cathedral of St. Sophia at Sofia in Bulgaria is another instance of much the same date.

CRUCIFORM BUILDINGS

Two distinct variations of this type occur, the free standing and the obscured or Greek cross forms. In the first the transepts project and the cross is at once visible. The type is to be seen in its most simple form in such a building as the mausoleum of Galla Placidia at Ravenna (*c.* 450), which has a dome at the crossing and four small arms of equal length.[1] In later days the type is quite common in Asia Minor, and we see examples in Greece. Of such a plan is the church of Kapnikaria at Athens, though extra chambers have been built in the corners, so that it has at first sight the appearance of a rectangular

[1] It has been suggested in connexion with this church that the cruciform plan first came to built churches from the catacomb tombs, where it was used during the earliest centuries of the Christian era.

building. Such chambers which fill no constructional purpose must be distinguished from the lower areas at the four corners of the obscured cross type.

The most famous example of a more elaborate version of the free standing cruciform plan of early date was the church of the Holy Apostles at Constantinople (536–46), now destroyed. Its chief characteristic was the five domes which roofed it, one at the crossing and one above each arm. The plan was closely copied for St. Mark's at Venice and elsewhere in the Byzantine area and even reached the West, for we see it in the twelfth-century church of St. Front at Périgueux in France. This is the type of multiple-domed church *par excellence*, and it must be distinguished from a later variety, especially common on Mount Athos, where one dome tops the crossing and others the side chapels, not the transepts, nave and choir, the actual arms of the cross.

The second variant of the cruciform building is known as the obscured or Greek cross plan. The cross is inscribed in a square, so that from the exterior the form of the cross is only visible above, the central aisle and transepts being carried up to a greater height than the side aisles. The place of origin of the group is disputed, yet it is so obviously a result of combined domical and cruciform construction that it may well have been arrived at independently in various places. It is thus the natural result of a crossing of two vaulted structures as in the baths of Caracalla at Rome or the natural elaboration of the Armenian apse-buttressed or lobed square (Fig. 3),[1] or the most obvious system of buttressing for the domed basilica. And with so many possible origins in view, it is beyond the scope of this chapter to make distinctions. All of them probably produced like results in different areas.

[1] A version of this is the trefoil apse, which Strzygowski attributes to Armenia and which other authorities, most notably Wiegand, assign to the Hellenistic area or to more than one source. It is so widespread that independent invention seems likely.

The dome is supported at first on piers, later more often on four columns. The four-angle chambers which are an essential part of the construction answer a natural demand of the Christian religion; those to the east serve as side chapels and are known as the Prothesis and the Diakonikon; those to the west form side aisles. They are roofed at first by vaults; in later times a small dome is often placed above each.

The origin of the type has already been noted when discussing the development of the domed basilica; we find it in common use by the eighth or ninth century. A fully developed example is the church at Skripu in Boeotia (873–4). By the eleventh century the type was well developed and widespread; a typical example is St. Theodore (Kilisse Djami) in Constantinople. Certain modifications take place which are of regional importance. Thus in Constantinople and the places most nearly dependent on the capital, Salonica, and Mount Athos, we usually see the dome supported on four columns, whereas in Greece, Anatolia, and Armenia there are two columns to the west, while the walls which separate the main apse from the side chapels are carried westwards to take the place of the two eastern columns. This is not the only feature in which Greek churches show eastern affinities from this time on, and Millet, in his detailed analysis of the Greek schools, has proved that they are generally more closely akin to those of Anatolia and the East than they are to those of Constantinople. An eastern feature which may result from this is the horse-shoe shaped apse, arrived at owing to the widening of the extremities of the walls when they have to serve the purpose of piers.

From the tenth century onwards no definitely new plans appear, but churches undergo a considerable development in structure and decoration. They tend to become smaller and higher; the windows are enlarged till they become tall niches, into the bases of which stone closure slabs are fitted; the

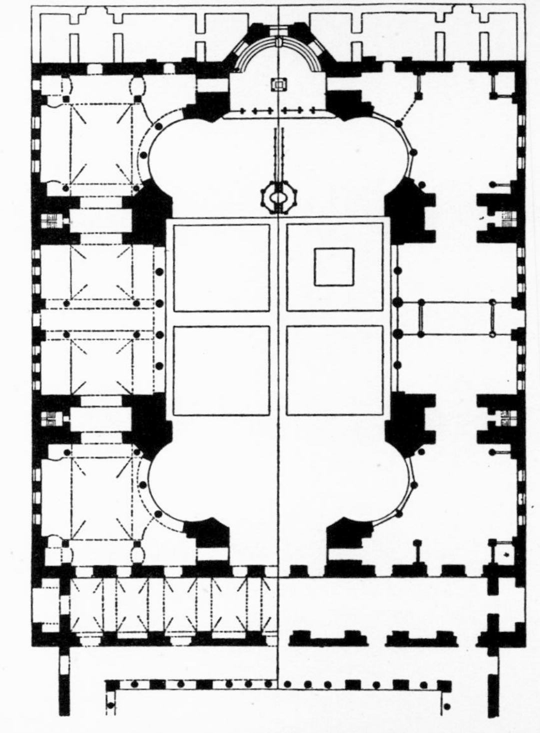

FIG. 5. Constantinople, S. Sophia. Plan (532–7)

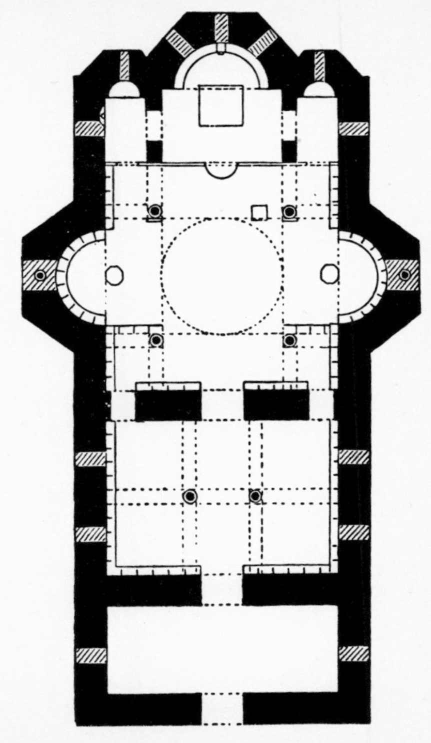

FIG. 6. A typical church on Mount Athos

domes are set upon tall, narrow drums;[1] the exteriors are generally richly decorated. Blank arcading, an eastern feature which was prominent in Sasanian art, is usual; ornamental brickwork on a smaller scale often plays an important part, and we find brick and stone being used to give a mosaic-like ornamental effect. This is particularly common in Bulgaria; there are superb examples at Tirnovo and at Mesembria of the twelfth and thirteenth centuries. We find blank arcading used with striking effect in the church of the Holy Apostles at Salonica (1312, Pl. 4, *a*) and that of the Virgin Pammacharistos at Constantinople (1315), and decorative brickwork was popular at Mistra. Here and on Athos glazed vessels were built into the walls to enliven the exterior; in Bulgaria it seems that special 'plates' were made for the purpose.[2] The westward spread of this niched and arcaded decoration can be traced from Sasanian Persia not only as far as the Byzantine world, but also in Spain, where it came by way of a southern route, and in the first Romanesque style of Italy and France, where it arrived by a northern one (see p. 228).

Each region develops its own particular type of church, though the plans are all fundamentally the same and all are essentially Byzantine. Thus on Mount Athos churches with long double naves are usual (Fig. 6) and a large, outer transverse narthex is often added. In Greece churches are small and of uniform plan, with small bema or choir, two small side chapels, and medium sized, three-aisled nave.

Unlike Greek architecture, where a sculptured frieze is an essential of the building, Byzantine architecture is in early times characterized by the plainness of its exteriors, which

[1] The earliest tall drums occur in Armenia, and even if all that Strzygowski attributes to this land cannot be relied upon, it is fairly certain that the idea of a tall drum came to the more western area from there.

[2] These retained the form of plates, but the bases were never finished, so that they could never have been used on a table. They offer an interesting instance of conservatism, an old form being retained for a new use, to which it was really ill suited.

give no herald of the magnificence within (Pl. 1, *a* and *b*). Both St. Sophia at Constantinople and St. Sophia at Salonica have this characteristic, and those who see such renowned buildings for the first time are usually disappointed. It seems that the classical idea was completely forgotten.[1] In the later periods, however, we have already noted a rich exterior decoration in brick in Greece and in the central area, and in view of recent research there can be no doubt that this was derived from the Sasanian art of Persia.[2] It was not due to a classical revival. In the parts of Asia Minor where brick was used we see a similar development; where stone was the building material, exterior decoration assumed rather a different character. Thus above the south door of the church of St. Sophia at Trebizond (XIIIth cent.) is a sculptured frieze, which Strzygowski thinks was due in spirit to Armenia. He regards the sculptures on the outside of the church at Achthamar on Lake Van (915–21) and those on the churches of Jurjiev-Polski (1230–4) and Vladimir (1190) in Russia as of the same family.[3] Of kindred inspirations are painted exteriors, and these were again popular in the Trebizond region, certainly from the tenth century onwards. An exceptionally charming example is a small church of the fifteenth century near the village of Kurt Boghan (Pl. 2, *b*). We see painted exteriors in an even more elaborate form in Russia and Roumania. Originally an Eastern feature (Mesopotamian or Persian), exterior painting reached these coun-

[1] Guyer, who has recently examined the trends and ideals of Byzantine art in detail, regards the importance which is laid upon interior decoration as one of the principal characteristics of Byzantine art. See his article, 'La rôle de l'art de la Syrie et de la Mesopotamie à l'époque byzantine', *Syria*, xiv, 1933, fasc. i, p. 58.

[2] See especially Puigh i Cadafalch, 'Decorative forms of the first Romanesque style; their diffusion by Moslem Art', in *Art Studies*, 6, 1928, p. 15. From the eleventh century onwards a number of features link up Greece and the East. See Diehl, *Manuel*, i, p. 467.

[3] *Die Baukunst der Armenier und Europa*, ii, p. 722. See also article by Alpatov in *Byzantion*, tome iv, 1929.

tries by way of the Caucasus, the region of Trebizond, and the northern shores of the Black Sea.

Certain other features of general interest may be noted. Thus open porticoes are a late characteristic, and probably point to western influence. The same is true of bell towers, since in the Orthodox East the service was announced, and is usually still announced to-day, by a rhythmical beating of a wooden bar, the simantron. A western entrance is usual, though small doors are occasionally added at the sides.

The interiors of Byzantine churches were always ornate; in early times they were as profusely decorated as the exteriors were plain. The columns were of the finest marble; piers and walls were covered below with polished slabs, above with mosaics and wall paintings; the capitals were delicately sculptured, and similar carving decorated the frame of the iconostasis or screen separating the eastern apse or holy place from the body of the church. In early times these screens were of stone; later, about the twelfth century, carved woodwork was more generally employed. On the iconostasis portable icons, panel paintings or mosaics, were fixed.[1] To the east was the altar, covered by a ciborium, or small domed canopy on four columns. In the area immediately to the west of the iconostasis was placed an ambon or pulpit of sculptured marble or wood; on either side were carved reading desks. Before the iconostasis or in appropriate niches, reliquaries, set in gorgeous frames of jewelled metal work or enamel, were preserved. Massive doors of wrought bronze or carved wood secured the entrance.

The larger orthodox churches of to-day in Greece or the Balkans retain something of the gorgeousness, as we see in St. Luke of Stiris in Phocis or in the monasteries of Mount Athos. But to-day ornateness has usually supplanted the real

[1] The profusion of icons which we see in Russia or in modern Greece was never attempted in Byzantine times; a few, portraying the Christ, the Virgin, or a patron Saint, would have been the only ones on a large scale.

glory, and it must be left to ourselves to recreate in our imaginations the dignity, the grandeur, and the charm of the Byzantine age. The architectural structure served not so much to house the treasures and mosaics as to envelop them like some superb garment. The beauty of the one enhanced the beauty of the other; separate, their perfection was none the less apparent, though it was less overwhelming at first sight.

BIBLIOGRAPHY

Résumés of the subject are given in various architectural histories, such as that of Jackson, *Byzantine and Romanesque Architecture*, Cambridge, 1913. But more useful and complete is the first chapter of Dalton's *East Christian Art*. For a summary of Strzygowski's researches see his *Origin of Christian Church Art*, 1923; for Rivoira's views see his *Lombardic Architecture*, 2nd edn., Oxford, 1933, and his *Moslem Architecture*, Oxford, 1918. For the question of origin of the pendentive and dome over square see Creswell, *Early Muslim Architecture*, 1932. The various detailed studies of regions or types are noted in the manuals, but three may be especially noted, namely van Millingen, *The Churches of Constantinople*; Lethaby and Swainson, *Santa Sophia*; and G. Millet, *L'École grecque dans l'architecture byzantine*. The most recent and complete survey is that of J. A. Hamilton, *Byzantine Architecture and Decoration*, London, 1934.

Chapter II

BYZANTINE MOSAICS

A. WALL MOSAICS

Introductory. The term mosaic is not a very satisfactory one, for it makes no distinction between the floor decoration composed of large cubes of coloured stones or marbles and the far more delicate work on walls, where tesserae of glass, paste, or some precious material such as mother of pearl, play the principal part. In this chapter we are concerned only with the second and more elaborate type, for though figure subjects appeared in floor mosaics of Greece, Rome, and the Hellenistic world,[1] they were extremely rare in Byzantine art. Mosaic floors were here in a different technique, known as opus sectile or opus Alexandrinum; they were geometrical in character, with animals or birds in small compartments sometimes added. In pre-Christian times mosaics were essentially a floor decoration, and their first transplantation to a position on the walls took place in the first and second centuries, when we find small niches at Pompeii adorned with glass mosaics, while soon after whole roofs were covered in this manner. The decoration of walls follows, the idea being arrived at, according to Strzygowski, in an attempt to imitate wall hangings. But painted walls or friezes of glazed bricks or mother of pearl inlay appear at such an early date in Mesopotamia, Crete, and Egypt, and the idea is such a natural one, that this rather strained explanation hardly seems necessary to account for an evolution which is in every way obvious.

Early in the Christian era a rapid elaboration took place, and numerous roof and wall mosaics of large proportions are already to be found in the Roman and early Byzantine art

[1] The important floor mosaics recently discovered at Jerash in Transjordania show buildings and other elaborate compositions.

of the third and following centuries. By the fifth century they have become general, and they remain so in Byzantine lands until the Empire becomes impoverished and patrons are no longer able to sustain the immense expense of furnishing a mosaic decoration for a whole building. Wall paintings then take their place, though portable mosaics of small dimensions, composed of minute cubes set in wax, were apparently fairly common as late as the thirteenth and fourteenth centuries (see p. 85). Throughout this long period mosaics are of primary importance and it is to them, and at a later date to painting, that the highest place must be assigned in a study of Byzantine art, just as it is to sculpture in Greece and to panel painting in Renaissance Italy that the student turns when in search of the characteristic and most accomplished art.

We have already stressed the fundamentally religious character of Byzantine art, and we have shown that its greatest achievement in architecture was the development of a plan suited above anything else to the demands of the Christian religion. We have shown also that the decoration of these buildings was concentrated within, and that the outside was left comparatively plain, in opposition to the practice universal in classical Greece. In the concentration of the decoration within the building and in its elaboration the idea at the back of the artist's mind was, however, twofold. First, he thought to glorify God by beautifying His house and by dedicating to Him the most sumptuous offering in his power. Secondly, his purpose was dogmatic. He had to instruct those who were illiterate or who were not sufficiently well equipped to understand the purpose of the ritual, by placing before them a series of pictures which would make clear to them the story of the Bible without the necessity of reading, and which would enable them to follow the ritual of the actual service with their eyes as well as with their ears. The first full series of such doctrinal mosaics appears in the church of the Holy Apostles, built at Constantinople between 536 and 546, and there the whole of our Lord's life could be followed scene by scene on the walls.

In addition to the intention of teaching and assisting the illiterate we can trace also a certain desire to overawe the spectator by an inconceivable splendour which would, when combined with the impression of the singing and the chanting as well as with the grandeur of the priests and vestments, leave him spellbound and astounded. And we see this desire fully rewarded in the tenth century, when Russian envoys sent to Constantinople by Vladimir were so impressed by the service at St. Sophia that they persuaded their sovereign to adopt Orthodox Christianity as the religion of their State. The interiors of the churches were thus covered entirely with mosaics or with paintings portraying saints, illustrating particular scenes from the Bible or decorating with ornamental designs surfaces which would otherwise have been left plain, such as the under side of an arch or the embrasure of a doorway.

In addition it may be noted that in developing the dome and vault as an essential feature of their architecture, the Byzantines aided the popularity of mosaic decoration more than they probably actually realized, for mosaics are best suited to a curved surface and to a building of complicated plan where the shining cubes take on and reflect the light in a far more effective manner than can ever be achieved on a flat ground or in a building such as the nave of a basilica, where the light is evenly distributed. At a later date when the rules of decoration became set, certain figures and certain scenes became identified almost as much with the shape of the area they covered as with their position according to the sequence of events in the Bible, and we thus usually find the four evangelists on the four pendentives of the dome, the Pantocrator in the dome itself, and the Saviour, and later the Virgin, in the eastern apse. Strzygowski has even made a summary classification of mosaics according to the shape and position of the area which they decorate,[1] and, though such a classification is not to be entirely relied on, the fact is important when considered with regard to the development of a fixed system of arrangement and a conservative iconography.

Of secular mosaics we know little, for practically all the monuments of this nature have been destroyed, but they were in composition, if not in actual subject, closely akin to the religious ones and their development followed the same lines. If we judge of them from contemporary secular ivories, it would appear that the Hellenistic element was usually uppermost; yet the only secular mosaic that survives, in the palace at Palermo in Sicily, is essentially eastern. We must hence conclude that, just as in the other arts, three main channels of influence are to be discerned, the Hellenistic, the Syrian or realist, and the eastern or formalist. It is even possible to distinguish and separate these one from the other at quite a late date, their influence having been conveyed principally by means of early manuscripts, which were copied in certain instances at a time when a complete fusion of elements had already taken place in other monuments.

Of these three elements the two of greatest importance in a study of Byzantine mosaics are the Hellenistic and the Semitic or Syrian. The one is refined, balanced, premeditated, and idealistic; it achieves its effect by means of shading and delicate gradation; it knows true perspective; it is romantic, in that it looks upon Christ as the carpenter's son and depicts Him as a youthful figure of 'antique' character, suggestive of one of the heroes of Greek mythology. The other strain is forceful and assertive, vivid in its colouring and realist in its conception; it represents figures frontally, and it achieves its effect by sudden contrasts, often amounting almost to ferocity; it places the chief importance upon inner meaning, yet

[1] See his *Origin of Christian Church Art*, p. 133.

seeks to some extent to impress, looking on Christ as an all-powerful king and depicting Him as an awesome, bearded figure, suggestive almost of one of those majestic gods of Semitic character of early Persia or Assyria. Linked with this tradition we find that of false perspective, where the figures in the distance or those of principal importance are enlarged, or that of vertical projection, where figures in the second rank are placed on an eminence which is either shown or imagined. These two trends are continually at variance, yet continually mingling one with the other, and we can trace them until the very end of Byzantine art. But in the greatest masterpieces of Byzantine mosaic something of the best is culled from each, and the two diverse elements are blended, thanks to the Byzantine genius, to form a delicate, subtle, yet forceful whole, which could never have been achieved had only one of the influences been at work.

These are the two main trends; but a third must also be noted, namely the eastern or non-representational, the influence of which Strzygowski sees not only in such a decoration as that in the apse of a small church in the oasis of Khargeh in Egypt, where eight-pointed stars connect octagons to form a repeat pattern over the whole apse, but also in the mosaics of Santa Constanza (Pl. 3, *a*) or San Clemente at Rome, where the work is fundamentally non-representational in conception. In the Roman examples it is hard to see any influence which it is impossible to attribute to the antique tradition, even if the assumption of an eastern origin be more tempting. Eastern traits are exemplified in these early mosaics, according to Strzygowski not only in such purely non-representational compositions, but also in others where landscape is stressed in opposition to figures, and where we see a complicated symbolism consisting of clouds and water, the earth, the phoenix, sheep in a flowered landscape or similar abstract subjects. A good example is offered by the apse in SS. Cosmo and Damian at Rome, where clouds and water form the background and sheep appear below (Pl. 4, *b*). These motives are, for him, to be attributed to Mazdaean influence, and though a contact with Persia can be certainly established as late as the fifth or sixth centuries, an eastern influence coming by way of early Christianity and the catacombs seems the more probable. But we would hardly go as far as Strzygowski and assert that all the earlier mosaics of Rome are of this character and that the Mazdaean symbolism was gradually superseded by religious representation. That symbolism is in general of eastern origin is, however, certain, and a somewhat different symbolism which characterizes the iconoclast age, where we see the cross forming the principal decoration of the church, is again to be attributed to the influence of the non-representational art of the East, helped on now not by the secret nature forced on Christianity by oppression, but by the anti-representational feeling behind the iconoclast faith.

Before passing on to a consideration of the monuments, it will be well to note three distinct methods of depicting scenes which can be reconciled to some extent with the three groups which we have just distinguished, though two or even three of these methods may often be found together in one monument. They are the selective, the continuous, and the complementary. In the first one part of the event only is shown; it is selected because of its particular importance. This system is associated essentially with the Hellenistic influence in Byzantine art. In the second method all the scenes of a certain event are shown in succession before a continuous background, forming as it were a panorama. This system is obviously derived from the illustrated roll (rotulus); it was common in Roman and Hellenistic art and from there descended to the Byzantine. Wickhoff assigns its origin to Rome, but the recent discoveries in a synagogue at Dura show that this method was well known in Syria in the early third century, and the eastern Mediterranean seems a more likely place of origin. The third system is essentially Asiatic and may be considered with the Semitic or Syrian trend in art. Here we find a number of subsidiary scenes shown around and as a border to the main one, as for instance in the Nativity at Kahrieh Djami, Constantinople, where the annunciation of the glad tidings to the shepherds can be seen above the main scene, to the right (Pl. 11, *a*).

In studying the mosaics of the Byzantine world two periods of primary importance have hitherto been distinguished, the first from the fourth to the seventh centuries, the second from the ninth century to the thirteenth; the two are separated by the iconoclast age. But recent research suggests that this intermediary period was by no means as barren as has hitherto been supposed. Records speak with fervour of the mosaics which were executed in the royal palace at Constantinople, and the superb work done for the caliph Walid at Damascus (*c.* 715) must for ever stand as the example *par excellence* of iconoclast art, although it was executed for a Moslem ruler before the commencement of the actual iconoclast period. It must have been the work of a Byzantine designer, and in part also that of Byzantine craftsmen, and it alone justifies us in classing the eighth and ninth centuries as a third great period (Pl. 6, *b*). To these may be added a fourth and last age, boasting but one major example in mosaic, Kahrieh Djami at Constantinople. But there is a vast material in the realm of wall painting and, as the exploration of churches goes on, more mosaics which are now hidden beneath plaster may well be disclosed.

In the first age Rome, Ravenna, and Salonica are the principal areas that concern us; in the second Syria is the most important; in the third the Greek mainland, the region of Constantinople, the north of Italy, and Sicily harbour the most material. For the fourth it is Constantinople alone that concerns us. It will be well to examine briefly the more important monuments in chronological order, noting as we proceed the features which are characteristic of each period.

FIRST PERIOD. IV–VII CENTURIES

In Italy this group falls aptly into two divisions, the one where classical feeling is uppermost, the other where the Byzantine style has been definitely imposed. Between the two are naturally a number of intermediary examples. In Rome there are four churches which contain decorations of major importance; the first three are chiefly in the antique style. Of these Sta Constanza (324–6), a rotunda surrounded by a ring, was once probably the most elaborate. The mosaics which adorned the dome are no longer to be seen, but we know of them from drawings and descriptions. They showed scenes from the Bible—principally from the Old Testament—which were bounded by a river. In this Strzygowski sees Mazdaean influence, and eastern traits are certainly apparent, though they probably arrived in a very roundabout manner. The ring vault is divided into twelve compartments, the opposites having identical designs, so that there are six distinct and elaborate compositions of continuous floral motives with figures interspersed (Pl. 3, *a*). They are in a purely Pompeiian style and, though in the main non-representational, can hardly be regarded as eastern. The technique is finished and accomplished and the design competent, but though the work belongs to the Christian period, there is nothing in it that can be called Byzantine. Characteristic of the early date is the white background; later we see blue and later still gold invariably employed.

The apse mosaic at Sta Pudenziana (fourth century)[1] shows our Lord enthroned between the Apostles Peter and Paul, who each head a group of five apostles. Behind them

[1] The date is disputed by the authorities, some saying 384–98, others 402–17. See Dalton, *B.A. and A.*, p. 336.

is an elaborate architectural composition which undoubtedly follows a manuscript model; it is an example of what we have called the continuous system, and we must bear it in mind, for a similar model must have served for the mosaics in St. George at Salonica and for the far more elaborate composition at Damascus.

In Sta Maria Maggiore the mosaics are of two main periods. The earliest, those in the nave, date from between 352 and 366. They show Old Testament scenes. The backgrounds are in the light colour characteristic of early work and the mosaics are definitely inspired by the antique, showing no oriental influence. We see in them in fact an attempt to preserve the Pompeiian impressionistic style in a new medium. The technique is somewhat crude, and, though they have been admired as the most perfect example of Christian classic art,[1] they are not entirely satisfactory as a church decoration; they prove in fact that Christian and classical art were essentially at variance, and that the former could not develop from the decadence of the latter without a very strong and fresh inspiration from without. More pleasing are the mosaics of the triumphal arch of 432–40, which show scenes from the New Testament (Pl. 4, *a*). Here the classical element has been to a great extent superseded, and we see in the competence of the work and in the inner content of the subject the birth of a new style which heralds the really great work of a future date. The apse mosaic, of the fourth or fifth century, was very severely restored in 1295; the original was apparently non-representational in character, as is the untouched portion of it at the sides to-day. Strzygowski sees here Mazdaean symbolism, and the eastern non-representational influence can hardly be questioned, though, as in the case of Sta Constanza, it probably came by way of a

[1] See Richter and Taylor, *The Golden Age of Christian Classic Art*, a large monograph on this church with a number of coloured plates. They suggest that the mosaics are perhaps even earlier in date.

very devious route. A similar symbolic and non-representational scene is preserved in the apse of S. Clemente; it is dated to 1299, but must follow a fifth-century original very exactly.

With the apse mosaics of SS. Cosmo and Damian (526–30) we find the Byzantine style firmly imposed, though the antique tradition lingers. The Christ is bearded; the costumes are treated in the Byzantine linear manner, and the faces show that elongation which was later to become characteristic, first of Byzantine art and then of the paintings of El Greco (Pl. 4, *b*). In St. Lorenzo-without-the-walls (578–80) we see the Byzantine style even more firmly established, but the artist did not properly assimilate the Byzantine feeling, for the result is wooden and rigid and lacks Byzantine dignity and delicacy.[1]

Ravenna. At Ravenna we see the same gradual intrusion of Byzantine influence, and it was indeed by way of Ravenna that this influence came to Rome. Whence it came is a point

[1] Other mosaics in Rome of less outstanding importance may be noted briefly. The apse of the small chapel of SS. Rufinus and Secundus in the Lateran executed in the fourth century bears a formalistic acanthus composition, comparable to that of Sta Maria Maggiore. Similar motives appear in stucco work of an earlier date. St. Sabina was formerly elaborately decorated—an inscription of the fifth century is all that remains to-day. The elaborate fifth-century decoration of St. Paul-without-the-walls was destroyed by the fire of 1823, but the mosaics were restored to represent the original scheme as closely as possible. In the Lateran Baptistry (640–2) a few small compositions of earlier date survive though the main mosaics are of the seventh century. In the apse of St. Agnese-without-the-walls (625–38) the patron saint of the church takes the place of precedence at the centre of the apse. The work is oriental in character. Mosaics in S. Teodoro are to be dated *c.* 550. Of the seventh century or later is the figure of Christ in St. Peter's. Of the seventh century are two saints and a cross in the apse of S. Stefano Rotondo. Mosaics in Sta Maria in Cosmedin are dated between 705 and 707; in Sta Maria in Domnica and in S. Praxede between 817 and 824, and in S. Marco between 827 and 844. Other mosaics of pre-twelfth century date survive in S. Pietro-in-Vincoli and the oratory of John VII and the Triclinium of the Lateran. Later mosaics such as those in Sta Maria in Trastevere, dated 1145, though Byzantine in style and iconography, cannot be considered here.

which is more disputed, Wulff maintaining that all the eastern influence came by way of Constantinople, others thinking that much of it travelled direct from Syria. Though direct Syrian influence is in some cases hardly to be denied, the formative role played by Constantinople has already been stressed and it is to that city that the principal influence is to be assigned.

The mosaics of Ravenna are to be divided into three distinct periods, that of Galla Placidia (388–450), that of Theodoric (493–526), and that of Justinian (527–65). The most striking monument of the first age is the mausoleum of Galla Placidia (*c.* 450), a small cruciform building, containing a rich decoration on a brilliant, deep-blue ground which achieves quite a different effect to the light grounds of earlier date. It is one of the most complete and most thoroughly successful mosaic decorations of early times. Figures and ornamental compositions alternate one with the other. Strzygowski sees here the Mazdaean landscape; Van Marle states categorically that there is no eastern influence; and he is probably right in so far as contemporary eastern influence is concerned. But how much of those ornamental scenes which we see so often in Roman and Hellenistic art is to be attributed to eastern influence culled in the Hellenistic and not in the Byzantine period is a wider and more complicated question which art historians are still debating and which it is impossible to answer here.

To the same period belong the dome mosaics of the Baptistry of the Orthodox, S. Giovanni in Fonte (425–30), with the Apostles above, architectural compositions below, and the baptism at the centre of the dome. The architectural compositions are important, for they show the influence of Hellenistic or Pompeiian models which are paralleled in St. George at Salonica and later at Damascus. There is little definite Byzantine influence, though certain minor features, such as the apostles' crowns, are eastern. Strzygowski sees an

Iranian element in the foliate candelabra designs for the origin of which we must look to Sasanian Persia, and for the development to Christian Syria.[1]

To the second age belong the Arian Baptistry, Sta Maria in Cosmedin (*c.* 520), where traces of Byzantine influence appear, though the work is not of a very high quality, and the scriptural scenes along the nave walls of S. Apollinare Nuovo (520–30). The other mosaics here are probably slightly later, and we see in them the definite meeting of the two main currents. The women at the well are essentially antique; the bearded or Byzantine type of Christ appears, however, in the Judgement scene, and He is larger than the other figures, and takes on the character of the oriental king, not of the youthful pagan hero.

In the third period eastern influence is firmly established, and S. Vitale (526–47) is a purely Byzantine—no longer an antique—Christian church in architecture and sculpture. In the mosaics, however, the fusion is not quite complete, for the Christ in the apse is beardless, the court scenes on either side are still rather Roman, and certain elements such as the profuse jewelling are eastern (Pl. 3, *b*). The angels at the table of Abraham are again Roman figures, though the colouring, composition, and feeling are Byzantine.

The apse mosaics of S. Apollinare in Classe (535–49) show a symbolic representation of the Transfiguration, the large cross which occupies the central position representing the Transfigured Christ. This symbolism is essentially Semitic in character, and we see it coming in again with the iconoclast period. It probably came to Italy from Syria with Christianity, for it is to be observed in the catacombs at a very early date. Other mosaics in the church, which belong to the time of Bishop Repartus (672–7), show the decline of

[1] They appear, for instance, as the result of Syrian elaboration in the Bethlehem mosaic and in those of the Dome of the Rock at Jerusalem (691–2).

the art at Ravenna, for with the seventh century this city cedes its importance to Rome.[1]

Elsewhere in Italy there are interesting mosaics in the Baptistry of Soter at Naples (470–90), where portions of large profusely decorated scenes in the antique tradition are preserved. The work was probably due to local artists, as it is much more primitive than what we see farther to the north, as for instance at Parenzo (530–5). Here there are mosaics in the apse which some authorities regard as the finest in Italy. Though the Christ is beardless, marked eastern influence is apparent in other respects. This is the first instance of the Virgin occupying the principal position in the eastern apse.[2]

We have throughout this sketch of the mosaics of Italy called attention to the gradual intrusion of eastern features, such as the bearded Christ. They are features which are to be observed primarily in iconography, and they are to be traced back finally to Syria, whether they come directly from there or indirectly by way of Constantinople. But in addition

[1] Other mosaics in the city, of secondary importance, may be briefly noted. In the chapel of Tutti Santi a fragment shows the head of Justinian; the Archiepiscopal chapel is richly decorated, but the work has been much restored; the apse mosaic of St. Michael 'ad Frigiselo' (545) is now in the Kaiser Friedrich Museum at Berlin. The style is oriental, but the Christ is beardless, and the work may be attributed to an artist who sought to copy eastern work, but had not properly assimilated the feeling.

[2] Other work in Italy of this age may be noted. In the cathedral at Naples is a mosaic dated to 575, akin to that of the Transfiguration at Sinai (see p. 76, n. 1). Other work in Naples and the south of Italy has been recorded but has disappeared; architectural compositions like those in St. George at Salonica were apparently shown. At Milan the chapel of S. Aquilino, in the church of S. Lorenzo (*c.* 500), contains an apse mosaic showing Christ and the apostles in the antique manner. Oriental influence is to be seen in the fifth-century mosaics of San Vittore in Ciel d'Oro, close to S. Ambrogio in the same town. The basilica of Casaranello contains non-representational work of the fifth century, as does the chapel of Sta Matrona at San Prisco, Capua, of the same date. A bearded Christ also appears here.

to the concrete variations which are to be observed, a change of a more subtle character is also taking place; it is an entire change of style and of feeling, and it is to be attributed not to Syria, but to the new centre and focus of the civilized world, Constantinople; it is due not only to a fusion of diverse elements, but also to the birth of a new ideal and a new culture, the Byzantine. It is possible to calculate to some extent the degree to which culture and the whole outlook of life were altering in Constantinople and in the new Byzantine world by the study of all contemporary art, and it is clearly illustrated in the mosaics of Italy. But in the capital itself, unless surprising discoveries are made, we shall never be able to appreciate it to the full on the evidence of mosaics alone, since so little has survived. The work of cleaning the mosaics which has recently been begun in St. Sophia has indeed disclosed work of sixth-century date which belongs to the original decoration of the church, but of this only crosses and decorative compositions have up to now appeared. The great lunette in the narthex, showing the seated Christ with an emperor at His feet, is associated by Whittemore, who was responsible for bringing it to light, with Leo VI (886–912). And, as far as can be judged from reproductions of other mosaics in the building published when they were laid bare at a period of repair in 1849, there are no further large compositions which are earlier than the eighth century.[1]

After Constantinople the most important centre of Byzantine culture was Salonica, where more examples of the mosaic art have been spared to us than at the capital. A glance at the monuments shows that work here was technically superior to any that was done in Italy. The tesserae were more carefully graded and more cunningly set; the colours were more subtly blended, and careful attention was paid to shading.

[1] See Diehl, *Manuel*, i, p. 162, and ii, p. 505. For the recently uncovered work see Whittemore, *The Mosaics of St. Sophia at Istanbul*, Byzantine Institute publication, 1933.

Moreover, the designs from which the mosaicists worked were more forceful and more masterly.

The earliest work at Salonica is probably that recently discovered in the church of Hosios David, where the dream of Ezekiel is shown (Pl. 6, *a*). It is in the antique style, with beardless Christ, and is to be dated to the fifth, perhaps even to the fourth century.[1] In the Hellenistic manner again are the architectural compositions of the early fifth century in the drum of the rotunda of St. George, the fantastic buildings there being related not only to those which we see in Pompeiian frescoes, but also to large panorama-like compositions which were apparently in vogue in Syria and Alexandria, and which served as models for the Damascus mosaics.

Of much better quality, and of a more Byzantine character, are the mosaics of St. Demetrius, of the fifth and following centuries. Most famous is the portrait of St. Demetrius and the donors on the south pier of the apse, of the seventh century (Pl. 5). Similar compositions balance it on the other piers, and further panels lie hid beneath buttresses of later date which support the eastern faces of these piers. This work is probably the most accomplished of the earlier age, and we see the Hellenistic and Syrian traditions fused to form a style of the greatest beauty, executed in the most finished technique. Fine compositions which adorned the side aisles were entirely destroyed in the fire of 1917. This work was of the sixth and seventh centuries, small panels having been erected by a number of different donors.

No less fine, but of a more limited, purely decorative character are the mosaics which survive below the arches which separate the aisles of the great fifth-century basilica, Hagia Paraskevi (Eski Djuma). Charming floral compositions,

[1] For a summary note see Diehl and Morey in *Byzantion*, tome vii, fasc. 2, 1932. A full publication in modern Greek by Xyngopoulos appeared in *'Αρχαιολογικὸν Δελτίον*, 1929, p. 142.

wherein birds and animals are included, constitute the motives.[1]

II. THE ICONOCLAST PERIOD

It has been suggested that this age was not only a barren one, but that it also marked a definite separation between the fully fledged Byzantine of the ninth and following centuries and the age of formation which we have hitherto been discussing. But neither of these assertions can be entirely accepted. The separation is by no means a marked one; the fact that the Cyprus mosaics at Chiti and in the Panaghia Kanakaria have been dated with the aid of convincing evidence both to the sixth and to the ninth centuries is proof of this. And the barrenness of the age can no longer be accepted now that we know more intimately the superb, yet entirely non-representational decorations of the Dome of the Rock at Jerusalem (691–2) and of the Omayyad mosque at Damascus (715). These must, on stylistic grounds, be classed as monuments of iconoclast art, though they are actually to be dated before the commencement of the iconoclast period. And though Syrian workmen were employed, the Byzantine character of the work is not to be doubted.[2] At the Dome of the Rock we see formal decorative work, in

[1] Other mosaics of this age are in the monastery of St. Catherine on Mount Sinai, where the Transfiguration is shown in the apse. This little known monument, due to Justinian, is probably of considerable importance. Certain authorities have assigned two mosaics in Cyprus to the pre-iconoclast period, though they have been assigned by others to the ninth century. The more important, in the apse of the church at Chiti near Larnaca, shows the Virgin and Child between archangels. Both here and in the other mosaic in the Panaghia Kanakaria the work is fine, the technique careful, and the composition balanced. But the style is different from that of Salonica or the West, and we seem to be dealing with the product of a Syrian or Alexandrine workshop. See Wulff, *Koimesiskirche in Nicaia*, p. 200, and Dalton, *B.A. and A.*, p. 384. Traces of another mosaic survive in a small church in the Karpass, but none of the figures are preserved.

[2] The Syrian case has been ably put by Mlle Van Berchem in Creswell, *Early Muslim Architecture*. See also de Lorey, *Mon. Piot*, xxx, 1930.

which Persian and Hellenistic influences are curiously combined; no figure subjects, nor even any representational ones, are present. At Damascus we see, in addition to work akin to that in the Dome of the Rock, a number of huge scenic compositions of a fantastic character. Colonnades, basilicas, towers, balconies, niches rise up, one poised above the other, in intricate but admirably balanced confusion. Vine plants twist round the columns; a roof which appears almost Chinese tops a classical rotunda; trees spring as it were from windowed terraces; at the summit of all stands an Hellenistic temple. Elaborate shading in darker tones serves to accentuate the fantasy, yet to give it balance; huge trees looming up from behind the buildings suggest infinite possibilities of exploration, call up delightful visions of mossy terraces, springs, and fountains (Pl. 6, *b*). Hellenistic and eastern art are here as subtly combined as in any other mosaic or painting of the Christian east.[1]

To the iconoclast period elsewhere are to be assigned certain non-representational decorations in churches, such as the cross in the apse of St. Irene at Constantinople and a similar cross, which was later replaced by a figure of the Virgin, in the apse of St. Sophia at Salonica. To-day the Virgin is bordered by monograms of Constantine VI (780–97) and the Empress Irene and the name of Bishop Theophilus who was at Nicaea in 787. In view of the fact that these belong to the middle of the iconoclast age, it seems likely that the monograms are to be associated with the original cross

[1] Similar though less elaborate mosaics existed in the church of the Nativity at Bethlehem, but most of the work to be seen there now is later (1169). The eight-century work of the Omayyad mosque was copied at Damascus in the tomb of Baybars in the twelfth century. Remains of important mosaics of the fifth and sixth centuries have recently been unearthed at Jerash; as far as can be judged from fragments of wall mosaics and from more complete examples which adorned the floors of churches there, buildings and trees formed an important part of the decoration. See Crowfoot, *Churches at Jerash*, British School of Arch. at Jerusalem, Suppl. Papers III, 1931, p. 41.

and not with the later addition, the Virgin.[1] Wulff suggests that there was formerly a similar cross in the apse of the church of the Assumption at Nicaea.

III. THE NINTH TO THE TWELFTH CENTURIES

The post-iconoclast age is in many ways the most rich in mosaics, and it is in any case the most truly Byzantine. It embraces a very wide field, for Russia and Sicily were, during part of the period, within the Byzantine sphere, not to mention western Asia, Greece, and the Balkans. Work is now characterized by a sublime grandeur. We see awesome figures dominating dim interiors; we see an etherial elongation of the individual figure; we see the inclusion of a number of delightful balanced scenes in which the principal events of the Bible—most generally of the New Testament—are set forth. Their titles accompany the scenes, their names the figures, in Greek characters, and the lettering forms an integral part of the composition. The backgrounds are invariably gold, the colours sombre, yet brilliant. We have to deal with an art which is above all religious in character, which aims at illustrating the Bible story, and which avoids the affairs of this world in the sanctity of its dim interiors.

Certain monuments appear to have been erected immediately after the lifting of the iconoclast ban. Such are the mosaics of St. Sophia at Salonica, notably the Virgin in the apse and the Ascension in the dome,[2] or again those at the east end of the church of the Assumption at Nicaea, which were unfortunately destroyed during the War (Pl. 8, *b*).[3] Both

[1] Diehl, however, dates the Virgin to the eighth century, *Manuel*, i, p. 371.

[2] The date of the dome mosaics is disputed. Ainalov assigns them to the ninth century, Muratov to the tenth, and Diehl in part to the seventh and in part to the eleventh. Ainalov's suggestion is the most probable.

[3] Mosaics in the narthex of this church probably belonged to the period 1025–8. The importance of colouring in the study of these is noted by Wulff, *Koimesiskirche*, p. 308. To the same date belong a number of

here and at Salonica a figure of the Virgin seems to have been erected to replace the cross of iconoclast times.

Few surviving examples are to be assigned to the tenth century, but in the eleventh and twelfth we have more monuments, and though the two main influences which we distinguished in the first period, the Hellenistic and the Syrian, are by now subtly blended, it is nevertheless possible to distinguish two distinct currents in art. One of these is associated essentially with Constantinople; it is delicate and refined in character, and is suited to the demands of a highly civilized court. The other is seen in its most characteristic form in the monastic chapels of Cappadocia; it is forceful and dogmatic, often preoccupied with obscure scenes, and is the obvious result of an ascetic, essentially coarse, monastic life. In mosaics the full monastic style is never completely to the fore, since something of the elegance of the capital always penetrates this art. Yet the most monastic influence is sometimes to be traced and we see it in the decoration of the two churches of the monastery of St. Luke of Stiris in Phocis. A particularly complete cycle of the early eleventh century is preserved here.[1] The mosaics of Daphni, near Athens,

rather second-class mosaics in Rome, one of the best of which is that showing Christ between SS. Peter and Paul in the Vatican, which was probably executed by Byzantine workmen in 983 (see Schlumberger, *Epopée Byzantine*, i, p. 529). Probably of the ninth century, though van Marle assigns it to the twelfth, is the apse decoration of S. Ambrogio at Milan, an Italian imitation of a Byzantine monument. Other mosaics of secondary importance at Rome are those at SS. Nereus and Achilles in Domnica (817), St. Cecilia (*c.* 882), and St. Mark's (827–43). Though they show Byzantine influence to a greater or lesser degree, they can hardly be counted as Byzantine monuments. Of the same character are the mosaics of St. Germigny-des-Près in France.

[1] For dating of these and other eleventh- and twelfth-century mosaics see Diez and Demus, *Byzantine Mosaics in Greece*. Related to the St. Luke mosaics and of the same monastic character are those in the Nea Moni on Chios (1042–56) and in the dome of St. Sophia at Salonica. The mosaics of St. Sophia at Kiev (1037) are again related, but they are to some extent Slav in character. Remains of other mosaics of this period also exist in Kiev (1037–54).

on the other hand, of the later eleventh century, are more typically Constantinopolitan. They have suffered severely and, though somewhat over restored, they still constitute what is perhaps the most perfect monument of the age, for we see blended here in the most subtle manner possible the idealistic and the realistic, the romantic and the forceful. The picture of Christ Pantocrator which dominates the church from the dome is one of the most alluring and one of the finest conceptions of the Christ for which Christian art has been responsible (Pl. 7, *a*).

In Italy Venice was the most important centre of the mosaic art at this period. In spite of the fact that tesserae were undoubtedly made there from the ninth century onwards, Van Marle holds that none of the surviving work in St. Mark's is earlier than the twelfth century. Diehl, Millet, and others, on the contrary, assign certain compositions there, most notably the Ascension in the central dome and scenes illustrating seven episodes from the life of the Virgin in the north aisle, to the eleventh. Comparative material in Greece supports the eleventh-century dating, and it is safe to conclude that, from this time on, additions were made to the decoration at every period and in every style until the fifteenth century.[1]

Some very good work survives in the neighbourhood of Venice. At Murano there is a fine figure of the Virgin in the apse, which is to be dated to the twelfth century. At Torcello there are mosaics of three periods. The apostles in the apse belong to the eleventh century; the Virgin in the apse and the Last Judgement at the west end belong to the latter half of the twelfth; mosaics in the southern side apse, due to a hand working in the first period in the Ravennate or Adriatic manner, were much restored in the thirteenth century. Of all this the twelfth-century work in the apse is the best, the

[1] For a summary of the dating of mosaics in St. Mark's see Muratov, *La Peinture Byzantine*, p. 104.

Virgin and Child creating a supremely grand effect in their isolation before a plain gold background, unadorned by any subsidiary decoration (Pl. 9, *a*).[1]

Some of the richest work of the whole eleventh and twelfth centuries is to be seen, however, in Sicily. Of the decoration of the cathedral at Messina little survives, for it was restored in the thirteenth century and again ruined in 1908. In the apse of the church of St. Gregory in the same town mosaics of the Madonna and an archangel of the twelfth or thirteenth century are essentially Byzantine works. In the Martorana, Sta Maria dell'Ammiraglio (*c.* 1143), at Palermo, a fine Pantocrator dominates the church from the dome. The life of the Virgin is displayed on the vaulted roof, and other scenes appear on the walls, amongst them one showing the donor, the admiral George, at the feet of the Virgin (Pl. 9, *b*). The Palatine chapel in the same town (1143–60) contains a full cycle of scenes, both from the Old and the New Testaments. The work is good, but somewhat arid. At Cefalù the original mosaics of 1148 remain in the choir only. In the apse we see our Lord; below Him is the Virgin, and on the walls are saints. The work is the best in Sicily—it is also among the best of the twelfth century (Pl. 8, *a*). At Monreale (1174–82) a full decoration survives; it is Byzantine in style and appearance, but the inscriptions are in Latin, and it is obvious that decadence has already set in. The work is essentially provincial in character in opposition to that at Cefalù, which might well be assigned to Constantinople itself. The secular work which survives in a chamber of the palace and in the

[1] Some other mosaics of this age survive in Italy. Those in the cathedral of St. Just at Trieste are of the thirteenth century; those at Spoleto, in a purely Byzantine style, are dated to 1207; some of the twelfth century, formerly in S. Cipriano at Venice, are now in the Friedenskirche at Berlin. At Grottaferrata, a Greek monastery on Italian soil, mosaics of the end of the twelfth century are in the static, academic style which is typical of the west at this period. A Virgin orans and other fragments dated to 1112 are preserved in the cathedral at Ravenna.

villa of Ziza (1154–66) at Palermo is strikingly Persian in character, archers, birds, and fantastic animals being depicted, which are closely akin to those seen on Persian textiles. Much of the work which decorated the imperial palaces at Constantinople must have been of this type.[1]

In Greece the Communion of the Apostles at Serres in Macedonia is probably to be dated to the early twelfth century. Diez and Demus (op. cit., p. 116) suggest that it is to be regarded as an early manifestation of that revival in painting which is usually associated with the Palaeologue age. But it seems that works which show the new spirit of energy and vitality which characterizes this revival were executed as early as the middle of the twelfth century, and it may well be that Serres is a herald in mosaic akin to that which we see in painting at Nerez in Serbia (1164). At this period we see, in fact, a curious mingling of the old monumental and the new revival styles in contemporary monuments. Thirteenth-century mosaics showing the Christ Pantocrator and prophets in the Panaghia Paragoritissa at Arta, in Epirus, are thus in the old monumental style, whereas the Christ and twelve apostles in the dome of the Pamakaristos (Fetiyeh Djami) at Constantinople show the spirit of the revival (Pl. 7, *b*).[2]

The last age of mosaics is, apart from the few minor examples mentioned above, represented by one monument only, Kahrieh Djami at Constantinople (1310–20).[3] But this

[1] For an account of thirteenth- and fourteenth-century painting in Sicily, which follows on from the mosaics, see Lazarev, 'Early Italo-Byzantine Painting in Sicily', *Burlington Magazine*, lxiii, Dec. 1933, p. 279. He assigns the paintings of St. Gregory at Messina to the thirteenth century, whereas they have sometimes been regarded as of the eleventh.

[2] Two isolated figures (St. George and St. Demetrius) in the monastery of Xeropotamou on Athos are probably of the eleventh century; inferior work in Vatopedi on Athos must be assigned to the twelfth century. Medallions and a christological cycle in the choir of the Basilica of the Nativity of Bethlehem are dated to 1169. Mosaics recently discovered in the church of the Holy Apostles at Salonica (1312) are probably of much the same date as the building.

[3] A figure of the Pantocrator over the door of the narthex and a Deesis

monument is of the first importance, for it shows the new style of the revival in all its glory. A great change has been worked upon Byzantine art; a new lightness, a new and more human touch has come to the painter, and though none of the old ethereal sublimity is lacking, a greater energy, a fuller conception, has been born. This revival, or renaissance as it is usually called, is most familiar to us through the medium of the painter's brush, and we hence leave the fuller examination of it until the next chapter. But it would seem that Kahrieh Djami (the church of the Chora) could hardly have been the only example of this art in the mosaic technique. No novice's hand could work the marvels which we see wrought on so extensive a scale in this superb little church, which is in reality one of the most important monuments of Byzantine art. The majority of the scenes that have survived are in the inner and outer narthices; a full cycle of the life of Christ and another of the Virgin are preserved, though some of the scenes are badly battered. Among the most striking are the Nativity (Pl. 11, *a*) and the scene which shows the founder of the church, Theodore Metochites, presenting a model of it to our Lord (Pl. II, *b*). In the last few years a composition showing the Dormition of the Virgin has been discovered over the west door in the main body of the church (Pl. 10)[1] It is of the same date as the cycles, and shows the same excellent work, the same completeness of design and, above all, the same glorious colouring. This is the last extant monument of mural mosaic produced by the Byzantine civilization, and constitutes, in its excellence, an apt close to the long history which we have attempted to trace in all too summary a manner in this chapter.

(Christ, between the Virgin and St. John the Baptist) in the inner narthex belong to the year 1152.

[1] See Ebersolt in *Revue de l'Art*, 1921, tome v, p. 83 and lvi, p. 163; H. E. del Medico in *Byzantion*, tome vii, fasc. i, p. 23; and R. Byron, in the *Burlington Mag.* lxii, 1933, p. 41.

BIBLIOGRAPHY

Mosaics are fully dealt with in the manuals already referred to, namely Dalton, Diehl, Wulff, and Kauffmann. In addition may be cited Van Berchem and Cluzot, *Mosaïques chrétiennes*, Geneva, 1924, which deals chiefly with Italy, and gives a bibliography for that country. See also for Italy, Van Marle, *The Italian School of Painting*, vol. i, and Wilpert, *Die römischen Mosaiken und Malereien der kirchlichen Bauten vom iv. bis xiii. Jahrhundert*, 1917. The Damascus and Jerusalem mosaics are published in detail by Van Berchem in Creswell's *Early Muslim Architecture*. See also de Lorey, in *Monuments Piot*, vol. xxx, 1930, and in *Syria*, tome xii, 1931, fasc. 4, p. 326. Diez and Demus, *Byzantine Mosaics in Greece*, deal with Daphni, Hosios Lucas, and Nea Moni. For Salonica see Diehl, Saladin, Le Tourneau, *Les Églises de Salonique*, and also Uspenskij and Klougé, in the *Izvestiya of the Russian Archaeological Institute at Constantinople*, vol. xiv, part I. This is the fullest publication of the mosaics of St. Demetrius. For Nicaea see Wulff, *Koimesiskirche*, 1903. For Kahrieh Djami, see Schmidt, *Izvestiya of the Russian Institute at Constantinople*, vol. xi, 1906, with album of plates. Muratoff's *Peinture byzantine* is a general summary, but it must be remembered that he uses the word Byzantine principally to denote the antique tradition in Byzantine art. A small and cheap book, with useful plates, is Grabar's *Décoration byzantine*, 1928 (in series 'Architecture et Art').

B. MINIATURE MOSAICS

Miniature mosaics constitute one of the most delicate and successful of Byzantine minor arts, but so minute are the stone and glass tesserae and so fragile is the wax groundwork in which they are set, that very few examples have survived to the present day. True portable mosaics—as distinct from small-scale renderings of mural mosaics, with larger cubes set in plaster—were probably first made in the tenth or eleventh century; by the twelfth they were very popular, but even then they were considered as rare and precious.

The earliest dated examples that we know are to be assigned to the beginning of the twelfth century. One, a Madonna and Child in Sta Maria della Salute at Venice, bears an inscription on the back which attributes it to an artist named Theodosius, and to the year 1115. On the grounds of certain stylistic features, most notably the use of a single band of light-coloured tesserae to pick out the high-lights, it seems possible to group certain of the other known examples along with it, and to date them to the same period. Such early specimens are the Madonna and Child, sur-rounded by twelve saints, in the Stoclet collection in Brussels, which may even be of the eleventh century, and four examples on Mount Athos, a St. Anne and the Virgin at Vatopedi, a standing figure of Christ at Esphigmenou, a Virgin and Child at Chilandari, and a bust of St. Nicholas at Stavronikita. The St. John the Baptist in St. Mark's at Venice is probably also to be assigned to the twelfth century.

To the late thirteenth or early fourteenth century probably belong the superb Crucifixion in the Kaiser Friedrich Museum at Berlin (Pl. 12, *a*), the Transfiguration (Pl. 12, *b*) and the Ascension in the Louvre and the two panels in the Opera del Duomo at Florence, bearing the twelve feasts of the Church. The Annunciation in the Victoria and Albert Museum is to be assigned to the early fourteenth century. In these later examples we see a greater attempt at modelling, and the work is in general less severe and formal than in the twelfth century. We see, in fact, here, as in the other graphic arts, the inspiration of that revival which distinguishes the work of the Palaeologue age and sometimes also that of the late twelfth and the thirteenth centuries.

The fine Christ in the National Museum at Florence, which shows certain affinities with the mural mosaics of Sicily, is probably to be assigned to the twelfth century, while the small circular panel in the Louvre whereon St. George is represented, which is usually dated to the fourteenth century, should perhaps be assigned to the thirteenth. It shows a certain classic feeling which one would hardly expect to see in the fourteenth century.

BIBLIOGRAPHY

A list of miniature mosaics known in 1886 is given by E. Muntz, 'Les Mosaïques byzantines portatives', *Bulletin monumental*, vol. lii. Certain additions are made by Dalton, *B.A. and A.*, p. 430, and by Diehl, *Manuel*, ii, p. 563. To the examples that they cite may be added the Christ at Florence; the Crucifixion and a Christ in the Kaiser Friedrich Museum at Berlin; the Madonna and Saints in the Stoclet collection; the Ascension in the Louvre; two examples on Mount Sinai and one in the Lavra on Mount Athos in a poor condition. See Schlumberger, *Epopée*, iii, p. 521.

In addition to the works cited by Dalton, see Wulff, *Altchr. Kunst*, 1909, iii, pt. ii, Nos. 1989 and 1990, for the Berlin examples. Orsi, 'Quadretti bizantini a mosaico della Sicilia', in *Studi Bizantini*, Naples, 1924, for the Berlin Crucifixion. Vollbach, Salles, Duthuit, *L'Art byzantin*, Paris, 1933, pls. 73, 74, for the Florence diptych and p. 69 for further references. Kondakov, *Iconography of the Virgin*, ii, p. 285 (in Russian), notes the discovery of mosaic icons on Sinai. See also D. Talbot Rice, *Apollo*, Oct. 1933, for reproductions of a number of examples and for a discussion of dating.

Chapter III

BYZANTINE WALL-PAINTINGS

IN painting the same four periods may be distinguished as in the mosaic art; but here it is the last period, from the thirteenth to the sixteenth century, which is of primary importance. Some remarkably fine work of the third age from the ninth to the twelfth century has also been preserved, and, though no examples from the first two ages have survived on purely Byzantine soil, some note of early work in other areas must be made in order to understand properly the manifestations of a later age. In the Byzantine region true frescoes, that is to say decorations in which the paint is laid on the damp plaster, are hardly ever met with. We have to do with paintings in an oil or tempera medium, which were laid onto hard plaster. They must thus be termed wall-paintings; the word fresco is applicable in only a very few cases, note of which will be made as we proceed.

FIRST AND SECOND PERIODS. THIRD TO NINTH CENTURIES

Throughout this age there are three main regions that concern us, Italy, Syria, and Egypt, but the last of these is of purely local importance, as are some painted crypts of the fourth century in the 'antique' style in Bulgaria.

Italy. The earliest paintings in Italy follow the antique tradition in the main, in spite of a considerable Syrian influence in some of them, to be seen most notably in a love of symbolism and of the frontal pose. It is at this period, in fact, that an elaborate Christian symbolism is in greatest vogue, and certain creatures are universally adopted for representation, such as the fish, because the letters of its name *ἰχθύς* stand also for the phrase *'Ιησοῦς Χριστὸς θεοῦ υἱὸς Σωτήρ*, Jesus Christ, Son of God, Saviour, or the peacock, because its flesh was thought to be incorruptible. It is to this age too that we owe the creation of such essentially Christian types as the Orans, a figure in frontal pose with the arms upraised. Their popularity in later Byzantine art is considerable.

The earliest examples of these paintings come from the catacombs of Rome, most important of which are those of S. Commodilla. Work in the tomb of Turtura there (sixth century) is of a very high standard. Rather more Byzantine in style are paintings in the cemetery of Sta Generosa of the sixth century, where the names appear vertically beside each figure. This is a feature quite foreign to classical art, as is the representation of a large number of gems on costumes and head-dresses. Similar work appears in churches at this date, most notably in Sta Maria Antiqua and in the lower church of S. Clemente, where there are paintings dating from the fifth to the tenth centuries.

Van Marle (pp. 56 ff.) concludes that there were at this date in Italy, and especially in Rome, two distinct schools of painting which existed simultaneously, the one following more closely the antique tradition, the other basing itself more definitely on intrusive eastern and Byzantine elements. In the seventh century relationship between Rome and Byzantium becomes closer still in painting, but Van Marle insists that the Hellenistic or antique current did not dry up, but continued on its course uninterrupted from pre-Christian times until the days of the great masters of the thirteenth century (p. 61). That it did continue to some extent is not to be disputed; but the glory of upholding culture and of continually revivifying it over this long period is without question to be attributed to Byzantium and not to Rome.

The paintings of the seventh century, though we see in some a marked Byzantine influence, are in general more classical in feeling than are contemporary mosaics in Italy, and in one instance in Sta Maria Antiqua we find an 'antique' Annunciation superposed above a Madonna of earlier date which is more purely Byzantine in style. Van Marle's thesis of the coexistence of the two schools is thus well supported at this date; he cites a number of examples in vol. i, pp. 60 ff. Sta Maria Antiqua and S. Sabas are the most important monuments, though the catacombs were still used and we find there restorations done as late as the ninth century.

The iconoclast movement puts an end to the period of confluence of Byzantine and Roman work and we see in Italy a developing native art, but there is alongside it another progressive art due to a wave of exiles from Constantinople, driven to Italy on account of their adherence to the belief of representation in art. They established a definite colony in Rome, and the essentially Byzantine paintings in the chapel on the left of the choir in Sta Maria Antiqua are to be attributed to them. The Roman and Byzantine strains are in fact quite distinct during the eighth century and both produce good work, though it must be classed as of secondary importance. The native strain is for a time supported by anti-Byzantine social feeling, but by the ninth century the burden of the heritage of antiquity becomes too great for the feeble Italy of the period to support, and marked decline is to be observed. From now on an impoverished, almost a peasant art, is all that survives of the antique tradition. And this no longer concerns us. The Byzantine element, divorced from its root, tends also to decadence, though it is sustained to some extent by the Benedictine school of Monte Cassino, and is responsible for quite a number of not very accomplished wall-paintings during the ninth and even in later centuries. Most important of these are paintings in S. Angelo in Fomis (1056–86), where the Byzantine heritage is discernible though the work is primarily of a primitive monastic character.

But this survey has already brought us down to past the end of the second period which we noted under mosaics. Before tracing out the continuation of Italy's artistic history as far as painting is concerned, we must return to the East and to the first centuries of the Christian era.

Syria. We have had occasion to call repeated attention to the importance of the role played by the Syrian or Semitic strain in the development of Byzantine art and iconography, and we have already noted the eastern character of this role. The area to the east of the Mediterranean, owing to its ready connexion with the Red Sea and the Persian Gulf, drew the chief contents of its culture from Asia and the Orient. This it passed on after the elements had been affected by the Hellenistic culture of the region to the western Mediterranean area. Syria was in fact the great cultural entrepôt between East and West. But hitherto we have not been able to cite any large number of monuments in the sphere of painting on which to base these assumptions. It is in fact only within the last few years that any actual monuments of painting in Syria have been available. Recent research has, however, come to our aid in this respect, and there seems every possibility that our store will be further enriched within the course of the next few years.

It was indeed possible to trace the history of such definitely Syrian features as the frontal pose in other arts of the Christian age, or in tomb paintings of the pagan, like those of Palmyra. In 1918, however, a new monument, the temple of the Palmyrene Gods, dating from the year A.D. 85, was discovered at Dura on the middle Euphrates, which provided us with a prototype in painting. Here we see a number of figures standing with their faces towards the observer, engaged in a ritual scene in the temple, which is probably connected with the Mazdaean faith. Beside them are other figures, the most important of which are those of the three Palmyrene Gods; they are without doubt the prototypes of the popular warrior saints of later times, and the debt which eastern painting owes to such monuments is very considerable. Breasted remarks that with the overthrow of Zenobia (272) Christians were left a free hand in Syria. Temples of other rites were appropriated, and it is probable that many of them were adorned with paintings similar to those of A.D. 85 at Dura.[1]

Further paintings in a Christian chapel at Dura, which must be dated before A.D. 250, show the Good Shepherd bringing the lost sheep to the flock; the three Marys bringing myrrh to the tomb of our Lord; Christ walking on the water, and other miracles. This is the earliest figure of Christ that is known in Christian art. The frontal pose is universal; the names are written near the figures; the colours are bright and striking and the general effect is forcible and moving. There is a certain similarity to Roman work of the same date, and many of the features which we see common to the two must be derived from Syria, where art and culture were flourishing many years before Rome became an important cultural centre through the western spread of Greek influence.

The manner in which this art was developed in Syria in the early Christian period is shown elsewhere than in this chapel and in the temple of the Palmyrene Gods at Dura. In 1932 a further discovery of the first importance was made in the same city by the Yale University expedition. It was that of a synagogue, dated to the year 245, which was decorated throughout with paintings showing Old Testament scenes. And this was done in defiance of the Jewish dislike of depicting the human figure, in defiance of the iconoclast feelings so deeply embedded in the Semitic mind. It has just been noted that early Christian—even pagan—art in Rome owed a great deal to the East; here we see the counter-effect of Hellenistic culture on Semitic thought in Syria. The Hellenistic character is to be seen here in the animated scenes and in the elaborate buildings which form the background. They are the

[1] *Oriental Forerunners of Byzantine Painting*, p. 73. He also notes, p. 97, that the figures on the north wall at Dura display bright golden aureoles behind their heads showing that, like the deified emperors, they have already been associated with the Sun-cult. It was from such figures as these that the aureole passed over to Christian painting.

naturalistic prototypes of the more formally fantastic work which we see in the Damascus mosaics and in the architectural compositions which form the panorama-like background of Byzantine painting in the 'continuous' style (see p. 66). The figures too are mostly of a Hellenistic type, though the hand of a Persian artist can also be traced. Syrian influence is seen in the frontal pose of the figures, which is usual though not universal; in the system of vertical projection, where the figures in the background are raised as if on a hill; and in the enlarged size of the principal figures—Moses, for instance, is almost twice the size of his followers. In the centre of the wall is a niche with a single panel above it; on either side are three registers of paintings, separated by ornamental bands. Above is the cycle of Moses; in the middle that of the Ark of the Covenant. Below, to the right, is the life of Elijah; to the left that of Ezekiel. We see here, in fact, the first instance of Bible illustration; we see, on Syrian soil and in a Semitic synagogue, the first beginnings of Byzantine pictorial art, and there is no doubt that such important prototypes as these played a far greater role in its development than did ever the catacomb paintings of Rome or Alexandria, confined as they were to an antique mannerism and an obscure symbolism.[1]

Christian—and perhaps even Semitic—paintings must have been common in Syria from this time, though few examples are at present known to us. Christianity was the most popular religion until the eighth century. Churches of the seventh century at Hira, near Kufa in Mesopotamia, contained remains of an elaborate painted decoration,[2] and one fragment bore what was apparently an 'orans', though most of the work appeared to be of a decorative character. Moreover, the importance laid upon painting in Manichaean texts

[1] These synagogue paintings have not yet been fully published. For a preliminary note see *Byzantion*, viii, 1933, fasc. i, p. 375.

[2] See 'The Oxford Excavations at Hira', *Antiquity*, Oct. 1932, and also *Ars Islamica*, i 1934.

suggests that this art was widely practised in Mesopotamia and Persia at the end of the Sasanian era (late VIth and early VIIth cent.). M. Blochet's assertions that the twelfth-century Mesopotamian school of Islamic painting is entirely based upon Byzantine influence are considerably exaggerated,[1] though the presence of Byzantine traits is not to be questioned. They were conveyed both directly from contemporary or imported work, or indirectly, by way of Hellenistic elements incorporated in the art of the region at an earlier date.

The long duration of the Hellenistic style in Syria is amply shown by the paintings at Kuseir Amra (711–15), which are in the main Hellenistic in character, though we see Sasanian influence as well, most clearly exemplified in the ornamental borders.[2] The kings who were overcome by Islam are posed formally and frontally in the manner of the Dura temple paintings; naked female figures in another composition are naturalistic and purely Hellenistic.

The manifestations of Moslem painting which come as the immediate followers of the Damascus mosaics and the Kuseir Amra paintings are almost entirely unknown to us. The only examples of importance so far discovered are the ninth-century paintings of Samarra, and these, with their profuse figure decoration, seem akin in a sense to Kuseir Amra; they are the last survival of an old Hellenistic-Sasanian art which had outlived its period. Far Eastern affinities can also be traced, but they probably did not penetrate to the Byzantine art of the period.

Of Christian painting in Syria or Mesopotamia at a later date we have no examples, but the orientalized style instituted at Dura was carried on in Cappadocia and perhaps also in Armenia (see below).

[1] See his *Musulman Painting*, London, 1929.

[2] That the paintings are almost certainly of this date is shown by Creswell, *Early Muslim Architecture*, p. 262.

Egypt. The earliest paintings of Egypt that concern us are purely Hellenistic, and may be considered along with Roman work at Pompeii or at Boscoreale. The characteristic feature is an architectural landscape, which we see reproduced at a much later date in the Damascus mosaics. It has been suggested that these were derived from scenes made for the Hellenistic theatre, and Alexandria has been proposed as their original home.[1] But Pompeii with its numerous monuments furnishes a more obvious centre in which to study the development of early wall-painting.

Coptic paintings of the fourth century retain the Hellenistic manner to a great extent. Of a rather different style and of purely local importance are the fifth-century Coptic paintings, which gradually assimilate Syro-Palestinian types embodying the realism and forceful expression, the frontal pose, and the vertical projection of the Semitic strain. The paintings of Baouit are of this class; influence from Syria may well have come to the inland region by way of the old north Red Sea trade route, for the coastal area of Alexandria retains its purely Hellenistic character certainly until well on in the sixth century. In the sixth- and seventh-century Coptic work, for instance in the church of St. Jeremias at Saqqara, we see a commingling of the Syrian and the Hellenistic (Alexandrian) influences. This development is paralleled in textiles, which constitute in Egypt a far more important branch of art than do wall-paintings (see pp. 175 ff). In paintings of later date, most notably those in the monasteries of St. Anthony and St. Paul, of the thirteenth and following centuries, the Syrian style is completely dominant.

The Balkans. Few paintings of pre-eleventh-century date are known elsewhere, though decoration of certain churches in Bulgaria, most notably Perustica, suggest that quite a

[1] See E. de Lorey, 'Les Mosaïques de la Mosquée des Omayyades à Damas', *Syria*, 1931, tome xii, fasc. 4, p. 326, for a summary of this style and for further references.

considerable amount of material once existed in Macedonia. Some of it may be hidden below plaster overcoats of later date, though the greater part has probably perished. Grabar, who has studied these paintings in detail, regards them as of more than local importance, for they serve to give an idea of the Constantinopolitan art of the time. Moreover, certain elements which are typical of the art of Constantinople in the ninth and tenth centuries appear here, especially in colouring and drapery, and it is possible to trace in these Bulgarian paintings the evolution in iconography which was taking place at the capital, even if the work is itself inferior or in a different style.

THIRD PERIOD. NINTH TO TWELFTH CENTURIES

The examination which we have given to the monuments of neighbouring lands enables us to approach the paintings of the Byzantine area and of the Byzantine period proper with a secure foundation beneath our feet, since we have seen the blending of the Syrian and the Hellenistic streams at the very source. There are no monuments of this age in Constantinople itself, but five other areas concern us intimately, namely Cappadocia, Armenia, Russia, south Italy, and the Balkans. They deserve the detailed consideration of the student of Byzantine painting, yet we can do no more than summarize the more important monuments here. In addition we must call attention to Cyprus, where paintings which are dated to the twelfth century have recently been discovered.[1]

1. *Asia Minor*. The paintings of the rock-cut chapels and built churches of the Cappadocian region offer by far the widest series of monuments of the period. These chapels and churches, of which a vast quantity survive, are in the process

[1] See W. H. Buckler in *Journal of Hellenic Studies*, 1933, vol. liii, pt. i, p. 105, and in *Archaeologia*, 1934, vol. lxxxiii, p. 327. There is a continuous series of wall-paintings in the island from the twelfth to the sixteenth century, but much of the work is of a purely provincial character.

of being fully described and published by the Rev. Père Jerphanion, and it is impossible to mention the names of more than a few of the most typical here. Of the ninth century are paintings in the built church of Qaranleq, admirable examples of the crude but vigorous monastic art of the region, where we see perpetuated all the principal features which we classed as characteristic of the Semitic art of Syria at an earlier date. They are here again exemplified in a particular fondness for apocryphal scenes and in a taste for cycles, where scenes are portrayed following one another in a frieze.

More delicate and accomplished than Qaranleq are the paintings of Qeledjlar Kilisse of the mid-tenth century, where some of the finest work of the region is to be seen (Pl. 14, *a*). Paintings in the *new* church at Tokale Kilisse, of the second half of the tenth century, are in a good state of preservation, and a very full cycle survives (Pl. 13). Other monuments are to be dated between the ninth and twelfth centuries, though the most important are of the eleventh or twelfth. Another chapel at Qaranleq is thus of the second half of the eleventh, and Elmale, Gueremé, Tcharegli, and the chapel of St. Eustathius are all of the twelfth. No paintings were executed in Cappadocia after this century.

Some caves in the region of Latmos on the west coast of Asia Minor contain decorations akin to those of Cappadocia, though the standard of the work is inferior. They are dated by Wulff to the seventh or eighth centuries, and by Strzygowski to the eleventh. So conservative is the art that in the absence of actual written proof exact dating is by no means easy, but the earlier period seems on general grounds the more likely.

The influence exercised by the eastern art of Cappadocia on decoration in the Byzantine area from the tenth century onwards, more especially on certain rock-cut chapels in the Balkans and on the larger and more famous group in southern

Italy, will be considered later. It may be noted here, however, that Grabar considers that the Latmos caves exercised some effect on the development of early Bulgarian painting.

2. *Armenia.* Early paintings exist here at Thalish, Tekor, Ani,[1] and Achthamar, where a full New Testament cycle occurs. Other work probably survives which has not yet been published or recorded. The art is not native to the region; it was introduced through Syrian and Byzantine influence, though the former was from first to last preponderant. A similar style is to be seen in the manuscripts, and when more work comes to be done these will doubtless prove of great assistance for dating the wall-paintings. At present, however, the dates of the latter are not firmly established, and there is probably little that is earlier than the tenth century. Even at a later date little material is available, though a strongly marked local style seems to have been developed from the original models, which at once distinguishes Armenian work on stylistic grounds.[2] The distinction is made more obvious by the use of Armenian script in place of Greek. It is recorded that Armenian painters worked at Sohag in Egypt; but, apart from this, the role played by Armenia in the history of Byzantine painting in general was without doubt small.

3. *Russia.* From the late tenth century, when Christianity was adopted as the State religion, until the Mongolian invasion of Russia in the thirteenth century, painting was in the main in the central Byzantine or Constantinopolitan style, and Kiev, the most important centre, was in all essentials a purely Byzantine town at this period. An equally close Byzantine heritage is to be traced in the paintings of

[1] Paintings in the church of Tigrane Honentz are dated to 1215. See *L'Art byzantin chez les Slaves*, ii, fig. 24.

[2] See Rice, in G. Millet and D. Talbot Rice, *Peintures murales de la région de Trébizonde*, vol. i (forthcoming).

more northerly centres such as Pskov (St. Saviour, 1156), Vladimir (Cathedral, 1195), Staraya Ladoga (St. George, second half of XIIth cent.), and Novgorod (St. Saviour, 1195). In many cases the artists were actually Greeks, who emigrated from Constantinople and established themselves in Russia. Some of them painted in the conservative, monumental manner of the eleventh century; the work of others already shows that new spirit which is to be associated with the fourteenth-century revival of painting in Greek lands. Recent research has shown that there was also in existence in Russia before the Mongol invasion an art of less purely Byzantine character which Grabar calls the pre-Mongol.[1] The importance of this strain was considerable in early times, and its influence is to be traced throughout. But by the thirteenth century it has lost its individual character as a result of the penetrating Byzantine wave, and by the fourteenth it can no longer be distinguished as a separate element. From then on Russian art develops on its own lines, and though essentially a child of Byzantium its growth must form a separate study.[2]

4. *South Italy*. A number of rock-cut chapels and churches in this region of the tenth and following centuries survive, the decoration of which belongs to the Cappadocian family both as regards iconography and style. In the tenth century we see an art which is in general of a rude, monastic character; Greek and Latin inscriptions appear in contemporary monuments. In the twelfth century a freer style is

[1] *Problems of Restoration*, ii, Moscow, 1928, p. 102 (in Russian.) It is possible that pre-Mongol art owes its birth to an influence of the Syrian stream which penetrated by way of Cappadocia and the Caucasus. Paintings in Armenia and in the Greek monastery of Sumela near Trebizond serve as intermediary examples.

[2] Most important of the Greeks working in Russia was Theophanes the Greek; the most important of the Slav painters was Andrew Rublev. For the penetration of Greek styles in Russia see Bréhier, *L'Art byzantin*, p. 167. An excellent summary and a full bibliography of works on Russia are given in L. Réau, *L'Art russe*. The literature on the subject in Russian is considerable.

developed, especially round Brindisi, but Sta Maria delle Grazie at Carpignano, north of Otranto, contains what is probably to be classed as the best work. A further exploration and publication of the churches is in progress.[1]

5. *Greece and the Balkans.* Monuments which belong in spirit as well as in date to this middle period of Byzantine art are not numerous; most important are paintings of the eleventh century in the crypt of the church of St. Luke of Stiris in Phocis,[2] and paintings of the twelfth century in the church of Nemanja at Studenica, in Serbia.

Other work which must be included in this section as far as date is concerned is of a rather different character, for we see in it the birth of a new spirit which distinguishes it at once from the earlier monumental work, whether in a Hellenistic or in an eastern manner. It was originally supposed that this new style was not conceived until after the Latin conquest of Constantinople (1204): that the conquest constituted in fact a definite break between the old and the new styles. But recent research, more especially that of Okunev and Muratov, has brought to light certain monuments which are clear forerunners of the revival style, and which it is impossible to class with the more conservative work with which they are contemporary. Most important of them are the paintings at Nerez in Macedonia, dated to 1164, and executed under imperial patronage by an artist of Constantinople. The work is of the finest, the conception amazingly gentle, and it is marked by an essentially humanist comprehension, which lays stress on emotion and feeling and which is absent in the sublime, non-worldly, art of the middle period. The Deposition at Nerez shows this in the tender, compassionate attitude of the Virgin and other attendant

[1] See the work of Società Magna Grecia, Rome.

[2] Though they have long been visible these paintings have only recently been noticed. See Soteriou, 'Peintures murales byzantines de l'XIe siècle dans la crypte de St. Luc', *Actes du IIIe Congrès international des études byzantines*, Athènes, 1932, p. 389.

figures (Pl. 14, *b*). The same humanist conception is apparent in the paintings at Boiana in Bulgaria, dated to 1259, though the delicate ethereal quality which is to become a characteristic of the revival period is here supplanted by a more realist manner (Pl. 15, *a*). The artist is concerned with the expression of the living model rather than with that of the intensity of feeling underlying a great religious emotion as at Nerez. Other monuments, though closely akin to these in evolution, are rather later in date, and they may hence best be considered under the last period.

THE LAST PERIOD. THIRTEENTH TO FIFTEENTH CENTURIES

Certain paintings of this age are the direct descendants of the monumental work of the middle period, but the refinement and sublimity of the finest work, as exemplified in the Daphni mosaics, have given place to a somewhat wooden sterility, and paintings, though interesting, are seldom of any great artistic value. Examples are to be seen in Greece and in the Balkans. Most important are the paintings of the first decoration of the Metropolis at Mistra in the Peloponnese (*c.* 1310), those of Gradatz (1314), those at Žiča in Macedonia (XIVth cent.), and those of St. Clement (1295) and some in St. Sophia (1517) at Ochrida.[1] Churches were also doubtless decorated in this manner at Constantinople itself as a result of conservatism, but none of them have survived. Apart from paintings in the side aisle of Kahrieh Djami of the fourteenth century, of no unusually striking quality, and other fragmentary ones in a ruined church known as Odalar Djami, nothing in the capital has been preserved. We must judge of what was happening there on the evidence of contemporary work elsewhere, and a very wide area now concerns us. With the Latin conquest of Constantinople (1204) artists as well as members of the court were forced to fly the

[1] Okunev, in *Mélanges Diehl*, ii, pp. 117 and 127.

city, and they found refuge in every corner of the Byzantine world, establishing at Nicaea, in Greece, in the Balkans, and even at distant Trebizond, schools which inherited all the best that the capital could give. For the next century or so provincial churches can thus offer us the best of Byzantine art, whereas both before this date and later, in the fifteenth century, to judge of Constantinople from what has survived in the provinces is, as Berenson has remarked, rather like judging the best French impressionist work of the nineteenth century from that of imitators in England and Germany. For the reason stated above all the Byzantine sphere must be regarded as a whole, and not as a series of subdivisions and countries.

We have already noted that in addition to the more conservative strain a new manner in painting had already dawned by the second half of the twelfth century, and as the finest instance of this manner, Nerez (1164), was due to imperial patronage there is reason to believe that this revival was a Constantinopolitan, not merely a provincial manifestation. Before we trace this movement farther and consider the monuments which are the result of it in the late thirteenth and following centuries, however, it will be well to pause, in order to inquire into its origin and cause, and to attempt some explanation of the movement which is generally known by the rather unsatisfactory name of the Byzantine Renaissance.

Various theories have been put forward by different authorities. Kondakov and the earlier investigators thus attributed it to Italian influence of the fourteenth century, and a more recent writer, Ainalow, to some extent follows this theory.[1] But the movement is far too deeply set in Byzantine art to be explained in this manner, and manifestations of the revival are to be found, as Nerez proves,

[1] *Byzantine Painting in the Fourteenth Century*, Petrograd, 1917 (in Russian).

long before Italy had awakened from its torpor of the Middle Ages. The theory that the revival was due to the change of conditions brought about by the Latin conquest may be similarly dismissed.

Even less reliable is the explanation offered by Schmidt, and to some extent also by Strzygowski. They believe the new manner to be due to a revival of Hellenistic spirit, resulting from an unusually apt copying of Hellenistic and more especially Syrian originals of earlier date. It is for them in fact not a revival, but a recapitulation.[1] That no such explanation is possible is at once proved by a study of the material. Not only is the work of the revival essentially alive, and obviously due to the hands of artists who were innovators though they benefited at the same time from the long heritage that had gone before: in addition we see the repertory of scenes and the numbers of figures in each scene being increased, a large number of new scenes which were unknown in ancient times being depicted from now on in all but the smallest churches. The individual figures and the backgrounds again show a careful elaboration and attention which is in every way a change from and an advance on what had gone before.

Diehl, Millet, and others regard the revival as a fourteenth-century manifestation resulting to a certain extent from Italian influence, but more from a fresh mingling of the original styles within the Byzantine sphere and a revival of the old Hellenistic spirit. Their explanation is in the main correct, but recent discoveries prove, as we have attempted to show above, that they are wrong as to the date, and the new style is born well before the Palaeologue age, with which the majority of its monuments are associated. Their suggestion as to Italian influence is thus disproved, and the cause of the remingling of styles must be attributed to that

[1] 'La Renaissance de la peinture byzantine au XIVme siècle', *Revue Archéologique*, xx, 1912, ii, p. 127.

surprising energy of the Greek race, which was responsible for the birth and for the ninth-century renewal of Byzantine art.[1]

The monuments of the revival period may best be considered according to region, though as we proceed we find that two distinct schools, the Macedonian and the Cretan, are born which are in no way limited by political and racial frontiers. The history of these schools is very complicated; their distinction is due to the wide research of Professor Millet, and the student must turn to his exhaustive works to study them in detail.[2]

Greece. The most important paintings of this area, and indeed some of the finest of all Byzantine art, are preserved in a number of churches at Mistra in the Peloponnese. These paintings are not only superb works in themselves, but they are of the greatest importance in the history of the period, for it is here that we first see the separation of the two distinctive schools of the later age. The first of these, the Macedonian school of Millet, is to be seen in the second decoration of the Metropolitan church (St. Demetrius) dating from about 1320,[3] and again in the Brontocheion (second half of the XIVth cent.). The paintings are in style closely allied to the mosaics of Kahrieh Djami at Constantinople (1310–20). We see in both that formalist, idealized, yet humanist conception of which the Byzantines were such masters, combined with rich decorative backgrounds. The colours are bright and contrasting, and light shades are used on dark in large splashes to give relief and life. No attempt is made to reproduce the shades of nature—an ox in the Nativity in the

[1] The chief honour in pointing out the early date of the revival must be assigned to Muratov. See his *Peinture byzantine*, passim, and especially p. 113.

[2] See especially his chapters in A. Michel, *Histoire de l'art* and his *Iconographie de l'Évangile.*

[3] It will be remembered that the first decoration, *c.* 1310, was in a more conservative, retrospective style.

Brontocheion, for instance, is coloured bright green—yet the results are supremely successful.

At the Pantanassa (1428) we see the very flower of later Byzantine art. There is no attempt at naturalism, but the paintings are essentially humanist; we see the artist's vivid joy in his power to evoke not only religious emotion, but also the concrete beauty of the world. The Raising of Lazarus is perhaps the finest composition in the church; it is also one of the finest Byzantine paintings (Pl. 16). Comparable in merit, as well as in iconography and style, to much quattrocento work in Italy, it seems to the author to rank among the world's finest pictures. Yet to appreciate it fully the Western comprehension must be forgotten, for in the eyes of the West humanism and understanding were conditional upon naturalism. The formalist artist who worked at the Pantanassa is a standing proof of the falsity of this idea, for his art is in no way bounded by the decrees of nature, but is in spite of that none the less endowed with sincere sympathy and deep feeling (Pl. 17, *a*).

In the Peribleptos at Mistra (late XIVth or early XVth cent.) we see the birth of the second main school, the 'icon-painting' or Cretan. At the Peribleptos the iconography is essentially the same as in the Macedonian; it is only the style that is different. But as time goes on a characteristic Cretan iconography is developed which permits a distinction of monuments regardless of style. Two painters worked in the Peribleptos, and the more accomplished of them, to be distinguished by the minuteness and detail of his work, was a master of the first class (Pl. 17, *b*).

There are probably in the south of Greece numerous other monuments which will serve to supplement our knowledge of the painting of the period, but none of them have yet been fully investigated. Such are fourteenth-century churches at Geraki in the Morea.

On Mount Athos we see a complete distinction of the

schools arrived at by the fifteenth century. Interesting paintings survive in practically all the monasteries, though some of them have suffered considerably at the hands of later restorers. The more important Macedonian paintings are in the Protaton at Karyes (XIVth cent., restored 1540), the catholicon (monastery church) at Chilandari (*c.* 1302, severely restored in 1804), in the catholicon at Vatopedi (1312, restored 1819), and in the chapel of the Prodrome at Karyes (probably about 1400).[1] Among the fine paintings of the Protaton a fragmentary head of the Virgin shows exquisite work; it dates from the fourteenth century and is untouched by the hand of the restorer (Pl. 15, *b*). The name of a particular painter, Manuel Panselinos, is associated with the Macedonian school on Athos and in the region of Salonica, and, though he can hardly have been responsible for all the paintings which are attributed to him by popular tradition, the suggestion put forward by certain authorities that he was a fictitious person seems entirely groundless.

Of the Cretan paintings on Athos the most famous are at the refectory of the Lavra (1512); the catholicon of the Lavra (1535); the old catholicon of Xenophontos (1544 and 1563); the catholicon and refectory of Dionysiou (1547); the chapel of St. George in the monastery of St. Paul (1555); the chapel of St. Nicholas at the Lavra (1560); the catholicon at Docheriou (1568), and the refectory at Docheriou (XVIth cent.). Other monuments of the Cretan school are to be found all over the Greek mainland, as for instance in the Meteora monastery (1552), one of the largest foundations in the group of monasteries which bears the same name.

The manner of this work has changed considerably since the first hints of a distinct school were noted in the Peribleptos at Mistra. Colouring is to be distinguished by a greater brilliance; striking but amazingly varied tones characterize

[1] The date of the work in this chapel has been disputed. See R. Byron and D. Talbot Rice, *The Birth of Western Painting*, p. 119.

the artist's palette; the subjects and scenes are isolated and often framed in separate compartments; the frontal pose is usually adopted for individual figures and the iconography is in some ways allied to the East. The emotion and humanism which were so characteristic of the Mistra paintings have changed to a mysticism, the light delicacy to a severe excellence of quality.[1] White high-lights are in general use, in opposition to the western practice of modelling with the aid of shading. The names of a number of actual painters of this school are known to us. The most famous is Theophanes the Cretan, who decorated the Lavra—he must be distinguished from Theophanes the Greek who worked in Russia more than a century earlier—but Anthony, who painted the nave of Xenophontos, was an equally competent and perhaps a more original painter (Pl. 18, *a*). At a later date icons are more usually associated with this school than are wall-paintings, and it was in their production that the school attained its greatest success (see Ch. IV, A).

Serbia. Throughout the period that concerns us Serbia was established as an independent kingdom, but her culture was essentially Byzantine, and of the numerous churches which were erected under the patronage of her rulers and nobles a large number were painted by artists who were of Greek blood. The work at Nagoričino (1317) is thus signed by a Greek, Eutychios, and the inscriptions designating the scenes are in Greek. Elsewhere Slav inscriptions are the more usual, but even where this is the case the signatures, when present, are in Greek, and this suggests that an artist who wrote in Slav to please his patrons preferred to revert to his own language in order to sign his name.[2] As time goes

[1] For a discussion of factors responsible for the birth of this school see Bréhier, in *Mélanges Diehl*, ii, p. 9.

[2] Petkovič asserts that Greek signatures cannot be regarded as proof of the Greek nationality of the artist, as Greek was an ecclesiastical language like Latin in the West in the Middle Ages, and it would thus be used by a Slav painter. But these remarks, though true for the inscrip-

on, however, schools of painting are developed in Serbia itself and the later painters were often of Slav origin. A certain slavinization of the art is to be discerned, and by the fifteenth century three schools are to be distinguished, two of which are in part serbianized. Before discussing these, however, it will be well to trace the development of painting in Serbia from the twelfth-century church of Nerez, which is, as we have seen, the first monument now preserved of the revival style.

The next church with important paintings is Mileševo (1236), again in the new style; it heralds work of sixty years later in the second decoration of the Metropolis at Mistra. Morača is of similar date and character. Sopoćani (1250), Nagoričino (1317), Gračanica (*c.* 1320) and Dečani (church 1327, paintings a few years later) continue in the Macedonian style. A detail of the Crucifixion at Sopoćani must serve as an example for all these important monuments (Pl. 18, *b*). It is a painting of the highest quality, as are some recently discovered in St. Sophia at Ochrida. A small church at Vodoca in Macedonia, with fragmentary paintings of the thirteenth century, is included in the retrospective monumental group by certain authorities. But the emotional character of the scene of the forty martyrs, where the crowd is a living mass and where the agony of feeling is clearly shown in the expression and attitude of each figure, proves that the work here must also be assigned to the revival style (Pl. 19, *a*).[1]

These monuments are essentially Greek, and there is little that is definitely Slav about them. The style is carried on in a number of other churches, but there a certain Slav character is beginning to be developed, and the pure Macedonian may best be traced from now on under the heading Graeco-

tions, do not seem to apply to the signatures. See his article in *Mélanges Diehl*, ii, p. 136.

[1] K. Miatev, 'Les 40 martyrs; fragment de fresque à Vodoca', *L'Art byzantin chez les Slaves*, i, p. 102.

Slav school, originally suggested by Okunev. We see pure bright colours, clean drawing, harmonious composition, and graceful and well-proportioned figures. The faces are well modelled, the modelling being achieved by opposition of light and shade and not by the addition of white high-lights, a feature which is developed by the Cretan rather than by the Macedonian school and its branches. The principal monuments are the church of Milutin at Studenica (1314), the church of St. Nicholas at Luboten (1337), the church of St. Nicetas at Čučer (early XIVth cent., restored 1483–4), the church at Peć (*c.* 1310) and the church of Berende in Bulgaria (XIVth cent.).

Developing alongside this Graeco-Slav school we see another group, the monastic. It is also a branch of the Macedonian, but is less accomplished and less refined. It is characterized by more sombre colouring, less virile drawing, and rather graceless figures. The aim is in the main didactic, and a preference is shown for scenes of an obscure, apocryphal character. The most important monuments are Lesnovo (1349), Markov Manastir (late XIVth) and Matejič (late XIVth).

The Cretan school does not penetrate Serbia until the very end of the fourteenth century, but it then supersedes the Macedonian to a great extent. The most important monuments are Kalenić (1405–10), Ljubostinja (1405), Ravanica (1381), Manasija (1407), Rudenica (1410), and the churches of Kalotino (late XVth), Dragalevci (1476) and Arbanassi (1681) in Bulgaria. In the Cretan, as well as in the Macedonian paintings, portraiture is far developed, the founders or donors usually being shown in elaborate costumes, a detailed study of which would probably prove of great assistance in problems of dating.[1] The likenesses are, as far

[1] A similar love of portraiture also appears in manuscripts. See p. 136 f. Such features as the crosses on the robes of saints or ecclesiastical dignitaries, &c., are also of importance for dating. See Okunev in *Mélanges Diehl,* ii, p. 125.

as can be judged, very striking, and we see here a primitive portrait style which has reached in its development a stage akin to that shown by fifteenth-century work in England.

Bulgaria. We have already noted that thirteenth-century paintings in Bulgaria, more especially at Boiana (1259), show the vitality and humanism of the revival, but that stress is here laid on the expression of the face rather than on the underlying emotion. The true character of the Byzantine revival is in fact rather more obscured here than in Serbia, and the majority of the paintings were, from the foundation of the second Bulgarian empire (1186), the work of local Slav rather than of immigrant Greek artists. They follow earlier Byzantine models closely, however, and develop from them a number of local schools. The most characteristic of these was that responsible for the work at Boiana of 1259. A second school decorated the church of the Forty Martyrs at Tirnovo (late XIIIth), the capital of the empire, and a third was responsible for paintings in the church of SS. Peter and Paul (late XIVth) and in sixteen funerary chapels in the same town, and for work in the monastery of Bačkovo.[1] Paintings showing the Pantocrator and the twenty-two prophets in the church of St. George at Sofia (XIVth) are more closely related to the best fourteenth-century Byzantine work and the scene of the twenty-two prophets is supremely successful both in the rhythm of the composition and the vitality of the figures (Pl. 19, *b*).[2]

In addition to these major schools we see a more archaic

[1] Most of the paintings here are of the twelfth century. They are in true fresco and in a pure Byzantine style.

[2] For the distinctions of schools in Bulgarian painting see Protic in *L'Art byzantin chez les Slaves*, i, p. 92. He groups the Tirnovo work and that in St. George at Sofia together, but the two seem strikingly different. Tirnovo is essentially the work of a Slav artist; St. George is by a Greek or one who followed the Byzantine revival manner very closely.

peasant manner in certain small churches in the mountains, and an individualist style, where considerable western influence has penetrated, in the church of Poganovo (1500). Poganovo is a turning-point. It marks the end of the Byzantine dominance, though it is an isolated monument and many paintings which are actually later in date are more Byzantine in style.

Roumania. In central Roumania the most important early work is to be seen in the two royal churches at Curtea din Arges, which date from the fourteenth century and belong to the Macedonian school. There were a number of Greek artists in the country at this time, though native schools were soon formed, and after about 1400 Serbians took the place of the Greeks to a great extent. In the sixteenth century numerous churches with painted decorations both inside and out were erected, and we see fine work at Snagov, Hurezi, Humor, and elsewhere. In Moldavia and Bukovina paintings of the sixteenth century are numerous, and a few of earlier date may be noted. The most important are Dolhesti-Mari (1480), Popauti (end of XVth century), and Roman (1550). Stefanescu distinguishes two main influences at the basis of these, which first entered Wallachia in the mid-fourteenth century; they are that of Byzantine art coming from the south, and that of a peasant art of the locality. In the fifteenth century there is a certain amount of influence from Athos, and a further intrusive style is superimposed from the West. In an opposite direction the westward spread of Byzantine art is to be traced in Poland, though work here is generally more allied to that of Russia.

In Russia three main schools exist at this time, those of Vladimir, Novgorod, and Pskov. We shall discuss them briefly in a later chapter, and can do no more than mention the names here, though their importance in the general history of Byzantine art is of the greatest.

Other Schools. A rather different character marks paintings of the fifteenth and following centuries in the city and region of Trebizond. They show a mingling of Constantinopolitan and Cappadocian traits, though the eastern element is usually in the ascendant. What little remains of early work here, most notably in the church of St. Sophia, suggests that there was an important local art in the first days of the Comnene empire of Trebizond (1204–1461) which was probably established by immigrant artists from Constantinople. The most interesting monuments are the three caves of St. Savas, one dated to 1411, the bell tower of St. Sophia (1443), and the church of Kurt Boghan (XIVth cent.). Portions of a more extensive decoration survive in the Theokepastos monastery, but the paintings here have been much restored. At the Armenian monastery of Kaimakli, close to the city, there are two separate series of Armenian paintings, of very individualistic style, the one dated 1622, the other to the eighteenth or early nineteenth century. Kindred work apparently survives in Armenia proper and in Georgia. Certain paintings in Roumania would appear to be related to those at Trebizond; the influence probably travelled by way of south Russia.

From the seventeenth century onwards we see paintings in all the orthodox area, though they are seldom of any merit. The style has become wooden, the colouring poor, and the iconography fixed owing to the general use of a book known as the *Painters' Guide*. This was compiled by the monk Dionysius of Fourna, who lived at the end of the fourteenth century, though it was quite probably founded on an earlier original. Similar guides, the podliniki, were common in Russia from the sixteenth century onwards.[1]

[1] The best edition of the *Painters' Guide* is that of Papadopoulos-Kérameus, in Greek, published at St. Petersburg in 1909. A French translation appears in Didron, *Manuel d'Iconographie chrétienne*, Paris, 1845, and an English summary in Stokes's translation of Didron's book, under the title *Christian Iconography*, London, 1886, 2 vols.

BIBLIOGRAPHY

GENERAL WORKS.

Full summaries and bibliographies are given in the principal manuals. See in addition Millet, *L'Iconographie de l'Évangile*, Paris, 1916; Muratov, *La Peinture byzantine*, Paris, 1928; and Diehl, *La Peinture byzantine*, Paris, 1932. A novel aspect of Byzantine painting, which throws light on the Byzantine theatre, is brought out in the works of Madame Cottas, especially *L'Influence du drame 'Christos Paschon' sur l'art chrétien d'orient*, Paris, 1931.

For particular regions the following are the chief works:

ITALY.

Van Marle, op. cit., vol. i. Wilpert, op. cit. Bertaux, *L'Art dans l'Italie méridionale*, 1903–4. Publications of the Società Magna Grecia.

SYRIA.

Breasted, *Oriental Forerunners of Byzantine Painting*, Yale, 1924. Also articles in *Syria*, especially tome iii, 1922, p. 177. See also reports on the Dura excavations, Yale University.

EGYPT.

Quibell, *Excavations at Sakkara*, Cairo, 1908.

CAPPADOCIA.

Jerphanion, *Les Églises rupestres de la Cappadoce*. Paris, in course of publication. Two volumes of plates and one of text, of the three of plates and two of text announced, have so far appeared.

BULGARIA.

Grabar, *La Peinture religieuse en Bulgarie*, Paris, 1928. Filow, *L'Ancien Art bulgare*, large edn., Berne, 1919. A smaller one was published in Paris in 1922, and an entirely new edition in German appeared in 1932.

SERBIA.

N. Okunev, *Monumenta Artis Serbicae*, a series which began in 1928. Also publications of the Archaeological Society and the National Museum, especially *La Peinture serbe du moyen âge*, Beograd, 1930. Other volumes are in Serbian.

ROUMANIA.

A general summary is given by Iorga and Bals, in *L'Art roumain*, Paris, 1922. There are a number of monographs. See especially Henri, *Les Églises de la Moldavie du nord*, Paris, 1931. Stefanescu, *L'Évolution de la peinture religieuse en Bucovine et en Moldavie*, Paris, 1928; and the same author's *Contribution à l'étude des peintures murales valaques*, Paris, 1922.

MISTRA.

Millet, *Monuments byzantins de Mistra*, Paris, 1910. Bryon and Talbot Rice, *The Birth of Western Painting*, London, 1930.

ATHOS.

Millet, *Monuments de l'Athos*, Paris, 1927, vol. i. Byron and Rice, op. cit. Fichtner, *Wandmalereien der Athos-Klöster*, Berlin, 1931. Brokhaus, *Die Kunst in den Athos-Klöstern*, Leipzig, 1891.

Articles referring to one or other of these areas or to particular branches of the subject appear in *L'Art byzantin chez les Slaves*, Paris, 1930; *Mélanges Diehl*, Paris, 1930; *Mélanges Schlumberger*, Paris, and *Seminarium Kondakovianum*, Prague (periodically).

Chapter IV

PANEL PAINTING AND ICONOGRAPHY

A. PANEL PAINTING

THE history of Byzantine panel painting is a long one, but it is not until about the twelfth century that it assumes any very considerable importance in a general study of Byzantine art. It may be that much early material has perished; it may be that in the rich and more prosperous days of the empire such sumptuous products as enamels or miniature mosaics took the place of paintings except in the poorer households or churches; whatever the reason, there are few panels of early date in existence to-day which show first-class work.

The origin of the art is to be traced back to the tomb portraits of Graeco-Roman Egypt, where two main techniques can be distinguished, one in true painting done upon a ground of gesso, with a brush and with a tempera medium,[1] the other a more elaborate technique known as encaustic, where coloured waxes were skilfully 'drawn' by means of a hot metal rod. Though these encaustic paintings are important in the history of Coptic art, they hardly concern us, for the technique never seems to have been adopted in the Byzantine area proper. A number of examples, some of which are dated to as late as the seventh century, were formerly preserved in the Theological Academy at Kiev.

The earliest actual paintings on panel which are known to us outside Egypt belong to the sixth century. The most famous is a casket in the Lateran, on the lid of which the Crucifixion and other scenes are shown in a style which is rather eastern or Syrian.[2] Examples are equally scarce in the

[1] Yolk of egg is the most usual medium in early times; later various kinds of gums are employed. The yolk of egg gives a very different effect from the western tempera or white of egg medium.

[2] Diehl, *Manuel*, ii, p. 593, dates this to the tenth or eleventh century,

seventh century; two Coptic book covers in the Freer collection at Washington are among the more important.

With the exception of these few early examples, icons are the most common form of panel painting, and from now on it is primarily with them that we are concerned. In the iconoclastic period large icons of any sort were naturally excluded. But it seems probable that small icons which could be easily hidden were used a great deal by those who did not wish to court displeasure, but who had at the same time faith in religious pictures. The great popularity of the icon in the home, which to-day characterizes the Orthodox world, be it Slav or Greek, may even date from this period, when those who had faith in such pictures were not permitted to admire them in churches. A minute diptych from Constantinople, which was exhibited in London at the Courtauld Institute in 1933, may well belong to this period.[1]

Icons of the golden age of Byzantine art from the ninth to the twelfth centuries are not very numerous. A few panels survive in various places in Italy, but more important than these are the large icons of Russia, most of which have been brought to light owing to the recent activities in cleaning and to research in obscure monasteries. Some of these pictures were actual importations from Constantinople; others were made by Greeks working in Russia; others were again purely Russian products in the Byzantine manner. The most important is the twelfth-century picture known as 'Our Lady of Vladimir', an importation from Constantinople. It is one of the finest religious panel paintings in the world.[2]

A painting on silk at Trieste of the eleventh or twelfth

but there can be little doubt that Dalton is right in assigning it to the sixth century, *E.C.A.*, p. 264.

[1] A typescript catalogue of this exhibition can be consulted at the Courtauld Institute or at the Victoria and Albert Museum. See also 'Byzantine Paintings at the Courtauld Institute', in *The Connoisseur*, xci, March 1933, p. 184.

[2] See A. J. Anisimov, *Our Lady of Vladimir*, Prague, 1928.

century, showing St. Just, though it is not an icon in the narrowest sense of the word, deserves mention here, for it must be classed among the most perfect examples of mid-Byzantine painting. It shows the monumental Hellenistic tradition at its very best (Pl. 20, *a*).

It is with the thirteenth and fourteenth centuries, however, that panel paintings really come into their own in the Orthodox world, and from now on they are universally popular. Hitherto usually confined to single figures, we now find them depicting either single figures, the Christ, the Virgin or some saint, a group of figures, religious scenes, or even a number of scenes. The schools are akin to those which we have noted in discussing the wall-paintings, and the same painter was probably sometimes responsible for both icons and major decorations. Yet at first sight the art is, for the uninitiated, of an even more aloof character. It does not attempt to portray nature; it does not bother about anatomy or perspective; its colouring is seldom that to be seen in nature; it is not concerned with this world, but with the world of the spirit. Like the liturgy it repeats certain well-known forms; like an oft-seen play of Shakespeare, familiarity only helps us to appreciate it the more. These icons exhibit the greatest possible contrast to Italian painting; they are metallic, electric; high-lights are picked out in bright colours, where a westerner would shade; brightly contrasting colours are laid on and achieve a true colouristic effect; seldom are they in the nature of coloured drawings; there is no attempt at chiaroscuro. Western art goes in for shading and half tones; it appeals to sentiment; it is essentially secular in character in that it employs everyday figures to depict the imaginative, the religious, or the sublime. The icon, on the other hand, like some of the art of to-day, does not seek to please; its aim is spiritual and mental, and depends on conviction; it is fundamentally religious and exalts everyday life to the religious plane. To Buslaieff, an eminent Russian authority of the seventies, who was brought up in strictly Orthodox surroundings, Italian art seemed morally decadent, grossly material, and nauseatingly sentimental.[1] Thus, though icons may seem strange and unsympathetic to the uninitiated western, there is an opposite, yet nevertheless quite legitimate outlook.

To the thirteenth or early fourteenth century in Byzantine lands belong a series of important panels in the church of St. Clement at Ochrida, which are unfortunately obscured by metal frames covering all but the actual figures. A fine icon in four panels in the British Museum is fortunately not concealed in this way, though it needs cleaning; it must be of Byzantine workmanship, though it came from the Natron lakes in Egypt.[2] A few other examples exist in churches in Greece, but the largest collections are in the Byzantine and the Benaki Museums at Athens. A Crucifixion from Salonica in the former and a superb Transfiguration in the latter (Pl. 20, *b*) are both works of the very first quality. Further paintings will doubtless come to light when obscure churches in the more inaccessible regions of the mainland or in the islands are explored, and when craftsmen who can clean off repaintings become as proficient as those of Russia. An Ascension at Nicosia in Cyprus (frontispiece), one of the finest examples of early fifteenth-century work that have come down to us, was thus till recently hidden away, and entirely obscured by overpainting. In Russia there are many more examples of these centuries, but art was already beginning to develop along Slavonic lines, and its consideration is beyond the scope of this volume.

Fifteenth- and sixteenth-century icons in Greece are more numerous; there is in fact enough material to permit us to distinguish a number of schools, though the nature of all of

[1] *Études d'iconographie chrétienne en Russie*, French translation, Moscow, 1874, p. 20.

[2] Dalton, *E.C.A.*, p. 264, pl. XLV.

them has not yet been fully determined, since little study has been given to the subject. Further material survives in the Balkans. Icons related to the Macedonian school of wall-painting are, however, not nearly as common as are those related to the Cretan; the Cretan school is, in fact, as we have noted above, even better represented in icons than in wall-paintings. The history of the school must hence receive here a rather more detailed consideration than it was possible to give it in the last chapter.

The earliest paintings in Crete itself belong to the beginning of the fourteenth century; an artist by the name of Pagomenos decorated churches on the island from 1314 to 1328, and other painters continued down to about 1500. After this date paintings in the island become rare. These early painters followed a Byzantine tradition, somewhat influenced by locality, and it seems probable that the characteristic icon manner and the extensive use of white high-lights was developed in the island at this time.[1] In any case these features were already developed when the Peribleptos at Mistra (late XIVth or early XVth cent.) was decorated, though a distinctive Cretan iconography is only to be seen here in embryo. Certain influence was in fact exercised by Mistra, and it was probably by way of Mistra that the Cretan painters came to be the direct inheritors of the purest Byzantine tradition. Certain authorities regard Venetian influence as of great importance in the birth of the school. This is to be doubted, though at a later date Venice did exercise an effect on its further development in the south of Greece and in the islands. Before the intrusion of this influence, however, the style was developed at Mistra and in Greece, both on walls and panels. We have already noted the Cretan wall-paintings on Mount Athos and in the Balkans;

[1] It has been suggested that the white high-lights result from the curious lighting of the Cretan landscape, where the sun produces exactly similar effects on the rocks.

few panels have survived. At the same time the Cretan style was doubtless developed at Constantinople, which must have been the most important centre of panel painting. We can only judge of this development by examples we know from elsewhere, more especially from Russia. A number of Greek artists emigrated thither at this time, and in addition actual panels were imported from Constantinople. The artists founded schools and the paintings were copied locally, so that in the early fifteenth century a large number of Russian icons were of Cretan character and Cretan inspiration.

In the sixteenth century the painters of the Cretan school, working in Greece, on Athos, to some extent in Crete, and at Constantinople, produced a large number of icons which are to be distinguished by their brilliant colouring and superb quality. Among the finest is one showing the Old Testament Trinity—three angels entertained by the hospitable Abraham and his wife Sarah, who appear on either side—in the possession of Mr. Charles Seltman.[1] Many of the paintings of this date are actually signed, and when the study of the subject has progressed it will doubtless be possible to attribute others on stylistic grounds to individual painters. Certain Italian influences may have penetrated to this school, but they are of a minor character, and the pictures remain in essence Byzantine. On account of certain subdivisions which may be made it seems best to distinguish this, the main stem, by the name of Byzanto-Cretan.

Quite distinct from it is the school which is termed Italo-Cretan or Graeco-Italian by Kondakoff, Likhacheff, and others. To it belong the works of a number of Greeks who lived in Italy, such as Emmanuel Zanfurnari, the painter of the well-known death of St. Ephraim Syrus in the Vatican, who lived in the late sixteenth and early seventeenth cen-

[1] In Russia Rublev's famous painting of this subject has ever been regarded as one of the most important examples of Christian art. It was painted about 1420.

turies. Another version of the same subject, probably rather earlier in date, is in the Northwick collection in Gloucestershire. Another important work of this group is the reliquary of Cardinal Bessarion (1443), now in the picture gallery in Venice. This subdivision of the Cretan school is characterized by a rather sombre colouring and greater softness of touch, by the occasional use of shading in place of the hard lights so typical of Byzanto-Cretan work, and by a greater feeling for sentiment. It is best called by the name Italo-Cretan.

The Italo-Cretan school probably exercised a considerable influence in Greece, and more especially on Athos. But in the sixteenth and seventeenth centuries a further distinct Athonite school can be distinguished, in which strongly marked oriental affinities are to be observed, more notably in the black eyes, like pin heads, and in a love of bright colour and profuse, minute decoration.

Distinct again, though closely allied, are certain paintings of a more orientalized character than the Italo-Cretan. The masters responsible for these, most famous of whom was Angelos Bizamenos, worked in the south of Italy in the region of Otranto, and they were doubtless considerably influenced by the cave and church paintings of the region, which were, as we have shown (p. 98), more closely linked with Cappadocia than with the Byzantine region proper as far as style and iconography were concerned. Examples are mostly preserved in the south of Italy and in Greece, and the term Graeco-Italian may be set aside to describe them as a whole.

In Bulgaria an individual style seems to have been arrived at in the fifteenth century if not before, the most characteristic feature of which is a black background. Later we see a number of local schools in this country which can be distinguished without great difficulty.[1] Similar schools exist

[1] Filow, *L'Ancien Art bulgare*, small edition, Paris, 1922, p. 65.

in Serbia, though as yet little has been done to distinguish them, and at Venice we see another rather distinct group determined principally by the subject, namely the Madonna and Child. These are descended from the twelfth-century Byzantine originals of which Our Lady of Vladimir is an example; but at Venice the Byzantine dignity was gradually lost and a somewhat uncouth severity took its place. The name Veneto-Cretan can perhaps best serve to distinguish this group. A similar local school of Byzantine character existed in Sicily,[1] and there was an important one in Cyprus.

The study of Byzantine and post-Byzantine icons is as yet in its infancy, and a very great deal of work remains to be done before a final distinction of schools or any accuracy of dating on stylistic grounds can be attempted.

BIBLIOGRAPHY

For the most important general study of the subject see Wulff and Alpatov, *Denkmäler der Ikonenmalerei*, Dresden, 1925. For an outline in which Greece is considered as well as Russia see Kondakoff, *The Russian Icon*, Eng. trans., Oxford, 1927. The Prague edition is fuller, but it is in Russian. Full bibliographies are contained in these books. Kondakoff's and Likhacheff's numerous books published in Russia before the revolution are of basic importance. For a convenient summary of Russian icon painting see Muratoff, *Les Icones russes*, and for an attempt to distinguish the later groups of the Cretan school see an article by D. Talbot Rice, 'Some Schools of Greek Icon Painting' in *Apollo*, xvii, May 1933, p. 187. The new French translation of Soteriou's *Guide du Musée byzantin d'Athènes* is also useful.

[1] This school has been studied and its distinctive features tabulated by Lazarev, 'Early Italo-Byzantine painting in Sicily', *Burlington Magazine*, lxiii, Dec. 1933, p. 283. He shows that two Madonnas from Spain which have been variously attributed must belong to this group. There is little about them to warrant Berenson's suggestion, *Studies in Mediaeval Painting*, New Haven, 1930, ch. i, that they should be assigned to Constantinople, and when compared to the only authentic Constantinopolitan panel that we know, Our Lady of Vladimir, their provincial character is at once apparent.

B. ICONOGRAPHY

The bearing of this subject on the distinction of schools and the establishment of origins in Byzantine art has already been frequently alluded to, but in discussing the mosaics and painting our distinctions have been made more on grounds of style than on those of iconography. And though in many cases the two go together and combine as sure guides, in others they are opposed, and we see two works which are of the same style but which fall into two entirely different iconographical groups, the figures being differently disposed and the scene differently interpreted. Iconography travels from one region to another, being easily transported by means of sketches or manuscripts; it is not dependent on the individual. Style is of a more static nature and is often to be associated with some particular individual, invariably with some particular school or group of individuals. Further complications may arise when we find a painter who has been brought up in one iconographical tradition copying a model which belongs to an entirely opposite tradition; it is thus that we see Syrian and Hellenistic iconography as well as oriental and Hellenic feeling blended in the same monument, and thus that we sometimes see an oriental or Hellenistic model reproduced in the opposed manner; the result is a curious idiomatic confusion.

The iconography of the early periods belongs to two main groups, an eastern or Syrian and a western or Hellenic. In the middle period, the Golden Age, we find a third distinction, the Byzantine, definitely established. The general traits characteristic of each have already been noted at the beginning of the chapter on mosaics. There are in addition definite features which belong to each particular subject, to each particular scene of the Bible-story that is illustrated, and to each particular portrayal, be it saint, Christ, or Madonna. The study of certain scenes in detail has been undertaken in a number of monographs, but much further research remains to be done, both as regards the earlier and the more complicated later periods.[1] The subject has, however, been set on a sure footing by the amazingly wide and minute research of Gabriel Millet, dealing mainly with the later centuries and published in the long and important work *L'Iconographie de l'Évangile*. So wide are Millet's researches that it is impossible to summarize them here, but two scenes may be briefly described by way of example, the Annunciation and the Raising of Lazarus.[2] In the former, according to the Eastern or Palestinian conception of the fifth and sixth centuries, the Virgin is shown seated to the left of the picture, in the act of spinning. In Byzantine iconography of the sixth century she usually stands on the right of the picture. In Cappadocia she stands, but is still on the left. The positions change to some extent when the full face (Eastern) usurps the side position (Hellenic). In eleventh-century Byzantine ivories we find the Virgin's arms raised before her breast with the palms turned upwards. In the twelfth century the seated Virgin who spins becomes usual again, the original Palestinian type having been preserved in manuscripts and resurrected owing to a renewed popularity of the Apocrypha. From the fourteenth to the sixteenth century the standing Virgin, so characteristic of the eleventh century, is very rare; we see her instead in the sitting position, turned in the attitude, but no longer in the act of spinning, or turned towards the Angel with whom she speaks. Characteristic of this period is a raising of the hand to her head. Similar variations are to be noted with regard to the angel.

In the raising of Lazarus Jesus and but one or two followers are present before the sixth century; soon after He is followed

[1] See, for instance, Strzygowski, *Die Taufe Christi;* Kondakoff, *Iconography of the Virgin* and *Iconography of Christ*, both in Russian.

[2] For a summary study of many other scenes see Bréhier, *L'Art chrétien*, passim.

by a crowd. There are three main traditions. In the oriental tradition Jesus approaches from the left; two women kneel before Him; three men stand near the tomb, two of whom turn away, while the third holds his cloak to his nose—a realist feature which is essentially oriental and foreign to idealistic, Hellenic thought. In the Hellenic version Jesus comes from the right. In the typically Byzantine or Constantinopolitan version one man is shown undoing the bandages, whilst another lifts the stone lid of the tomb. The crowd of spectators is small; the apostles behind Jesus only come in with the twelfth century. In the fourteenth century the crowd, the apostles, the workmen, and the two women are all included. The Macedonian school, however, shows the crowd near the tomb, most of them looking at Jesus; one man kneels in an attitude of reverence as he unrolls the bandages. In the Cretan school there is often no sarcophagus; the man who unrolls the bandages leans less and turns his head; the crowd stands in the half-distance, and the town of Bethany is shown in the background.

It is largely owing to iconography that we have come to realize the wide harmonizing influence which Constantinople played on art, for there the eastern and Hellenic systems of representation were blended to form a Byzantine iconography as well as their manners to form Byzantine art. It was by an elaborate analysis of each scene and of each figure that Millet was able to make an original distinction of schools in the fourteenth century and to set the study of later Byzantine painting on a sure footing.[1] But even further discoveries were possible, for in addition to the early eastern and western divisions, and in addition to the Macedonian and Cretan 'schools' of the fourteenth and following centuries,

[1] In general lines the sureness of the footing established in his *Iconographie* is certain, but some authorities dispute details, and the fact of a unified Macedonian school is not generally accepted by Balkan writers. See, for instance, Grabar, *Peinture religieuse en Bulgarie*, and Petkovic, *Peinture serbe*.

Millet distinguished two cycles of subjects. These are of fundamental importance in church decoration, and their distinction helps us considerably in an analysis of any particular monument. They are known as the liturgical and the narrative cycles.

In the narrative cycle all the more important events of our Lord's life are included in early times; at Tokale Kilisse in Cappadocia there are thus six registers on the walls, with six scenes in each, thus making thirty-six scenes in all. At a later date, however, the miracles and legends of martyrs become detached to form subordinate groups, while the more important events are picked out for emphasis. The selection of the important scenes is determined according to one of two systems, the oriental and the Byzantine. In the one the Nativity and the Passion only appear and the Baptism, which is very important in other systems, is excluded. We see it in the wall-paintings of Cappadocia and also of Serbia, and there is every probability that the same selection applied to panel painting; we should thus expect to find that Serbian icons of the Baptism are rare. In the Byzantine system all the epochs of Christ's life are shown, but we see at different periods a varying number selected. Thus in early times seven were chosen because of the days of creation—it must be remembered that before the ninth century the Old Testament was more popular in art than the New. Later ten were chosen, because of the beatitudes, and from the fourteenth century we usually see twelve because of the apostles. In the twelfth century the events chosen are the Annunciation, Birth, Presentation, Baptism, Transfiguration, Entry into Jerusalem, Crucifixion, Resurrection, Ascension, and Pentecost. To make up the twelve in the fourteenth century two more were selected, the selection being determined by the importance of the Virgin or Christ in the particular instance. Thus if a church were dedicated to, or an icon adorned a chapel of the Virgin, the Visitation and the Dormition would be added;

if the patron were our Lord, choice would be made from the Incredulity of Thomas, the Descent from the Cross, or the Raising of Lazarus.

The events shown in the liturgical cycle, comprising the miracles of Christ, the lives of the Martyrs, and the miracles of the Virgin, are arranged in the church according to its shape and the space available. The order is determined by the sequence of events in our Lord's life or by that in which they appear in the daily lessons with which the painter's manual coincided;[1] if a full cycle could not be included, selection was made according to the importance of the events.

It will be seen that numerous features are thus available to assist the student in assigning to a particular school any monument under his consideration. But, important though the immense work of Millet is, the factor of style must not be forgotten, for it is this factor and this only which can distinguish an age, a region, or an individual master. It is in fact the amazingly fixed conservatism of iconography in Byzantine art which makes the study of its later manifestations so difficult, and endows them to an unprecedented degree with that sameness which any unfamiliar art must have until we get to know it intimately. A long familiarity is necessary before this impression of sameness can be overcome; but when once this has been done, variations of style can be appreciated quite easily. And, with a firm iconographical background established, a more elaborate study both of wall and of panel paintings (icons) from an aesthetic standpoint must come as an obvious corollary.

BIBLIOGRAPHY

Millet's *Iconographie de l'Évangile* is by far the most important work. Further references will be found there. See also Bréhier, *L'Art chrétien*.

[1] It seems likely that manuals for the guidance of wall-painters were compiled at an early date, though those which survive till to-day in Russia and Greece are comparatively late.

Chapter V

BYZANTINE BOOK ILLUMINATION

MANUSCRIPTS have probably received a more detailed attention from scholars than has any other branch of Byzantine art, and on account of this, as well as because quite a number of them are dated, the attribution of certain styles to definite periods is more reliable than in other branches. Hence we can often turn to a comparative study of the manuscripts for assistance in general problems of dating. In this respect the religious manuscripts are more important, for they develop along lines closely parallel to those we see in wall and panel painting. Secular ones are throughout much more classical in style, and we see in them far less change or advance than in the monuments of religious art.

Apart from the distinction between religious and secular manuscripts, a further distinction may be made in early times between the two principal types of book, the roll or rotulus, and the bound book or codex. The former, essentially a product of classical art, was only made in early times and was even then more popular for secular than for religious uses. It ceded its place to the codex at an early date, but had some influence on illustration, for the panorama-like backgrounds to which we have alluded above were obviously derived from it. Three types of workers were responsible for the production of these books, the copyist or calligrapher, the chrysographer, who did the headings to chapters and the more elaborate lettering, and the painter who was responsible for the actual miniatures. The writing is often beautiful and the headings frequently constitute decorative work of the first importance, but the miniatures must be our chief concern. It would seem that variations in style were from age to age often more considerable in them than in mosaics or wall-paintings, and that the art was in some ways rather more free, in spite of the fact that the Hellenistic tradition was usually uppermost. Manuscript illuminations were again less affected by the East than most of the other arts, and, although we see certain examples which belong to the Syrian family, middle eastern or non-representational features are to be traced only in the decorative headings.

Two distinct manners are to be observed here after the sixth century, as in wall-painting and mosaic, but they may here be more clearly identified geographically. One, the Alexandrine, keeps the rich and subtle draperies, the feeling for idealism and the love of noble attitudes of Hellenic art. It inspires the school of Constantinople and the narrative cycles which we have noted in mosaics and in wall-paintings; the two most typical examples are, according to Millet, the works of Gregory Nazianzus, of the ninth century, in the Bibliothèque Nationale (Gr. 510), and a gospel at Florence, written at Constantinople in the eleventh or twelfth century (Laurentian, vi, 23). The other style, usually known as the Antioch edition, is more purely Syrian, and we see here the search for truth, the realism, and the love of apocryphal events which characterizes the art of this area, as well as sometimes that love of picturesque and brightly coloured costumes, which is so characteristic of Eastern feeling in general; the most typical example is, according to Millet, a twelfth-century manuscript in the Bibliothèque Nationale (Gr. 74).[1]

To distinguish further between these families would necessitate a minute iconographical discussion which is beyond the scope of this chapter, but with the two variants clear in our minds we may pass on to an historical survey of the monuments. Here again two definite groups may be distinguished, one where the illustrations cover the full page

[1] For illustrations see Omont, *Miniatures des plus anciens Manuscrits grecs de la Bibliothèque Nationale*, Paris, 1929, and also the numerous volumes of his *Facsimiles des Manuscrits grecs de la Bibliothèque Nationale.*

and form a complete picture, where the figures are displayed before an extensive background; the other where the illustrations are marginal, and where figures only appear, as it were as mimes to the text. An example of the marginal class of early date is offered by the manuscript of the *Iliad* in the Ambrosian Library at Milan. In the earliest full-page illustrations we usually find the background formed by a continuous panorama, as for instance in the Joshua rotulus at the Vatican (V. Palat. Gr. 431). A characteristic technique, where little colour is employed, is used throughout, but two styles are to be distinguished, the one essentially antique and the other heralding the developed Byzantine. The date of this manuscript is somewhat disputed, but Ebersolt is probably right in considering it as of the fifth or sixth century (Pl. 21, *a*).[1]

One of the finest manuscripts of this age is the famous Genesis at Vienna;[2] it has been assigned to the fourth, fifth, and sixth centuries by different authorities, and to practically every region of the Christian world except Greece. Syrian and Ravennate affinities are both marked, and we see here a herald of the Byzantine style on account of which it is most tempting to assign the manuscript to Constantinople. The fifth or early sixth century would seem the most likely date. The style of the miniatures is naturalist, the manner antique, and the work is of the finest. Closely related and equally accomplished is the Rossano codex, which is to be assigned to the fifth or sixth, more probably to the latter, century.[3] The illustrations are on a more monumental scale than those of the Vienna Genesis; the colouring is brighter, and the style is perhaps more definitely Byzantine. The frontispiece to the table of canons shows a superbly bright geometrical

[1] *Miniatures*, p. 73, note 1. It was restored after the ninth century.

[2] Vidobon. Theol. Gr. 31; Hartel and Wickhoff, *Die Wiener Genesis*, Wien, 1895.

[3] Haseloff, *Codex Purpureus Rossanensis*, Berlin, 1898; H. Munoz, *Il Codice Purpureo di Rossano e il frammento Sinopense*, 1907.

composition, which is entirely foreign to the naturalist and impressionist Pompeiian style which is to be detected to a greater or lesser degree in most of the miniatures of this age; it shows rather the spirit of painting and sculpture of the Golden Age, when eastern influence had been fully assimilated, though we see similar geometrical work in the wall-paintings of Coptic Egypt. The manuscript is in certain iconographical respects eastern, and it has been assigned variously both to Egypt and Syria. The former is the more likely.

The Sinope fragment in Paris (Bibl. Nat. suppl. Gr. 1286) and the Cotton Genesis in the British Museum are akin in date and style to the Rossano codex. The Sinope fragment is, however, more definitely Syrian than its contemporaries; the Cotton Genesis may perhaps be assigned to Constantinople. In any case we see here the first instance of the use of thin gold lines to pick out the high-lights on the costumes, a custom which becomes very common in later Byzantine painting. It gives an effect akin to that obtained by the gold partitions of a cloisonné enamel. The antique tradition is more purely preserved in a fragment of the Quedlinburg Bible in the Berlin Library; the Syrian is to the fore in the important Rabula Gospels, written at Zagba in 586.[1]

Secular manuscripts of this age, though in general hardly as superb as the Rossanensis or the Vienna Genesis, were both numerous and important. An early Virgil in the Vatican (V. lat. 3867) contains miniatures rather akin to those of the Vienna Genesis, and shows antique miniature art at its best. There is something here which is suggestive of the Dura

[1] Strzygowski regarded certain of the miniatures in the Etchmiadzin manuscript as of the sixth century, though the manuscript itself is dated to 989. In a recent analysis Weitzmann has shown that the miniatures are to be attributed to the same date as the book. See his *Die armenische Buchmalerei des 10. und beginnenden 11. Jahrhunderts*, Bamberg, 1933. The style and the iconography are, however, essentially eastern.

synagogue paintings; and this is to be attributed to the Hellenistic elements which are common to both, rather than to a Syrian influence in the Virgil. Dioscorides' *Natural History* was much used; it contained numerous entertaining and often beautiful illustrations. The travels of Cosmas Indicopleustes, written in Egypt in the sixth century, were frequently copied; the oldest example now extant is that in the Vatican (V. Gr. 699), and it is probably to be assigned to the eighth or ninth century. The figures are shown in rather formal attitudes; the scenes are in several tableaux, one above the other, yet within the same borders, and there is a non-naturalistic, abstract tendency, typical of the Byzantine spirit. An eleventh-century copy in the Sinai monastery contains a remarkably fine abstract composition depicting the movement of the heavens round the earth (Pl. 21, *b*).

In the iconoclast period the most popular religious book was probably the psalms, copies being fully illustrated, and topical matter often being introduced into the illuminations. The wicked are thus depicted as iconoclasts in the ninth-century Khloudov psalter at Moscow.[1] Old Testament scenes also appear, but in no particular order and in the margins, without backgrounds. Some of the figures are very Hellenistic in appearance, but Byzantine traits are now firmly established, in spite of a certain artificial reversion to the antique, which is to be observed from time to time, especially in secular work.

Architectural and geometric compositions are usual at this period to frame the titles, and a few copies of the Gospels have similar compositions in place of the usual portraits of the Evangelists at the head of each. Ornamental borders are much developed, as this form of art meets with especial favour owing to the iconoclast ban, and the elaboration of

[1] This seems the most likely date, though it follows an earlier original closely. Ebersolt even thinks it may belong to the seventh century. See Bréhier, *Art byzantin*, p. 58.

animals and birds is almost suggestive of the Celtic, though it is not carried to such extremes of fantasy.

In the ninth century the discourses of Gregory Nazianzus are especially popular, though there are strikingly different illustrations in different copies. Thus one in the Ambrosian library at Milan (Ambr. 49–50) has marginal illustrations, whereas one at Paris (Bibl. Nat. Gr. 510) contains forty-six plates. These vary considerably in merit and in the style, which is antique in some, and Byzantine in others. The finest is perhaps that of the Christ enthroned, and we see here in a developed state those trends which are later to be traced as characteristic of the Macedonian school in Byzantine painting. It is such manuscripts as these that show us the continuity of Byzantine art and disprove beyond question those theories of an extensive Italian influence which have been put forward to account for the Byzantine Renaissance of the thirteenth century. The Paris manuscript is to be dated to the reign of Basil the Macedonian (867–96), who appears in the frontispiece between Gabriel and Elias.

From the tenth to the twelfth centuries a vast quantity of manuscripts both religious and secular were illustrated, and a large number of them have survived to this day. Psalters both with marginal and with full-page illustrations are plentiful. Among the most important examples of the latter class is that in the Marcian library at Venice (Marcian Gr. 17) made for Basil II (976–1025), and that in the Vatican of much the same date (V. Palat. Gr. 381). This psalter is perhaps rather more antique in style than that of Basil II, but it is nevertheless definitely Byzantine, and its somewhat ascetic character is effective and pleasing in its delicate accomplishment (Pl. 22, *a*). Numerous other full-page psalters of the same period exist, and they are often more fully illustrated than that of Basil II. Marginal psalters show a similar tendency towards asceticism, which is in general effective, though certain authorities are inclined to regret the loss of classical ideals. A fine example of this class is in the British Museum (Add. 19352); it was executed at Constantinople in 1066.

Octateuchs, or volumes comprising the first eight books of the Old Testament, were now popular, as were illustrated editions of the prophets and certain theological writings. In the former we find numerous, though not always very elaborate, illustrations; the frontispiece of the Smyrna Octateuch, showing the Ancient of Days holding the world, is one of the most important. The illustrations of the latter retain perhaps a more antique style. Most important of the theological works are the Menologion, where the exploits of the saints are recorded in the order of the ecclesiastical calendar. A fine manuscript executed for Basil II in the Vatican (V. Gr. 1613) was illustrated by eight different painters, working in a fairly uniform style.

Homilies of the various saints were also illustrated and they usually contained, in addition to the religious miniatures, the portraits of the patron. Thus a copy of the Homilies of St. John Chrysostom in Paris (Bibl. Nat. Coislin, 79), executed for Nicephoras III (1078–81), contains four repetitions of the Emperor's portrait; in the first he is shown between St. John Chrysostom and the archangel Michael (Pl. 22, *b*). Examples of the homilies of the monk James of Kokkinobaphos in the Vatican (V. Gr. 1162) and at Paris (Bibl. Nat. Gr. 1208) contain fine frontispieces showing the church of the Holy Apostles at Constantinople, which are of interest to the topographer; but the chief importance of this work lies in the interpretation of the text and illustrations recently arrived at by Bréhier.[1] According to him the text of this work reproduces the words of an old religious dialogue

[1] See his *Art byzantin*, p. 63, and more especially 'Les Miniatures des Homélies du moine Jacques et le théâtre religieux à Byzance', *Monuments Piot*, xxiv, 1921.

play, and the miniatures are virtually sketches for the scenes before which the actors stood. Further research on the lines instituted by Bréhier in this connexion has led to the identification of other dramas and scenes; the well-known Akathistos hymn with its twenty-four episodes from the life of the Virgin is probably of such an origin, and Madame Cottas has studied in detail a further drama, the *Christos Paschon*, and its influence on art, both with regard to manuscripts and wall-paintings. Further investigations on the lines of those conducted by Bréhier and Cottas will probably produce important results regarding the history, not only of the Byzantine, but also of the whole European theatre.[1]

But most common of all books and most typical of the age are the *Tetrevangelia* (four gospels) and the *Evangelesteria* (liturgical gospels). Practically all of them contained the portraits of the Evangelists at the commencement of their respective gospels, portraits which are derived, according to Diehl, from a Hellenistic custom of illustrating the author. They exhibit great differences of style and colouring. Sometimes the Evangelists are shown standing, as in the copy of the year 964 in Paris (Bibl. Nat. Gr. 70); but more often they are seated. Figures of emperors, the Christ, the Virgin, and so on, are added in the more elaborate copies, and occasionally scenes occur either in the margin (e.g. Bibl. Nat. Gr. 115) or as full-page illustrations (e.g. Vatican, Urbin, Gr. 2). These full-page illustrations are usually very closely related to contemporary wall-paintings, and they doubtless often served as the models from which the wall-painters worked. It is possible in fact to distinguish two distinct manners in the manuscripts purely on colouristic and stylistic grounds, which are akin to the Macedonian and

[1] See her book *L'Influence du drame 'Christos Paschon' sur l'art chrétien d'orient*, Paris, 1931. The subject is dealt with in general by her in *Le Théâtre à Byzance*, Paris, 1931, and also by Bréhier, in *Journal des Savants*, août et septembre, 1913.

Cretan schools which we have already noted in the wall and panel paintings.[1]

In general this middle period is characterized by a lavish use of gold, both for backgrounds and for picking out the high-lights on costumes; jewels are freely imitated on the costumes; the colours are rarely naturalistic, being more often bright and daring, and invariably effective; elaborate

Fig. 7. KUFIC SCRIPT
from a manuscript of the Homilies of
John Chrysostom

borders are introduced wherever possible. The art is in fact essentially artificial, cultured, and urban; there is nothing idyllic or naturalistic about it, and this urban spirit—characteristic of Persian culture and painting—serves as another indication of the oriental spirit which we see concretely in the love of brightness or in the actual introduction of Kufic as an ornamental motive (see Fig. 7). The influence of Arabic script is also often to be traced in more elaborate ornament, where it has been fully assimilated, not merely copied.[2]

Later manuscripts, though they are in general fully illustrated, are not usually as fine as wall-paintings or icons, though the superb miniatures in a manuscript of John

[1] In the Bodleian, Seld. 6. Supra and Baroc. 19 are thus clearly Macedonian, while Baroc. 31 and Cromw. 16 are Cretan.

[2] For instance on the canons of concordance of a Gospel, Bibl. Nat. Suppl. Gr. 75, fol. 2, Ebersolt, *Miniatures*, pl. XLI, No. 2.

Cantacuzenos in Paris (Bibl. Nat. Gr. 1242) are worthy to rank with the best products of any age; the Transfiguration is a superb picture (Pl. 23). Copies of the Gospels or similar religious works invariably contain portraits of the authors, the Evangelists, or particular saints, as well as elaborate ornamental frames for the canons of the Church. The small pictorial handbooks or menologia are especially common; they are picture-books which serve as church calendars, and were hence turned out in large numbers, as were illustrated versions of the Akathist hymn. These books are usually small in size, and paper is as often employed as parchment. Blue and gold are the favourite colours in the illustrations. A few secular manuscripts exist with scenes in the classical manner. One at Madrid of the historian Skylitzes contains over six hundred miniatures illustrating Byzantine history from 811 to the middle of the eleventh century.

A characteristic of the last period is a taste for portraiture, to be seen in the pictures of the patrons; they are often enough drawn from actual life. Those of emperors are common, but they often tend to be formal and stereotyped; those of other individuals are more spontaneous and more varied. One of the most alive and original is that of the High Admiral Apocaucos on the title-page of an Hippocrates (Bibl. Nat. Gr. 2144). He sits on a wooden chair with a reading-desk beside him; his costume is of the finest woven silk, a number of actual examples of the type of stuff being preserved to-day in our museums and treasuries. The Lincoln College Typicon, now in the Bodleian at Oxford, contains ten full-page portraits in addition to miniatures of the Virgin, &c., and similar portraits frequently appear in wall-paintings. They are all in a fine, primitive, portraitist style, akin, as far as the stage of development is concerned, to that of English portrait painting of the Tudor period, though, of course, no actual relationship is suggested.

Through the twelfth, thirteenth, and fourteenth centuries

a number of manuscripts were written and illustrated in the Balkans, the finest probably being Bulgarian, with miniatures either purely Byzantine or akin to local wall-paintings, and the text in old Bulgar. Such a one in the Vatican, dated between 1356 and 1362, contains a translation of Constantine Manasses, an historical writer; another, in the British Museum, is now known as the Curzon Gospels. These Balkan manuscripts are little known, but it is probable that none of them are of more than secondary importance. Armenian illumination has been more fully studied; it follows along lines fairly closely parallel to the Byzantine, though the work is of the oriental family throughout. In late times a very large quantity of manuscripts were produced in a traditional style. The work is in general of secondary merit.

BIBLIOGRAPHY

Chapters on illuminations appear in the various manuals, where references to earlier works are given. The most compact yet fully illustrated monograph is that of Ebersolt, *La Miniature byzantine*, Paris, 1926. Of first importance are Gerstinger, *Die griechische Buchmalerei*, Wien, 1926, and Omont's *Miniatures des manuscrits grecs de la Bibliothèque Nationale*, Paris, 1929. A few publications have appeared since the bibliographies in the above works were compiled. Such are: Diehl in *Art Studies*, v, 1927, p. 9, who publishes an Évangéliaire of the Empress Catherine, of the first half of the eleventh century, in the Phanar Library at Constantinople; Munoz, *Studi bizantini*, Naples, 1924, p. 200, who published three codices in the Serail at Constantinople, which were not illustrated by Blass, *Hermes*, xxiii, p. 218; and Willoughby, in the *Art Bulletin*, xv, No. 1, March 1933, who publishes the Rockefeller-McCormick New Testament (Codex 2400). See also J. J. Tikanen, *Studien über die Farbengebung in der mittelalterlichen Buchmalerei*, edited by Tancred Borenius, Helsingfors, 1933.

For Armenian work see Macler's various books, more especially *Miniatures arméniennes*, Paris, 1913.

Chapter VI

MAJOR SCULPTURE

A. STONE

THE study of Byzantine sculpture is still in its infancy, and it is only of recent years that sufficient material has become available to permit anything like a comprehensive survey. Recent excavations and researches in the Near East, more especially since the War, have, however, filled the museums of Constantinople, Sofia, and Athens, and there is to-day enough material to show us at a glance that this art changed more than any other during the period of development between the fourth and sixth centuries, and continued to change until the ninth century or even later. A change in Roman sculpture had in fact set in even before the Christian era,[1] and we can trace its course by way of such monuments as the arch of Galerius at Salonica (298), the arch of Constantine at Rome, and the Theodosius column (386), the base of Theodosius (390),[2] and the column of Arcadius (403) at Constantinople. It is to be seen in ornament even more fully than in representational work, and the sixth-century columns from Antioch, now in the square of St. Mark's at Venice, are not only among the most striking, but also some of the most easily accessible monuments in which the change is illustrated.

This change is to be attributed to the penetration of eastern ideals and methods, which came to the Hellenistic area principally by way of northern Mesopotamia and Syria.

[1] Riegl regarded it as due to a development from within and not to eastern influence exerted from without. But the fact of eastern influence is now no longer to be doubted.

[2] That the base is of this date and not almost a century earlier as suggested by Wace and Traquair is shown by L'Orange, *Studien zur Geschichte des spätantiken Porträts*, Oslo, 1933, pp. 66 ff. For the column see second report on *British Academy Excavations at Constantinople*, Oxford, 1929.

More than one route and more than one version of the change can be traced, and we see the simultaneous penetration of Semitic realism in figure sculpture, of the low-relief, formalized representational system which is probably of Persian origin,[1] and of that surface covering, non-representational 'all-over' style which Strzygowski traces to the Altai-Iran region and regards as so important both in Byzantine and in north European art.

In every case Syria played an intermediary part, and Strzygowski is thus wrong when in his later work he takes from Syria the important role he assigned to it in his earlier researches. The farther East must not be forgotten; but Syria is the principal and most important centre.

But if this eastern spirit, whether formal, realist, or even purely non-representational, is to the fore in monumental as well as in architectural sculpture after the sixth century, recent discoveries show that the Hellenic tradition was not entirely lost sight of by the tenth and following centuries. Figure reliefs which show a supreme delicacy and a definite humanistic feeling were executed at this time, though geometrical and formalistic compositions are better known to-day owing to the fact that when Byzantine churches were turned into mosques by the conquering Turks these reliefs were retained, whereas most of those depicting the human or saintly form were probably destroyed.

But before passing on to a consideration of these reliefs, the eastern traits which are found definitely established by the time of Justinian may be summarized. We find non-representational features expressed in the use of the silhouette, as well as in the actual presence of formalistic patterns in place of objective shapes. The sculpture is thus akin to

[1] Representational reliefs in low salience and with a formal, even geometric, feeling are characteristic of the sculpture of Achaemenid Persia in the fifth century B.C. There is reason to suppose that such works had a definite though indirect influence on the development of a similar style in the Christian East about a thousand years later.

painting; it is to be seen from a distance, not to be touched; there is little appreciation of true perspective; owing to the nature of the art statuary and even high relief are avoided. The aim of the artist was to seek the inward significance behind the appearance, and Eric Gill's description of his own methods can be safely applied here. 'What is important', he writes, 'is what the workman has in mind, not what some model has in his body', or again, 'a work of sculpture may resemble other things or it may not, but such resemblance is accidental, not substantive'.[1]

Such features are already to be traced in certain of the more formal architectural sculptures of the fourth and fifth centuries; numerous capitals and some of the sarcophagi of Ravenna serve as examples. But at this date Latin, Hellenistic, Semitic, or eastern non-representational features are usually separate and distinct, not fused as at a later date. Thus in the important group of sarcophagi known as the Lydian or Sidamara, we see a pure Hellenic feeling surviving in the figures, whereas the ornamental work at the sides is more or less completely eastern in conception and effect. An extremely fine and fairly typical example in the Berlin Museum, which must be assigned to the fourth century, has been frequently reproduced;[2] a more complete but less delicate one recently discovered at Synnada in Asia Minor is illustrated here (Pl. 24, *a*). The same eastern and Hellenistic traits appear together in the well-known ambon or pulpit of the sixth century, formerly at Salonica, but now in the Constantinople Museum (Pl. 24, *b*).

Certain statues and portrait busts, on the other hand, are of a purely Roman character. The colossal bronze statue, probably of Valentinian I (364–74) at Barletta is the most

[1] *Eric Gill*, in Contemporary British Artists Series, 1927, Introduction, p. 14.

[2] For the Berlin fragment see Dalton, *E.C.A.* pl. XXIX. Other sarcophagi of the type are in the Ottoman Museum at Constantinople; see Mendel, *Catalogue*, vol. i.

striking example. A similar one of Justinian, now destroyed, stood at Constantinople, and a number of others survive to-day in various museums.[1] The large imperial sarcophagi of porphyry now on the terrace of the Ottoman Museum at Constantinople, are again romanized works; they may have been carved at Constantinople, though the material was certainly imported from Egypt, and a suggestion has been put forward that the majority of carvings in this material were executed on the banks of the Nile before exportation. Of porphyry again are the figures of tetrarchs of about 300 built into the wall of St. Mark's at Venice or the inferior version of the same subject in the Vatican. Certain authorities note even in these an incipient change of feeling which heralds the definite Byzantine style. It is, however, a change which might produce vigorous, but hardly refined results, and the tetrarchs seem to be much more Coptic in feeling than they are Byzantine. They may well have been carved in Egypt, for they are typical of the Christian art of that country, energetic yet rough and often second rate.[2]

In other examples we see the Hellenistic element most clearly defined. The side of an ambon in the Ottoman Museum, which is probably to be assigned to the sixth century (Pl. 25, *a*), is thus clearly Hellenic in spirit, as is a slab of the eleventh century in the Byzantine Museum at Athens bearing Jason and the bull.[3] The most common

[1] Excellent illustrations of these and of other early 'romanized' work fill the first half of Peirce and Tyler's *Art byzantin*, vol. i. For the lost statue of Justinian see Diehl, *Manuel*, i, p. 280, and for mention of occasional later survivals of these secular statues see Ebersolt, *Les Arts somptuaires*, p. 131.

[2] L'Orange, op. cit., pp. 17 and 24, also thinks they are of Egyptian workmanship.

[3] No. 175, *Guide du Musée*, fig. 28*b*. See also Bréhier, *Nouvelles Recherches*, pp. 20 ff., for this and similar Hellenistic slabs. We see in eleventh-century Greece not only a marked survival of this style, but also a marked intrusion of an oriental manner, due to the importation of Sasanian models, probably textiles.

type of fourth-century capital which is best known as the Theodosian is again clearly of Hellenistic descent (Pl. 27, *a*). Less purely Hellenistic are some heads which have a curious style of their own. A head from Ephesus now at Vienna shows this character, and another at Milan, which is sometimes called that of Theodora, falls into the same group (Pl. 26, *c*). It is almost certainly to be assigned to the age of Justinian. These heads show certain affinities with Palmyrene sculpture, but the influence responsible for their character is more probably to be attributed to Anatolia.

A survival of similar feeling is to be observed in the fine heads from a ciborium arch recently discovered in the church of St. Mary Panachrantos at Constantinople, now in the Ottoman Museum (Pl. 26, *a*), or again in a smaller fragment bearing an angel in the same museum (Pl. 26, *b*, Mendel No. 75). Dalton and Rivoira date the latter to the sixth century, though now that we are beginning to realize the excellence of the sculpture of the second Golden Age (IXth–XIIth cent.) Mendel's dating to the eleventh century seems equally probable. On similar grounds it seems possible that the Panachrantos sculpture is to be assigned to the tenth century, the date at which the church was reconstructed. Both these works show the force, lightness, and delicacy of the best Byzantine art; we see it again in the superb sixth-century Constantinopolitan capital, now in the Ottoman Museum, bearing winged horses (Pl. 27, *b*). A work like Archbishop Theodore's sarcophagus at Ravenna, which must date from about 688, is more definitely Italo-Byzantine in character.

Typical of the fifth and early sixth centuries again, but in another strain, is the rather heavier and coarser work which we see in three reliefs from the church of the Studion at Constantinople, in the St. Peter relief at Berlin, or in a relief in the Ottoman Museum showing the sacrifice of Abraham. One of the Studion reliefs showing the entry into Jerusalem is illustrated here (Pl. 25, *b*). These were probably executed at

Constantinople, though some very fine work in this forceful style is also to be assigned to Syria, more especially Antioch. Examples in major sculpture from the city are offered by the two front columns of the ciborium of St. Mark's at Venice, which date from the sixth century.

Another class of decoration to be seen in work of the age of Justinian is most aptly illustrated by capitals like those in the church of SS. Sergius and Bacchus at Constantinople or those in S. Vitale and S. Apollinare in Classe at Ravenna. They are distinguished by their deep undercutting and forceful movement—most successful is the type known as the wind-blown acanthus (Pl. 27, *c*). Numerous other examples are to be seen at Salonica, in western Asia Minor, at Constantinople, or in Greece. The undercutting of the ornament, its 'all-over' character, and its general formalistic feeling are essentially eastern, but the volutes of the classical capital here remain, whereas in another type, which is perhaps more characteristically Byzantine, they have disappeared (Pl. 27, *d*). Capitals of this form were evolved entirely owing to the demands of Byzantine architecture (see p. 46). Shadow work of the type that we see here is further developed in the ornamentation of closure slabs, until they are pierced completely through. Such slabs appear in St. Sophia at Constantinople, in S. Vitale at Ravenna, and elsewhere in the sixth century, though they are seldom found at a later date. More common in the smaller churches, however, are closure slabs with decoration in low relief; it is usually of a geometric character.

The various styles of the sixth century are developed in the seventh, but as yet we cannot estimate the extent of the development, for there are few monuments that can be definitely assigned to the age. In the iconoclast period the elaboration of the non-representational style is somewhat artificially assisted by the religious ban on the representation of the saintly or divine form, but on the other hand the

Hellenic vein seems to have survived in secular art. It was in fact this secular art that maintained the figural tradition, and in the ninth and following centuries we see a developed religious figure sculpture blossoming with amazing vigour. We have already suggested that the Panachrantos arch is to be assigned to post-iconoclast times and, though this particular assignation may be disputed, there can be no doubt of the date of a large group of closure slabs of the finest workmanship, distinguished by their low relief. The geometric motives of an earlier age continue in use—fine examples of the tenth or eleventh century are preserved at St. Mark's at Venice, at Constantinople, or in numerous places in Greece—and similar slabs with animal ornament, usually of Persian inspiration, are common. But some of the finest of all are the slabs bearing the figures of saints, angels, or of the Virgin, usually in the 'orans' position. There are a large number of examples of these slabs in the museums of Constantinople and Athens, and others appear in Italy. The finest specimen of the class is probably the mutilated slab bearing the Virgin orans, found by the French in the neighbourhood of the Serail at Constantinople in 1922, and now in the Ottoman Museum. It is to be assigned to the eleventh century (Pl. 28).[1]

In addition to the slabs with low-relief ornament we see examples decorated by means of other techniques. Thus in some cases the ground is cut away and the design left in reserve. The incised portions were probably usually filled in with some coloured material. A number of specimens, now in the Ottoman Museum, were found during excavations in the church of St. Mary Panachrantos at Constantinople; they probably belong to the tenth or eleventh century.

[1] There is a similar Madonna in Santa Maria in Porto at Ravenna, though the style is somewhat westernized, and other interesting slabs in a western-Byzantine manner are preserved in the church of Caorle near Venice. Important work at Volo in the pure Byzantine manner is published in the *Bulletin de Correspondance hellénique*, 1920, vols. vii–ix, p. 181.

Low-relief work akin to that which we see from the ninth to the twelfth centuries appears also in the Palaeologue age. The relief, however, tends to become lower and lower as time proceeds, till a system which is no more than engraving supplants that of carving. Results thus achieved, though they cannot lay any claim to be first-class works of art, are sometimes not without charm, as the seated figure of Christ in the Metropolis at Mistra shows (XIVth cent.). In some cases, however, modelling was more carefully attempted, and an interesting example of the thirteenth or early fourteenth century is offered by the reliefs above the south door of St. Sophia at Trebizond, which show scenes from Genesis. The iconography is here eastern in the main, and the reliefs may be related to the earlier ones which adorn the outside of the remarkable church of Achthamar on Lake Van (915–21).[1]

The ornament of this last age is characterized by a very profuse decoration in low relief, which often shows marked oriental affinities, due either to the presence of Islamic craftsmen or to a local copying of Islamic designs. Plaited and twisted work of Islamic character is thus common, and the employment of a Kufic script as the most usual border is general. Some attractive slabs bearing ornament of this type are preserved in the Byzantine Museum at Athens; others are to be seen in the Balkans, but the most striking are probably those built into a church at Volo in Thessaly.[2] Designs which are closely related appear on contemporary textiles, woodwork, and ceramics.

As far as we can tell the evolution which we have attempted

[1] Achthamar, as an Armenian, not a Byzantine building, is beyond the scope of this volume, though it is of the first importance in a comparative study of East Christian sculpture. For illustrations and references see Strzygowski, *Origin of Christian Church Art*, p. 63, &c. For the Trebizond reliefs see M. Alpatov, 'Les Reliefs de Ste-Sophie de Trébizond', *Byzantion*, iv, 1927–8, p. 407.

[2] See N. J. Giannopoulos and G. Millet, in *Bulletin de Correspondance Hellénique*, 1920, vols. vii–ix, pp. 181 ff.

to trace in this chapter was in the main due to the artistic influence of Constantinople and to the proximity of the fine marble quarries of the Proconnesus. The style was made universal throughout the Empire not only because artistic impulse was centred to a great extent at the capital, but also because actual finished works were exported from the quarries of the Marmora in large numbers. Certain capitals and sarcophagi of the sixth and probably also of the fifth century at Ravenna are thus of Proconnesian marble and workmanship, as are those of many another area. But other centres played a part; sculptors travelled from place to place, and designs were easily transportable, so that the actual provenance of a work is primarily to be determined by the character of the marble itself. Thus we shall only be able to tell the exact extent of the role played by Constantinople when analysis of the material has been undertaken on a wide scale. Until this has been done, it is impossible to attempt any final system of grouping or classification according to region.

BIBLIOGRAPHY

The manuals all give satisfactory outlines of the subject, and the student is referred to them for detailed references and bibliographies. In addition the following may be noted. For the early period there are excellent photographs in Peirce and Tyler's *Art byzantin*. Laurent's 'Delphes chrétien', in *B.C.H.* xxiii, 1899, p. 207, contains an important study of sixth-century sculpture. There is a vast quantity of information in Mendel's *Catalogue des Sculptures du Musée ottoman*, 3 vols., and his dating is probably the most reliable. Most of the Byzantine material is in vol. ii. See also his *Catalogue du Musée de Brousse*, 1908, and Soterio's *Guide du Musée byzantin d'Athènes*, 1932. The most important work on later Byzantine sculpture is undoubtedly that of Bréhier, 'Étude sur la sculpture byzantine', in *Nouvelles Archives des Missions scientifiques*, nouvelle série, fasc. 3, tome xx, 1911, and his Nouvelles Recherches, in vol. xxi, fasc. 9, of the same periodical, year 1916. For a catalogue of the more recent acquisitions in the Ottoman Museum see Arif Müfit, in *Jahrbuch des deutschen Archäol. Instituts, Archäol. Anzeiger*, 1931.

B. WOOD

Though probably at one time very important, sculpture in wood of early date is now practically unknown to us, owing to the fragile nature of the material. Coptic woodwork—a fair quantity of which has been preserved in the dry climate of Egypt—is beyond our scope,[1] though it suggests that friezes and iconostases of wood were used as well as those of stone in some of the smaller, if not in the larger Byzantine churches in early times, and that they were decorated with religious scenes as well as with decorative compositions. There must also have been a number of elaborate carved doors like those at Santa Sabina in Rome, an extremely important monument of the sixth century. It is divided into eighteen panels, bearing religious scenes. The iconography is Syrian. That the majority of these doors have long since perished is suggested by the pitiable state of such a late example as the fine wooden door in the church of the Nativity at Bethlehem, which belongs to the year 1227.[2] A few smaller carvings in wood which belong to the middle period survive, but none of them is of great importance. To the Palaeologue period and to post-imperial days are to be assigned a large number of carved thrones and iconostases, wood having entirely supplanted stone for these purposes. Some of them show fine work in a rather rococo style. The iconostases were often gilt; a characteristic example of the eighteenth century from a church in Cyprus is to be seen in the Victoria and Albert Museum. A few wood carvings on a smaller scale are akin to ivories; none of them is of the first importance. Carvings in other materials are again on a small, not a large, scale.

[1] Strzygowski, *Koptische Kunst, Cat. gen. des. ant. égyptiennes du Museé du Caire*, 1904. Also Millet, in Michel's *Histoire de l'art*, i, p. 257.

[2] Photos appear in the Byz. Research Fund monograph on the church, 1910, fig. 3, and in Vincent et Abel, *Bethléem*, Paris, 1914, fig. 40, p. 101.

Chapter VII

MINOR SCULPTURE

A. IVORIES

BYZANTINE ivories can very conveniently be considered under two divisions, an early and a late. In the early division we are concerned with a number of definite groups, which can be determined both according to the nature of the object and upon stylistic grounds, though it is by no means easy to be sure of the provenance of more than a few individual examples. In the other division there is far less deviation from the norm, but two main groups, the secular and the religious, must be distinguished. Before passing on to a discussion of these groups and periods, however, it may be noted that in general ivory carving probably takes longer to evolve than most other arts, and a purely Byzantine style is only arrived at in the ninth century, after the iconoclast period. Even then, when the style is firmly established in religious art, secular ivories continue in a very pagan character, and a whole group of secular caskets, which are sometimes assigned to the iconoclast period, but which are more probably of the ninth, tenth, and eleventh centuries, are completely different both in subject and in feeling from contemporary religious plaques. But with the eleventh, if not even with the tenth century, the secular style falls into the background, and the more truly Byzantine religious work appears during the remaining centuries of the Empire and is imitated in Greece, Russia, and the Balkans after the arrival of the Turks in western Europe.

In a study of the early ivories the fields that concern us are somewhat more limited than are those which we dealt with under paintings. Only two are of primary importance, namely Antioch and Alexandria. The work of both these centres was at first of a definitely Hellenistic character, but as time proceeded it became more and more affected by Syrian influence. By the fourth century ivories associated with Antioch are thus already to be distinguished by their forceful, realist style; those of Alexandria remain much more purely Hellenic and idealist until the sixth century, when Syrian influence comes in with such force that in the course of a few years a new and distinct Syro-Alexandrine manner has become supreme in the former stronghold of Hellenism. Certain of the early ivories that survive may be definitely assigned to one of these cities or the other. The superb diptych of the Symmachi and Nicomachi, of the end of the fourth century, divided between the Victoria and Albert and the Cluny Museums, is thus typical of the pure Hellenic style of Alexandria, untouched by Syrian influence (Pl. 29, *a*), while the famous Berlin pyxis, of the mid-fourth century, is typical of the early work of Antioch (Pl. 30, *a*). The earlier penetration of the realist Syrian style will be at once perceived in the pyxis, and it stands in strong contrast to the idealism of the Symmachi leaf. The Brescia casket, of the mid-fourth century, may again be assigned to Antioch. Examples which illustrate the penetration of the Syrian manner at Alexandria are more numerous. The more important are: panels with the personifications of Rome and Constantinople at Vienna, a panel at Berlin bearing Apollo, one of the fourth century with the sleeping guards and the two Marys at the Tomb in the Trivulce collection at Milan, one with Apollo and Daphne at Ravenna, and others inserted in the pulpit at Aix-la-Chapelle.[1]

The full flower of the syrianized Hellenistic style is illustrated by the ivories attached to the so-called throne of Maximian at Ravenna which belong to the early sixth century.

[1] Strzygowski considers that the composite ivory in the Louvre, known as the Barberini diptych, is also Alexandrine. Others assign it to Constantinople, and the capital seems the more likely home for so important a piece of definitely imperial character. It bears a mounted figure, perhaps Constantine or perhaps Anastasius.

With them must be associated the book covers formerly at Etchmiadzin and now in the Bibliothèque Nationale, two panels bearing gospel scenes in the Fitzwilliam Museum at Cambridge, a panel with the Baptism and one bearing St. Maenas in the British Museum, a plaque bearing St. Paul in the Cluny Museum, and others in the Louvre, at Brussels, Tongres, Berlin, and in Russia, of the sixth and seventh centuries. Though this group is easily to be distinguished on stylistic grounds, it is by no means easy to establish the place of its origin, and though it is certainly not to be assigned to Rome or Constantinople, it might just as well belong to the syrianized Alexandria as to Antioch. Until further material be unearthed in one or other of these cities, or until further researches elucidate the problem, it seems most satisfactory to designate the group by the name of Syro-Hellenistic.

Though Antioch and Alexandria are to be considered as the main type-stations of the eastern and southern Mediterranean until the sixth century, the areas respectively dependent on them are also important, and Syro-Palestinian and Egyptian or Coptic schools are also to be distinguished. Coptic work, though at first allied to some extent to the Alexandrine, soon develops along definite lines of its own, which make its products easily distinguishable by the sixth or seventh century. It is characterized by a rather florid, naturalistic manner, and is essentially a provincial art. Though not without merit, it can hardly rank with contemporary, even less with the later, Byzantine work. The Syro-Palestinian school remains, on the other hand, more closely allied to the central region; and owing to the importance of Palestine for pilgrim traffic, and the ease with which ivories could be transported, it probably exercised a considerable influence both on Italy and on Constantinople. Jerusalem seems the most likely centre for this school. A diptych with Passion scenes at Milan, a panel with the Ascension and the two Marys at Munich, and others from a casket carved about 400, which bear Passion scenes, in the British Museum, are to be assigned to it. There was, as we know, a Palestinian colony at Rome as early as the fifth and sixth centuries, and ivory carvers who worked in their national tradition probably travelled from place to place at this time; to such a travelling Palestinian workman are probably to be assigned the doors of Santa Sabina at Rome (see p. 147).

Another distinct group of ivories, comprising a book cover at Milan, casket panels in the Victoria and Albert Museum, two panels of a diptych, one in Berlin and one at Nevers, and a pyxis at Rome, is assigned by Wulff to Antioch, by Haseloff to Rome or Milan, and by Baldwin Smith to Provence. The panels bearing Passion scenes in the British Museum, which we have here associated with Palestine, are also included in the Provence group by Baldwin Smith. Though his case for Provence is well supported, Milan, or perhaps Rome, would seem a more likely home, since it is certain that ivory carvers worked in both these areas, and one of the groups that have been distinguished must undoubtedly be assigned there.

A further group associated by Dalton with Egypt and by Wulff with Edessa comprises a book cover, showing our Lord between St. Peter and St. Paul, from Murano and now at Ravenna, a panel from a book cover in the British Museum, showing the Adoration and the Nativity (Pl. 30, *b*), the Daniel pyxis in the British Museum, and panels at Paris, Bologna, and Moscow. The British Museum panel shows such marked Syrian features that the north of Syria seems a fairly certain home for the group, though so definite an assignation as Edessa seems as yet hardly justified.

Another group of early ivories, namely the consular diptychs, is determined by shape and function. About fifty of these survive, and they extend from the beginning of the fifth century till the abolition of the Consulate in 541. Only six of them were made for Rome; the others are Constantinopolitan, and were probably mostly made there, though the style of some of them is distinctly Roman, and they serve to illustrate the continuity of early imperial art which existed at the new capital. Some are in fact doubtless of Latin workmanship; others show certain oriental features, which suggest that they are the work of immigrant Syrian carvers, while some again show the distinctive mannerism of Constantinople. The diptych of Probus (406), now at Aosta, is thus essentially Roman in style, feeling, and appearance; the leaf of the fifth or sixth century in the Bargello at Florence suggests Alexandrine Hellenism, while the fifth- or sixth-century leaf bearing the Archangel Michael in the British Museum (Pl. 29, *b*) shows the superb quality, the extreme neatness of work, and the delicate feeling which herald the style of the ninth and following centuries. These features are, above anything else, the hall-mark of the capital, and this and other kindred examples serve as ample proof that the art of Constantinople at this age was not merely an eclectic art, as Dalton and others have suggested. Alexandrine, Antiochene, and Roman traits appear, yet even if the features characteristic of one or other of these are uppermost in certain instances, a subtle blending of influences is in process. This blending has not always gone as far in ivory carving by the sixth century as it has in the other arts, but the Byzantine manner is nevertheless already conceived, and we see it bursting forth into early flower in the seventh, and into full flower in the ninth centuries.

From now on it is Constantinople and her immediate dependencies, such as Salonica, that concern us, since Antioch and Alexandria produce no work of importance. Certain forms which were characteristic of the first age, such as the pyxis and the composite diptych with a number of panels like that known as the Barberini ivory in Paris (see p. 149, note 1), drop out of use, while acanthus and similar floral borders become less general. Single panels, diptychs and triptychs are now practically the only forms which are to be seen in religious art, and they bear figures which stand isolated upon a flat ground, with their names cut on either side of the head. Their character is in general pictorial rather than monumental, and the study of these religious ivories is from now on closely linked with that of painting; yet their merits as ivory carvings are none the less considerable, and the summary manner in which they have sometimes been passed over by art-historians is entirely unjustified, as even a most cursory glance at a number of specimens or reproductions cannot fail to show. But before passing on to a discussion and classification, it will be well to consider secular ivories of the iconoclast period and succeeding centuries which retain more purely antique and Hellenistic traits.

Secular Ivories. Most important of these ivories are the caskets, the decoration of which retains classical features to a marked degree. Their characteristic feature is the rosette, and these form an essential part of the ornament of practically every example. The forms again are remarkably constant, flat-topped and pyramidal-topped caskets of rectangular shape being universal; polygonal caskets are later and do not fall into this particular group. The caskets are either made entirely of ivory or consist of a wooden frame, to which small ivory or bone plaques are affixed; ivory is more usual in the tenth and eleventh centuries and bone in the twelfth. The majority were doubtless marriage caskets intended to hold the bride's jewellery; a few, more especially the later ones, were intended for ecclesiastical use. Goldschmidt and Weitzmann, in their recent exhaustive study, consider that the majority were made in Constantinople, and they are without question correct, in spite of the cases which have been put forward in favour of northern Italy or the Adriatic coast by certain earlier authorities; for the caskets are obviously of a single group and of so rich a character that no society but the most civilized and prosperous of the world could possibly have been responsible for their production. And at this period it was to Constantinople that the whole of Europe looked as the centre of civilization.

The most famous and probably the most beautiful example of the group is the Veroli casket in the Victoria and Albert Museum, which Goldschmidt and Weitzmann assign to the tenth or eleventh and certain other authorities to the ninth century (Pl. 31, *a*). Here the relief is high; the plastic feeling is marked; the composition is superbly balanced and free, while the work is of the highest quality. Classical scenes of the same character appear on most of the earlier examples; caskets of the twelfth century often bear such religious subjects as Paradise scenes or figures of Adam and Eve. New Testament scenes are unusual, though a very fine rosette casket of the twelfth century in the National Museum at Florence is composed of small panels bearing busts of Evangelists and Apostles; it is the last important example of the group and shows affinities with later plaques and diptychs as well as with the caskets (Pl. 31, *c*).

Of a rather different character is the fine casket of the tenth or eleventh century at Troyes; it lacks the rosettes, being decorated on the top and sides with mounted warriors and at the ends with fantastic birds (Pl. 31, *b*). The warriors show the influence of antique and perhaps also of Sasanian art; the birds at the ends are distinctly Chinese in character, and are due to the influence of textiles—an influence comparable to that produced on contemporary Persian pottery. The twelve-sided casket at Sens is again unusual. It is generally dated to the tenth century, but Goldschmidt and Weitzmann assign it to the eleventh or twelfth. The eleventh century would seem the more probable date. Dalton sees here a western work which translates East Christian ideals into a new language, but it is more probably Byzantine, affected to some extent by foreign influence; to venture a suggestion as to more exact provenance would be unwise in the present state of our knowledge.

Another class of secular work determined by its form consists of the large, elaborately carved tusks known as oliphants which first appear in the iconoclast period. A number of them are known from the eighth century onwards; a few bear circus scenes; one has a religious decoration, but by far the largest number bear an animal or beast ornament, set in a network of circles, suggestive of Eastern textile designs. Similar ornaments appear on Islamic ivories—mostly caskets from Sicily and Spain—and it would seem that both these and the Byzantine oliphants which bear these motives are influenced alike by Sasanian models. So similar are they at times that it is difficult to be certain whether they are actually Byzantine or Islamic. Others were in addition made in the West, in imitation of Islamic or of Byzantine originals, but these can usually be distinguished by the unfamiliar copyist feeling to be discerned in the treatment of the decoration. It has been suggested that the subject of the ornament may give some clue as to the use to which these horns were put, and that those bearing circus scenes were intended for the Hippodrome; those bearing religious motives for an ecclesiastical use; and those bearing animals for employment in the chase; the majority in any case were certainly used in hunting.

Religious Ivories. It is in the religious ivories of this age that the Byzantine genius appears in its most characteristic form. Some of them are perhaps rather too aloof in tone and too stereotyped in appearance, but others have a sublime quality which has seldom been achieved and never excelled in any other art or country. The most marked feature of these ivories are the slight and rather elongated figures, which give an impression of a general detachment from life and things of every day. A curiously ethereal quality is combined with a very minute and exact technique. From the traces of colouring and gilding which remain on certain specimens, it seems likely that some if not all of them were coloured. The subjects depicted are either single figures of Christ, the Virgin, or saints, groups of several such figures, or scenes from the New Testament, which usually appear singly or in pairs upon individual panels. The backs are often adorned with formal designs, such as a cross, from the base of which spring up stylized acanthus leaves. The iconography of saints and scenes is identical with that to be seen in contemporary painting, both in manuscripts, on panels, and on walls.

The most difficult problems connected with the study of these ivories are those of dating, for the Byzantine manner, when once established, remains peculiarly constant, and it is often hard to assign objects to a definite date between the ninth and the twelfth century, much less to a half-century or a decade. One of the few exactly dated pieces is an ivory at Berlin showing the coronation of Leo VI (886–911), but the work is poor and the style though vigorous is unpleasing. More important, and of far better quality, is a panel on a reliquary at Cortona, which is dated by an inscription to the reign of Nicephoras Phocas (963–9). It is closely related in style to the famous centre-piece of a triptych in the Bibliothèque Nationale, showing the coronation of Romanus and Eudoxia (Pl. 33, *b*). Recent research suggests that the usual assignation of this ivory to Romanus IV (1068–71) is incorrect, and that in reality it belongs to the time of Romanus II who was crowned in 959. The similarity which it shows with the Cortona plaque makes this supposition probable, and it is further borne out by a stylistic study of all the work of the age. If certain rather second-class ivories, such as the panel in the Cluny Museum showing the blessing of Otto II and Theophano (*c.* 972) be left aside, in fact, it seems that a fairly accurate dating may be arrived at by a study of style.

Among the earlier ivories, to be assigned to the end of the ninth or the early tenth century, may be cited the two fragmentary plaques in the Victoria and Albert Museum, one bearing the Virgin and Child, the other the Christ (Pl. 32, *a*). The latter undoubtedly belongs to the period immediately succeeding the iconoclast age; in it are to be seen all the features which characterize the best Byzantine art, though the supreme delicacy which is to be associated with eleventh-century work has not as yet supplanted the virile energy of the ninth. The same style is to be discerned in the large triptych in the Palazzo Venezia at Rome, which bears an inscription referring to an Emperor or prince named Constantine. It can hardly be more than half a century later, and Constantine Porphyrogenitus (913–59) would seem more likely than Constantine VIII (963–1028) or any of the eleventh-century princes of that name.[1] We have suggested that the Romanus ivory is also to be assigned to the mid-tenth century, and a fine plaque in the Gualino collection at Turin, bearing the Christ and a small figure of St. Peter, is probably only slightly later.

To the end of the tenth or the early eleventh century may be assigned the seated figure of Christ in the Louvre; a similar one in the Bodleian at Oxford is probably only slightly later, while that in the Victoria and Albert belongs rather to the early twelfth century. To the middle of the eleventh may be assigned the Harbaville triptych in the Louvre, one of the finest of Byzantine ivories (Pl. 34, *a*). It is distinguished by its supreme delicacy of feeling, while the strength and energy of such a ninth-century example as the Victoria and Albert Christ (Pl. 32, *a*) have in no way been lost. It is a masterly rendering, full of life and vigour, of a composition which would seem monotonous from any hand but that of a great master. The fine figure of St. John the Baptist at Liverpool may again be assigned to the eleventh or to the early days of the twelfth century, as may the Utrecht

[1] For an illustration and a translation of the inscription see Vollbach, Salles, Duthuit, *Art byzantin*, pl. 37, and p. 50.

Madonna and Child (Pl. 32, *b*) and the statuette of the same subject in the Victoria and Albert. This is practically the only example of free-standing Byzantine sculpture on a minor scale that is known. To much the same date belong leaves of diptychs bearing saints at Venice, Vienna, and Dresden[1] and numerous other plaques with scenes, such as that bearing the Nativity, the Transfiguration, the Raising of Lazarus, the Marys at the Tomb, and Christ with the Marys in the garden, in the Victoria and Albert Museum; that bearing the Entry into Jerusalem in the Kaiser Friedrich Museum; or that with the two Marys and the Anastasis at Dresden. To the very end of the eleventh or to the twelfth century may be assigned the ivory bearing the Baptist and SS. Philip, Stephen, Andrew, and Thomas in medallions in the Victoria and Albert (Pl. 33, *a*). It is a fine example of the exquisite quality and delicacy of the age, and shows affinities with the casket at Florence which we mentioned above (p. 154). Numerous other plaques exist in public and private collections, but space forbids us to call attention to them here.

A quantity of smaller objects in ivory and bone such as buttons and spatulae do not deserve any close attention from the artistic point of view, though small plaques intended for attaching to caskets or other objects often show elaborate work. Some, which bear a purely geometrical ornament, were commonest in Palaeologue times, though they were popular from the eleventh century onwards; others, bearing elaborate and often fantastic birds, animals, or griffins of essentially oriental character appear at their best in the eleventh or twelfth century. These plaques were probably turned out in large numbers both at Constantinople and Salonica, and they were frequently copied in the West.

To the Palaeologue period belong certain plaques akin to

[1] For the Dresden plaque and the most recent discussion of the other two see Diehl, in *Art Studies*, v, 1927, p. 3.

those of the twelfth century, though the work is in general of much less fine quality, and bone is more usual than ivory; morse (or walrus tooth) probably imported from Europe was also employed. Small crosses for attachment to necklaces are especially common; the execution is often quite good, but the figures lack vigour and the ornament tends to be stereotyped or somewhat over-profuse. This tendency is exaggerated as time proceeds, and in post-imperial days ivories from the Balkans of the fifteenth and sixteenth centuries, and more especially those from Roumania, though not lacking in interest, can hardly be considered as of more than secondary importance. The traditions of the middle period were upheld for a time on Mount Athos, and though the profusion of ornament which we see in the Balkans is avoided, the work soon becomes arid and lifeless.

B. STEATITE AND OTHER MATERIALS

Plaques of steatite or similar soft stones, both large 'icons' bearing a number of figures or scenes, and smaller pendants with a figure of the Virgin or some saint, are common from the tenth or eleventh century onwards; in Palaeologue times they come into special prominence owing to the poverty of the Empire and the difficulty of obtaining so expensive a material as ivory for the panels or a more precious one such as gold for a pendant. Though the work is often of secondary quality, a few surviving examples are very fine, and more were probably distinguished originally by a delicacy of execution which can now no longer be appreciated owing to the softness of the material, which suffers very easily from attrition.

One of the earliest and finest examples is the small head of an emperor in the Kaiser Friedrich Museum; it is to be assigned to the tenth or early eleventh century (Pl. 34, *c*). To the eleventh century belong the fine Archangel Michael at Florence and the Hetoimasia or Preparation of the Throne in the collection of the Comtesse de Béhague in Paris (Pl.

34, *b*). In both these examples the relief is high and the style vigorous. Of the same date is probably a very fine plaque bearing St. Theodore Stratelates in the Chersonese Museum.[1] To the twelfth century may be assigned the twelve feasts at Toledo, while the rather smaller panel of the same subject in the Monastery of Vatopedi on Athos is probably of early Palaeologue times. Slightly later again is another version of the subject in the church of St. Clement at Ochrida. Other examples in public and private collections are too numerous to mention individually, though those in the British Museum and the Louvre may be noted as the collections are easily accessible. The majority are on a rather small scale and are characterized by low relief.

Occasionally compositions or pastes were employed, imitating steatite or some more precious material such as lapis. A very fine figure of Christ in actual lapis, with inlaid lettering in gold, from the St. Denis treasure, is preserved in the Louvre. It is to be dated to the eleventh or twelfth century.

It is impossible here to call attention to the numerous small engraved gems for which Byzantine art was responsible; most of them belong to the first and second periods. The fine cameo, probably of Honorius and Maria, in the Rothschild collection, to be dated to about 395, the rock-crystal lions' heads in the Cluny Museum, of the fourth or fifth century, and a sapphire of the tenth century bearing the head of Christ, in the Feuardent collection, may, however, be noted.[2]

BIBLIOGRAPHY

Except for certain recent works, full bibliographies and general summaries of the subject are given in the manuals. Wulff, and Dalton in *East Christian Art*, give special attention to the early ivories, and the student should consult Dalton's later work in addition to *Byzantine Art and Archaeology*, owing to certain opinions which are changed or cast aside. For the early ivories see also

[1] See *L'Art byzantin chez les Slaves*, ii, p. 35.

[2] See Vollbach, Salles, Duthuit, *Art byzantin*, pls. 40, 41, and 49.

Delbrueck, *Die Consulardiptychen*, Berlin and Leipzig, 1929, and for the lates ones Goldschmidt and Weitzmann, *Die byzantinischen Elfenbeinskulpturen des X.–XIII. Jahrhunderts*, Berlin, 1931. Only the first volume of this great work is as yet published; it deals with the rosette caskets in a full and masterly manner. The second volume will deal with plaques, diptychs, &c. Schlumberger's *Épopée byzantine*, though it does not deal with the arts, contains a large number of unpublished or little known ivories as illustrations, and original material is included in Vollbach, Salles, Duthuit, *Art byzantin*, and in Miss Longhurst's *Catalogue of Carvings in Ivory in the Victoria and Albert Museum*, Part I, 1927; both these contain more general information than is usual in a catalogue of individual objects.

Chapter VIII

METAL WORK AND ENAMELS

A. VESSELS

THE early vessels known to us can be classed in a single group, most of them being made of silver. They were apparently in fairly universal employment and were transported long distances either as loot or for purposes of trade. Thus Byzantine as well as Sasanian silver plate has been discovered in south Russia, where it was probably used as a means of barter to obtain furs; an important example is the plate from south Russia formerly in the Stroganoff collection bearing a jewelled cross at the centre. Alexandria and Antioch were probably the main centres of manufacture, though silver plates were also made at Constantinople, a supposition supported by the story of Shapur quoted on page 197.

Most of these silver vessels are ecclesiastical; their origin can be traced from Roman work and the secular imperial disks of silver, which were given as presents in early Byzantine times, are their closest relations. Eight such disks are known, the most famous being those of Theodosius at Madrid and of Justinian at Leningrad.[1] They show close affinities with the sculpture of the period, as for instance with that on the base of the Theodosius obelisk at Constantinople (390).

Ecclesiastical plate of various dates between the fourth and seventh centuries has been preserved in quite large quantities, more than one important hoard having been unearthed in the last forty years or so. The Esquiline treasure in the British Museum has certain eastern affinities, but Dalton thinks that it is to be attributed to Alexandria; the same is probably true of the Traprain treasure in the Edinburgh Museum. A fine paten, bearing the Communion of the

[1] See Peirce and Tyler, *L'Art byzantin*, vol. i, pls. 35, 36, 37. They illustrate the disk of Valentinian II (375–92) and also that of Aspar (434).

Apostles, from Riha on the Orontes and now in the Bliss collection at Washington, shows the Syrian realist and the Hellenistic idealist styles combined (Pl. 35, *a*); it is probably to be assigned to Antioch, and shows the work of the sixth century at its best. Bréhier also attributes the treasures found at Lampsacus on the Hellespont, and in Cyprus, to Antioch, but Dalton considers that the latter, which is known as the Kyrenia treasure, and is now divided between the British Museum, the Nicosia Museum, and New York, was actually made in Cyprus. The former opinion seems the more probable, since Antioch was an important cultural and artistic centre, whereas Cyprus was primarily agricultural and residential. Its proximity to the Syrian coast also makes the Antiochene origin likely. These treasures, which probably belong to the fifth century, comprise plates, patens, chalices, and spoons, all of which invariably bear hall-marks of single letters or monograms. The decorations are usually in relief—the dish from Kyrenia illustrated here (Pl. 35, *b*) is a fine example; they are sometimes also incised and filled with niello. A fine paten from Lampsacus, now in the Ottoman Museum, is decorated in this manner.

Of rather more elaborate character is the famous chalice discovered near Antioch in 1910, bearing an open-work decoration. Its date and even its authenticity have been much disputed, but consensus of opinion now votes for its genuineness; it is probably to be assigned to the fourth century, but it is not by any means so superb a piece of work as has often been suggested. A smaller chalice and an embossed book cover were brought to light at the same time. They are probably to be dated to the fourth or early fifth century. Somewhat similar workmanship was doubtless employed on the famous altar of St. Sophia, of which we have written accounts only.

Church plate of silver, with decoration in relief or engraved, was apparently in more or less universal employment till the ninth or tenth century, when a new and more elaborate type comes into vogue, superb examples of which are preserved in the treasury of St. Mark's at Venice. Metal, precious stones, and enamels are now employed on the same object, the most gorgeous and sumptuous results being obtained. The bodies of these vessels are more often of some precious stone such as agate, sardonyx, or alabaster than of metal; the stems of the chalices are of gold or silver-gilt; enamels and precious stones are set around the rims in mounts of metal (Pl. 36, *a*). Glass was occasionally employed in a similar manner (see p. 192). No Byzantine examples of work in rock crystal, such superb specimens of which belong to contemporary Moslem art, have, however, come down to us. A fine eight-lobed paten of the eleventh century at Halberstadt may be noted, and Clarke bought the fragments of another made of agate from a gem-cutter in Constantinople in about 1810.[1] For sheer excellence and beauty few things have ever been made that can equal the six-lobed alabaster paten with enamel at the centre in the treasury of St. Mark's (Pl. 36, *b*).

That sumptuous work was also occasionally executed at Constantinople in the Palaeologue period is proved by the fine chalice of Manuel Palaeologos (1391–1425) in the monastery of Vatopedi on Mount Athos, but treasures of this nature were rare, and later work in Greece and the Balkans, more especially Roumania, is usually of secondary quality. Fine, but perhaps somewhat over-ornate church plate of Byzantine type was common in Russia till the art of that land was modified by west-European influence.

BIBLIOGRAPHY

For the early silver plate see especially Dalton, *Catalogue of Early Christian Antiquities in the British Museum*; Ebersolt, 'Le Trésor de Stûma', in *Revue Archéologique*, xvii, 1911, ii, p. 407; and

[1] E. D. Clarke, *Travels in various Countries*, London, 1811, ii, p. 10.

Bréhier, 'Les Trésors d'argentine syrienne et l'école artistique d'Antioch', in *Gazette des Beaux Arts*, 1920. Excellent reproductions are also given in Peirce and Tyler, *L'Art byzantin*. For the middle period see especially Pasini, *Il tesoro di San Marco*, Ebersolt, *Les Arts somptuaires de Byzance*, Paris, 1923, and the same author's *Les Sanctuaires de Byzance*, Paris, 1921.

B. METAL WORK IN RELIEF

A number of bronze statues of Roman style occur in the early period; the most important of them is that usually attributed to the emperor Valentinian I (364–74) at Barletta. After the fifth century the free-standing statue is almost entirely superseded by the bas-relief, and the scale is much reduced. Work of the fifth to the ninth centuries is in fact illustrated only by the silver vessels already discussed. Other examples on which figured relief decoration appears are the seventh-century lead ampullae from the holy places in Palestine, some of which are preserved at Monza, or the small bronze lamps and censers of about the seventh century, which bear New Testament scenes.

In the post-iconoclast period relief work is much more popular, and we see more than one technique elaborated. Large-scale work is used for the decoration of doors, such as those of the ninth century at St. Sophia in Constantinople; and Clavijo records that two silver-gilt doors, large enough for a man on horseback to ride through, were taken by Tamerlane from Brusa and erected outside the tent of his chief wife at Samarkand.[1] Small plaques of bronze or copper bearing cast figures were also made, single panels, diptychs, and triptychs occurring. A beautiful triptych of

[1] He describes them as follows: 'These double doors were covered with plates of silver gilt ornamented with patterns in blue enamel work, having insets that were very finely made in gold plate. In one door was figured an image of St. Peter, while in the other was St. Paul, each saint having a book in his hand.' He also mentions a cabinet decorated with enamel work, and a wooden screen covered with plates of silver gilt. Broadway Travellers Series, p. 269.

the eleventh or twelfth century in the Victoria and Albert Museum is one of the finest specimens (Pl. 37, *a*).

More common, however, is work in the embossed or repoussé technique, which is often carried to a high pitch of excellence. The earliest example is probably the gold cross in St. Peter's presented by Justin II; crosses at Ravenna and Monza are only slightly later. Among the earlier reliquaries decorated in this way the finest are probably those of Jaucourt near Troyes, Brescia, and Alba Fucense. In the middle period the technique is especially popular for plaques intended for attachment to book covers, icons, or reliquaries, the thin metal which this hammering out necessitates being unsuitable for use unless attached to some stronger base. Examples are numerous from the tenth to the twelfth centuries. The superb Nicephoras Phocas Bible cover in the Lavra on Athos, bearing the standing figure of Christ, provides us with a point of departure, for it is not earlier than 970 (Pl. 37, *b*). A fine plaque bearing the Deesis (Christ, the Virgin, and the Baptist) is probably not more than a century later; it is attached to a book cover in the John Rylands Library at Manchester (Pl. 38, *a*). A standing figure of the Virgin with the Child on her arm in the Victoria and Albert Museum may again be assigned to the late eleventh century;[1] other good work of the tenth, eleventh, and twelfth centuries is preserved in the treasury of St. Mark's at Venice, the most notable being some book covers with figure and purely ornamental decoration, and an artophorion or reliquary in the form of a church for containing the Eucharistic bread. Later fourteenth-century examples of these appear in Roumania and Greece; the most important is probably that in the monastery of Dionysiou on Mount Athos.

Among other examples of the work of the middle period may be cited the staurothekes or flat rectangular reliquaries,

[1] This has been regilt in a very unpleasant manner in recent times, though there can be little doubt as to the authenticity of the metal work.

intended to contain a fragment of the True Cross. An example in repoussé from the treasure of St. Denis is now in the Louvre; repoussé figures are associated with enamel ones on the Estergom reliquary in Hungary (Pl. 40, *b*); an interesting and little known example now at Urbino and formerly at Murano is decorated entirely in repoussé (Pl. 38, *b*).[1] In the twelfth century icon frames begin to appear, and they continue in use until the present day, covering the backgrounds and sometimes even the whole pictures with the exception of the faces. There is a twelfth-century example in St. Mark's, and some which are probably to be ascribed to the thirteenth century are preserved in the church of St. Clement at Ochrida in Macedonia. Much work was done in Italy in imitation of the Byzantine—a cross in the church of S. Francesco at Assisi serves as an example—and the technique was even further developed in Georgia. A cross formerly at Nicorzminda (Pl. 39, *b*) and the side wings of the Gelat icon may be cited.[2] Icons and crosses in repoussé work are perhaps more numerous there than specimens of any other type. At a later date, namely in the fifteenth and sixteenth centuries, a large number of book covers were produced in Roumania, but the work has lost the balance and excellence of the Byzantine. Important examples are preserved at Neamtu and at Brancoveanu in Roumania and in the monastery of Dionysiou on Athos.

BIBLIOGRAPHY

For the early examples see the manuals, more especially Dalton, and also Ebersolt, *Les Arts somptuaires de Byzance*. Later specimens have not as yet been studied in full detail, but some of the repoussé work will shortly be published by the author in *Apollo*.

[1] See Luigi Serra, in the *Burlington Magazine*, xxxv, 1919, p. 105.

[2] Kondakov, *Georgia*, p. 27, fig. 11 (in Russian). This is the most important source for the Georgian work. See also T. Talbot Rice, 'Georgian Art in the Middle Ages', *Asiatic Review*, April 1929, and 'The role of Georgia in the art of the Middle Ages', *Asiatic Review*, Jan. 1930.

C. ORNAMENTS AND JEWELLERY

Finger-rings of gold, silver, copper, and bronze, with engraved inscriptions or with stones or pastes set in the bezel, are common throughout the whole period. Constantinople was the main centre, but they were doubtless also produced in every large town. They usually bear monograms or symbols of a religious character, such as fish, or occasionally figures of saints. Ear-rings, brooches, and necklaces sometimes show very excellent workmanship, but only very few examples have come down to us, since such objects were not usually placed in the tombs as in the pagan world and, being of valuable material, they were probably in most cases melted down at the sack of Constantinople by the crusaders (1204). Gold work, filigree, and especially orfèvrerie cloisonné, where gems or pastes are set in little frames or clasps on the main background, were types of work favoured by the rich. Cameos were again essentially a luxury product, and they appear only in the first period.

In general we know far less about Byzantine jewellery in early times than we do of pagan, and at a later date purely ornamental jewellery was much more of a Gothic than a Byzantine art. In the Byzantine world, in fact, only objects of a religious character seem to have been universally popular, and these were more in the nature of talismans than adornments, so that each person would only possess a single specimen. Most important of these were pendant crosses of gold, silver, copper, or enamel. They usually open so as to contain the relics of some saint. A famous example is the Beresford Hope cross in the Victoria and Albert Museum (Pl. 39, *a*). Crucifixes, as in the western world, were never made.

Under this heading attention may be drawn to certain small figures of cast metal, most of which are to be dated before the sixth century.

BIBLIOGRAPHY

See the manuals, especially Dalton, *B.A. and A.* Photographs of some interesting jewellery, some Byzantine and some Gothic, appear in Vollbach, Salles, Duthuit, *Art byzantin*, Pls. 49 and 54.

D. COINS AND SEALS

The Byzantine coinage may be most conveniently considered to begin with the reign of Arcadius I (395–407). It comes to an end with that of John VIII (1425–48), since no coins have as yet been found that can be attributed to the last ruler of the Empire, Constantine XI. Though the superb portraiture and exquisite die-cutting which make of ancient Greek coins one of the choicest of the arts are not apparent in Byzantine work, we do not find that the East Christian coinage takes on a purely stereotyped character as has sometimes been suggested. The imperial portraits, though they follow a strict convention, are generally full of life and spirit: other subjects, most of which are of a religious nature, comprising figures of Christ, the Virgin, or certain saints, often show an extreme delicacy of feeling, conception, and execution. Byzantine coins are in fact invariably interesting and quite often beautiful, and hence they deserve the attention of the art historian, though their study is too detailed to be undertaken here. Their importance to the archaeologist, numismatist, and historian of events is obvious.

Somewhat allied to coins are the lead seals or bullae which were in such common use. They usually bear an inscription upon one face and a figure on the other. These figures are both of an imperial and a religious character, and as the work is often excellent and as there are many dated examples, they help us, on stylistic grounds, to a dating of carvings in ivory or other forms of metal work on a larger scale.

BIBLIOGRAPHY

The fullest publication of coins is Wroth's *Catalogue of Imperial Byzantine Coins in the British Museum.* Sabatier's *Description générale des Monnaies byzantines*, 1862, is now almost unprocurable. An excellent handbook in three parts by H. Goodacre is published by Spink.

The standard work on seals is Schlumberger, *Sigillographie*; there are articles by the same author in his *Mélanges d'archéologie byzantine*, Paris, 1895. A more recent work is C. H. Constantopoulos, *Byzantine Lead Seals*, Athens, 1930 (in Greek).

E. ENAMELS

The art of enamelling was no new one when the Byzantine Empire was born, superb examples having been produced in Egypt, in the western half of the Roman Empire, and in the East. But in the first centuries of its existence the new culture produced nothing of strikingly original character, though literary evidence suggests that enamelling was done from the fourth century onwards. An ear-ring in the Louvre is perhaps to be assigned to this period, and a clasp from an ivory binding in Milan Cathedral was made, according to Kondakov, before the days of Justinian. It is of red and light-green enamel, which in places turns to emerald-green or violet. Of the treasures in enamel which were set up by the same emperor in St. Sophia nothing has survived, though a few examples preserved in western museums and treasuries are of much the same date; they serve to give us some idea of the art at this time. Such are the well-known reliquary of St. Radegond at Poitiers, a fine cross in the Vatican, bearing various scenes, and perhaps also the Beresford Hope cross in the Victoria and Albert Museum (Pl. 39, *a*).[1]

Enamels from other areas and of early date are in the champlevé or encrusted technique on copper or bronze grounds, but it would appear that the very first Byzantine efforts were on gold grounds and in the cloisonné technique, and it was this system that was so superbly developed by the Byzantines between the ninth and thirteenth centuries. The

[1] Some authorities consider these as of ninth-century date. Diehl, however, takes them to be early. See his *Manuel*, i, p. 307, fig. 153.

work is to be distinguished by the small cloisons or partitions which separate the enamel pigments. These wire-like partitions are bent so as to outline the desired contour and are then soldered edgeways to the ground, which is sometimes also beaten out slightly to give greater depth. Their height, according to Kondakov, is a valuable criterion for dating. In the sixth and the following centuries there are but few examples; in the eleventh century one millimetre would appear to be the usual height; in the thirteenth they are often as much as two millimetres high. The colouring also differs somewhat from century to century. Thus in the iconoclast age the colours are dark and lack variety, translucent emerald greens, blues, and purples predominating, while purple is often used for the hair, and the flesh tints are waxen or greenish. In the tenth and eleventh centuries pure bright colours are usual, sky and turquoise blue, violet, and bright purple being usual, with pinkish flesh tints. In the twelfth century white and turquoise blue predominate; red and light-coloured shades are only used here and there. In the thirteenth century we see a copper-green ground and white lettering as the characteristic features; in the fourteenth the colours are misty and of a very vitreous quality, bright tones such as deep blue, bright yellow, red, and vermilion being most popular, though in spite of this variety the work somehow lacks brightness and depth. Work on a small scale is further usually to be associated with the eleventh century, while the best drawing and drapery are to be found in the tenth.

A few small enamels of decorative character are perhaps to be attributed to the iconoclast period, but the Golden Age of the art really begins in the tenth century. Important enamels are mentioned in contemporary records of the reign of Constantine Porphyrogenitus (911–59), and slightly later we find Basil II (976–1025) as a great patron of the art. Constantinople was certainly the chief source of manufacture at this time, though in the twelfth and thirteenth centuries a few examples appear to come from Sicily, while others, more closely akin to the Constantinopolitan ones, were also made in Georgia. Usually—owing to the exigencies of the technique and the expense of the materials—enamels were on a small scale, medallions or plaques for attachment to other objects such as book covers, metal crosses, chalices, reliquaries, or even ceremonial garments being most usual. Sometimes a whole object is composed of a single enamel, as for instance in the case of small reliquary crosses intended to be hung around the neck. The most famous of these is the Beresford Hope cross in the Victoria and Albert Museum, which we here assign to the sixth century. Occasionally larger enamels in the encrusted technique appear, where a whole figure is composed of enamel: painted, as it were, in enamel, not a coloured drawing, like the cloisonné work. Such examples are the tenth-century book covers bearing the archangel Michael and the tenth-eleventh century Virgin known as the Madonna of St. Mark's, both in St. Mark's treasury at Venice. They antedate examples of the same technique in Europe by some centuries.

Figure subjects of a religious character constitute the most usual decoration. It is often possible to date them on iconographical and stylistic evidence by comparison with other arts, as well as on the technical grounds to which we have already called attention. Other enamels are dated more exactly historically. Such are the fine cross at Copenhagen from the tomb of Queen Dagmar, who died in 1212; the Limburg reliquary which bears an inscription relating to Constantine and Romanus (919–44); the crown in the Budapest Museum which bears enamels of Constantine Monomachus (1042–54). The enamels on the royal crown of Hungary, one of which bears a portrait of the Emperor Constantine Ducas[1]

[1] The first detailed photograph of this appeared in the *Illustrated London News* for 22 Feb. 1930.

(1060–7), and some enamels on the icon at Khakuli in Georgia which show Christ crowning the same emperor. By far the richest collection is preserved in St. Mark's at Venice, where plaques of the first quality of every size and shape occur. A Crucifixion on a book binding is perhaps the finest example (Pl. 40, *a*). A large number of enamels of different dates and varying quality are also attached to the Palo d'Oro, a screen of Gothic workmanship in St. Mark's.[1] A plaque bearing a dancing girl of very eastern character, from the crown at Budapest, is preserved in the Victoria and Albert Museum; this and the Beresford Hope cross are easily accessible and show the art at its best. They should be inspected, for no photograph can do justice to the exquisite quality and colouring of this art. Exceptionally fine work appears on the staurotheke or reliquary for a fragment of the True Cross at Estergom in Hungary (Pl. 40, *b*), which is to be dated to the twelfth century, and again on a cross in Cosenza Cathedral of the same date.[2] A cross of Georgian workmanship which bears three medallions of the very best eleventh-century Byzantine enamel was formerly at the monastery of Nicorzminda in Georgia (Pl. 39, *b*). Numerous other enamels were preserved in that country until 1917, some of which were Byzantine, but many more of local workmanship. The quality of this local work is often quite as good as that done at Constantinople. The present whereabouts of most of these enamels is uncertain.

Some liturgical fans at Serres in Macedonia, which belong to the sixteenth century, represent a local survival of the art; elsewhere in Greece and the Balkans any late enamels that exist are in the champlevé technique and usually show attractive, though rather second-class work. In Russia, on the other hand, enamelling of this type was carried to a high pitch of excellence. In the nineteenth and early twentieth

[1] For an account of this see Diehl, *Manuel*, ii, p. 701.
[2] See Vollbach, Salles, Duthuit, *Art byzantin*, pls. 61 ff.

centuries a large number of very fine forgeries of Byzantine work were put on the market, more especially in Russia, which were said to be due to the hands of an Armenian family.

BIBLIOGRAPHY

Kondakov's *Histoire et monuments des émaux byzantins*, 1892, in French and German, is the standard work, but excellent summaries appear in the manuals, especially in Dalton, *Byzantine Art and Archaeology*. See also Ebersolt, *Les Arts somptuaires de Byzance*, for a general summary. Dalton, in the *Burlington Magazine*, xxi, 1912, pp. 3, 65, 127, 219, 290, describes the superb pieces in the Pierpont Morgan collection, with excellent coloured plates; H. P. Mitchell, *Burl. Mag.*, xl, 1922, p. 64, publishes the Victoria and Albert and Budapest dancing girls. The most recent general work on enamelling by a practising expert is Tenischeva's *Enamels and Incrustation*, Seminarium Kondakovianum, Prague, 1930 (in Russian).

Chapter IX

TEXTILES

IN the history of Byzantine art textiles form a very important group, not only on account of their own excellence, but also because they served as convenient models for other techniques. They could be easily transported from region to region, and were hence frequently imitated, in carving, on metal work, in paintings, or on pottery, and it was without doubt by means of textiles that a great number of the motives which we find developed in the Byzantine art of the sixth century and again in that of the eighth to the twelfth centuries were conveyed thither from Egypt or the East. The eagle design on a fragment of pottery excavated by the British Academy expedition at Constantinople in 1927 serves as an excellent instance of a textile design imitated in pottery (Fig. 13); the rosettes which appear on a whole group of ivory caskets (Pl. 31, *a*) were probably first used on stuffs, while the majority of the consular diptychs of earlier times show us contemporary textile designs reproduced on the costumes of the figures. A similar instance occurs on the well-known relief of Chosroes II (590–628) at Taq-i-Bostan in Persia, and it is this above anything else that enables us to assign certain textiles which have survived to this day in the West to Sasanian Persia rather than to Byzantium or to Egypt.

Were it not for these concrete reproductions in stone, ivory, or some other solid material, our knowledge of such fragile things as textiles in early times would be but very one-sided, for it is only from Egypt that any extensive quantity has been recovered. Here they were invariably employed for burial purposes; they were manufactured on a very wide scale, and in addition the dry soil served to preserve them admirably. There is in fact a wealth of material, dating from classical times till about the eighth century, most of which is definitely Hellenistic in design; Greeks as well as Egyptians were often employed as weavers. Three main periods may be distinguished in Christian times: the Graeco-Roman, from the third to the fifth centuries, the transitional period, from the fifth to the sixth, and the Coptic period from the sixth century onwards. The last is of local interest and does not concern us here; the two former played a role of the very first importance in the development of the Byzantine textile art.

In the first period linen or wool are the most common materials, the linen forming the groundwork, the wool the decoration; tapestry weaving or embroidery is usual, though looped weaving is also often employed to give greater thickness to the costumes. Figure subjects, such as pagan gods, mythological scenes, animals and fish, or purely geometrical patterns form the decorations; a thin, line-drawing style, with simple colouring is characteristic. In the second period (fifth and sixth centuries) flowers and baskets of fruit and Christian symbols such as the XP cross are introduced into the pagan scenes, and Christian scenes and figure subjects become more usual. The colouring is in general rather brighter than in the preceding age. Dyed stuffs, where the design was drawn out in a 'resist' before the material was dipped, are also quite common. It is in this period also that silks begin to become popular. We first see them as small panels for attaching to costumes, in two colours only, a pale design on a purple ground; but soon other colours become popular, and by the sixth century a number of polychrome panels are known which are without question of Egyptian manufacture. Others, however, which bear figured designs on a large scale, are more probably to be attributed to western Asia, and it is with the study of them that our first real problems begin.

Strzygowski thinks that these figured silks are to be

attributed wellnigh entirely to Persia, where there was doubtless a long-established textile industry of which we know little owing to the destruction of all material by damp.[1] Von Falke, on the other hand, considers that Persia only learnt to make figured silks in the time of Shapur, owing to the introduction of foreign weavers, Greeks or Egyptians, after the campaign of 355–60. For him the development of silk weaving is due to the long-established tradition in Egypt, and it is only in the designs that Persia contributed anything new. In the absence of actual material from Persian soil it is hard to affirm which of them is correct, nor does the question concern us very nearly in a study of Byzantine textiles, for there can be no doubt that the technique which was adopted by the Byzantine weavers was that generally employed in Egypt, and that it came to them from Egypt together with a number of important motives of design. But they owed in addition a very great deal to Sasanian Persia, for it is to that country that are to be assigned all the vast number of animals, birds, or fantastic beasts, all those riders and horsemen framed in medallions and usually shown in pairs, back to back or confronted, with the sacred tree or *hom* motive between them. The Persian designs probably penetrated to Egypt at the same time that they penetrated to Constantinople and to Syria, for by the sixth century much in the general disposition of Egyptian work is of a very Iranian appearance. And even if the Sasanians only began to make textiles of importance in the fourth century, it is only natural to find that their art affects the region to the west for the next two or three hundred years, for the cultivation of silk was an Eastern monopoly and all silk had to come to the West by way of Persia. Until about 552, when legend records that two monks of Khotan sold the secret of cultivation to Justinian, the silk trade presented one of the most important diplomatic problems of the day. We find, moreover, that

[1] *Altai Iran*, p. 79.

Sasanian designs were even carried to China and copied there, though there was an old-established silk industry in the country from Han times onwards (206 B.C.–A.D. 265), which employed different techniques to those which we see in western Asia.

The earlier pagan textiles which are to be assigned definitely to Egypt must be passed over briefly; the superb painted triumph of Dionysos in the Louvre (IVth cent.), the woven linen textile showing Nereids and marine monsters in the Bliss collection at Washington (IVth to Vth cent.), and the linen showing a seated divinity (VIth cent.) in the same collection, must, however, be noted.[1] Of Egyptian manufacture, but Christian in character, is a printed stuff of the fifth or sixth century in the Edinburgh Museum, showing the Hetoimasia or Preparation of the Throne. To Egypt again has been attributed an important linen textile in the Rockefeller collection bearing a bearded military saint (Pl. 41, *a*). On account of analogies which it shows with the seated divinity in the Bliss collection, Peirce and Tyler date this textile to the last quarter of the fifth century.[2] But the saint is so strikingly Byzantine in appearance, we see here so complete a fusion of the Semitic and Hellenistic trends, that one is tempted at first sight to assign the textile to Constantinople and to a later date. A final decision will only be possible when more comparative material is known.

The superb textile of the first half of the sixth century in the Vatican which shows the Annunciation and the Birth of Christ, framed in medallions, in green, gold-brown, and white, on a red ground (Pl. 42, *a*), is attributed by von Falke to Alexandria, but the style is exactly what one would expect to see at Constantinople. Oriental influence is to be dis-

[1] For illustrations see Vollbach, Salles, Duthuit, *Art byzantin*, pls. 81, 83, and 84.

[2] Peirce and Tyler, *Art byzantin*, i, p. 92, pl. 155.

cerned here in the bejewelled throne on which the Madonna sits, and though certain authorities consider that it is a Hellenistic feature, it is probably to Persian influence that the framing of scenes in circles is to be attributed. The Hellenistic tradition proper prefers to devote to each scene a whole panel, or at most to enclose it within a rectangular frame. We see the circles again enclosing a four-horse chariot or quadriga in gold on a purple-blue ground on the fine silk, part of which is at Aix-la-Chapelle and part in the Cluny Museum at Paris (Pl. 41, *b*). It is to be dated to the sixth century and is very probably of Constantinopolitan workmanship.

As time progresses the use of circles to frame different figural compositions becomes more and more popular, and with the seventh century we see an introduction of very pure Iranian motives into Byzantine textile art. Constantinople is by now the most important centre of manufacture, and it is possible to assign to that city certain definite types, both on historical and on stylistic grounds. Thus the royal workshops there held a monopoly of the imperial purple, while certain of the creations of this and subsequent centuries show so marked an individuality and so developed a quality that it is only possible to assign them to the capital. Syria, though important as an area of cultivation of silk, was conquered by Islam in 636 and Egypt fell soon after; as a result both Syrian and Egyptian work soon began to take on a definitely Islamic character, though, as the conquering Arabs were devoid of a culture themselves, Persian and Byzantine elements form the basis of the art. Byzantine and Moslem textiles thus have in common many motives which they both owe alike to Sasanian Persia or to Egypt. It is often impossible to distinguish works of the one culture or the other for the first century or so of the Islamic era, but distinctive elements are soon developed, and after about the ninth century classification becomes somewhat less difficult. Islamic work is characterized in general by an elaboration of detail and of line which is in the days of decline over-exaggerated; inscriptions, first in Kufic and later in flowing Nastalic, are often added. The Byzantine style, on the other hand, can be distinguished by its monumental manner, its restraint, the strength of conception of design, and its rather more severe colour schemes. Occasionally inscriptions in Greek are added, and the pieces that bear these furnish us with absolutely sure criteria for attribution and dating.

To separate Byzantine from Persian work between the seventh and ninth centuries is, however, rather less easy, for a very pure Sasanian style penetrated to the former area and survived in the latter after the Islamic conquest. Some of the superb textiles of these centuries which have been preserved in the West in the treasuries of various cathedrals are thus still assigned somewhat divergently by the different authorities, some to the one and some to the other country. The fine textile of the seventh or eighth century at Nancy, for instance, which bears two lions confronted with the *hom* between them, in the usual circle, was shown both at the Persian exhibition in London and at the Byzantine exhibition at Paris in 1931,[1] while a silk of the eleventh century bearing confronted horses in medallions in the treasury at Sens has again been claimed for both countries.

The Nancy textile is probably Persian; the Sens one may be Byzantine. Other textiles of the age are without doubt Byzantine; they show the style of the capital at its best, and their colouring is distinct from that usually to be seen on Persian products. They now constitute some of the most important monuments of Byzantine art that have survived; how much they were valued in Byzantine times is aptly illustrated by a passage in the so-called chronicle of Nestor, where it is recorded that the Byzantine emperor John Zimisces (969–76) tried to prevent Sviatoslav of Russia from invading

[1] Vollbach, Salles, Duthuit, *Art byzantin*, pl. 99.

his territory by sending him presents of gold and textiles.[1] A few examples of these superb works may be noted. The shroud of St. Victor at Sens, of the eighth century, shows a man holding a lion in either hand (Pl. 42, *b*); the old Mesopotamian motive of Gilgamesh is thus reproduced.[2] Closely related to this, and of the eighth or ninth century, is a textile showing a similar figure holding two elephants by their trunks in the Bliss collection at Washington.[3] This textile has been attributed to Persia by some authorities, but its similarity to the Sens example shows that it is more probably Byzantine. A stuff with an inscription in Greek bearing four lions in Siegburg and another in Düsseldorf are dated to the reign of Basil II and Constantine (976–1028). The elaborate textile bearing elephants in medallions from the tomb of Charlemagne probably belongs to the latter part of the same century (Pl. 43, *a*); it must have been placed in the tomb when it was first opened in the Ottonian period. To the tenth or eleventh century belong a fine lion in the Amsterdam Museum, another at Maestricht, and stuffs bearing double-headed eagles and two eagles confronted in circular medallions at Berlin.[4] Of much the same date is the white silk damask known as the shroud of St. Siviard at Sens, which shows winged gryphons in medallions (Pl. 43, *b*). It is one of the most delicate and most perfect textiles of all time, but for force of design, for balance, and for dignity, it must perhaps rank after the glorious silk at Auxerre bearing eagles and rosettes (Pl. 44).

During all this period Constantinople was without doubt the most important centre of production, for the royal looms were situated there, and the larger stuffs, especially those bearing eagles, are definitely 'imperial'. But certain other

[1] Schlumberger, *Épopée*, i, p. 155.

[2] Diehl, *Manuel*, i, p. 271, assigns the textile to the sixth century, but the later date is more probable.

[3] Vollbach, Salles, Duthuit, pl. 88.

[4] Vollbach, Salles, Duthuit, pls. 93, 94, 95.

places were noted for the manufacture of textiles, the most important being Cyprus and the towns of Thebes and Corinth in Greece. It was from these towns that weavers were deported to Sicily in the twelfth century, and they founded a flourishing industry in the island, which was responsible for some first-class work both for Christian and for Islamic patrons. One of the most notable of Sicilian textiles is that in the Schatzkammer at Vienna, dated to 1134; akin to it, but not quite so fine, is the so-called mantle of Charlemagne at Metz (Pl. 45, *a*). Both were probably made at Palermo. Of better quality is the silk bearing eagles confronted and gryphons back to back in medallions composed of a Kufic design, known as the shroud of St. Potentien at Sens. No photograph can do justice to the colour and quality of this great stuff, four and a half medallions in height by two and two halves in width. An interesting banner bearing a figure of St. Michael, dated to 1141, is preserved in the monastery of Santa Croce at Avellana. It is also to be assigned to Sicily.[1]

Many of these stuffs, more especially those bearing animal motives, were intended for use as hangings. Some were perhaps used in churches after the iconoclast period—we read that Michael III (842–67) sent a stuff to Pope Nicholas I which bore figures of Christ and the Apostles; others again were made up into costumes, and we can get a good idea of these by means of contemporary paintings. Alexius V (1204) thus wears a purple garment in an illumination,[2] while the High Admiral Apocaucos is clothed in a stuff with lions in medallions in the well-known miniature of about 1340 in the Bibliothèque Nationale. After the iconoclast period royal costumes were profusely adorned with precious stones—the dress of Manuel I Comnenus (1143–80) was described as a meadow covered with flowers by contemporary writers—

[1] Published by Luigi Serra in the *Burlington Magazine*, xxxiv, 1919, p. 152.
[2] Gerstinger, *Die griechische Buchmalerei*, Wien, 1926.

and even hangings were decorated in this way. Embroideries were also probably in use, though we know little of them before the Palaeologue period. From that time on this technique was much elaborated for the decoration of epitaphioi or altar-cloths bearing the Body of our Lord which were used on Good Friday. They are found all over the Orthodox world from this time onward, and it is not always easy to date them on stylistic grounds alone, though the best work is usually found before the fifteenth century. A very fine one dated 1407 is in the Victoria and Albert Museum (Pl. 45, *b*); another dated 1437 is in the monastery of Neamtu in Roumania, and there are a number of fourteenth- and fifteenth-century examples at Putna in the same country. Others are preserved on Athos, but by far the finest on Greek soil is the fourteenth-century example from Salonica now in the Byzantine Museum at Athens.[1] Dalmatics and other ecclesiastical garments are common in the fifteenth, sixteenth, and seventeenth centuries, though the work is of varying quality. Fine Greek and Island embroideries may be considered as the ultimate descendants of the Byzantine textile art, and the velvets and stuffs of Venice and the rest of Italy are also closely related. Owing to the popularity of Sasanian motives in both Byzantine and Moslem art, however, it is not always possible to attribute such designs in the West to one culture or the other without the aid of additional evidence.

BIBLIOGRAPHY

Von Falke's great book, *Kunstgeschichte der Seidenweberei*, first published in two volumes in 1913, but reissued in one in 1921, must always remain the standard work on the subject. See also the usual manuals where bibliographies are given. For Egypt the four volumes of the *Victoria and Albert Museum Catalogue* are indispensable; Vollbach and Kuehnel, *Late Antique, Coptic and Islamic Textiles of Egypt in the German State Museum*, 1929, is a more recent

[1] *Guide du Musée byzantin d'Athènes*, 1932, p. 134, figs. 78, 80, 81.

and fuller work. See in addition for the Sens textiles Chartraire, 'Tissus anciens du Trésor de la Cathédrale de Sens', in *Revue de l'Art chrétien*, 1911, p. 277, and for those in England, W. R. Lethaby, 'Byzantine Silks in London Museums', *Burlington Magazine*, xxiv, 1913–14. Ebersolt, *Les Arts somptuaires de Byzance*, Paris, 1923, is also useful.

Chapter X

CERAMICS, GLASS, AND INCRUSTATION

A. CERAMICS

BYZANTINE pottery is a subject about which our knowledge has until recently been very incomplete; even now, though we are familiar with the wares which were used from about the tenth century onwards, we know practically nothing of early Byzantine ceramics. So far as we can tell, potteries of Roman type, plain unglazed wares, or wares with a green or blue, lead or tin glaze, and a moulded or impressed decoration were used; a fragmentary bowl of this class from Constantinople, in the author's possession, with a deep green glaze is probably to be dated to the sixth or seventh century. Whether Samian ware was manufactured by the Byzantines is uncertain, for only a very few fragments have up to now been discovered on Byzantine sites. A highly polished red ware very akin to it, which must have been imported, was, however, used in Sasanian—and apparently also in early Islamic—times in Mesopotamia. Somewhat similar vessels were manufactured in Egypt, and the Copts developed a fine painted, but unglazed ware of their own, the best specimens of which belong to about the seventh century. Small unglazed lamps of Roman form, and pilgrim flasks like those found in such numbers at the shrine of St. Maenas are also common from the time of the foundation of Constantinople till the eighth century or thereabouts. The only glazed vessel of essentially Byzantine type and of any importance or individuality is the so-called bowl of Constantine in the British Museum, which was almost certainly manufactured in Egypt.[1]

From the ninth or tenth century onwards, however, potteries of various types begin to appear, some of them of a very

[1] Dalton, *Catalogue of the Early Christian Antiquities in the British Museum*, 1901, pl. XXXIII, and p. 159.

individual character, some closely related to wares known in Persia and in Egypt. We cannot enter here into the discussion as to which of these countries first employed certain types of glaze and decoration; suffice it to say that a definitely Iranian influence is to be observed in more than one group of Byzantine ceramics, both in design and in technique. The similarities in individual examples will be briefly noted here; the whole question will be discussed at greater length by the author in the forthcoming *Survey of Persian Art*.

The earliest group of importance consists of a pottery of white body with polychrome decoration in thick upstanding colours, comprising brown, green, yellow, black, and red. Gold and perhaps silver pigments were also used. Vessels of numerous forms were made, and plaques for the decoration of walls are also common. Examples of both types have been discovered at Constantinople, where they date from the tenth to twelfth centuries, and again at Preslav and Patleina in Bulgaria, where they belong to the ninth and tenth. The discovery of pigments and wasters at these sites proves that the wares were manufactured there; they were probably also made at the capital, though no kilns or wasters have been found to support this supposition. The designs comprise geometrical and plant motives both of Hellenistic and of Sasanian character, and Islamic influence is indicated by the presence of a Kufic script on certain examples.[1] The most elaborate and important specimen of the ware is the portrait icon of St. Theodore of the ninth or tenth century at Patleina in Bulgaria (Pl. 47, *a*).

To the tenth and eleventh centuries is to be assigned a group of white-bodied vessels covered with a green or yellowish glaze, but no slip, and bearing an impressed decoration. The designs vary in quality; a very fine example showing an eagle at the base of a fragmentary bowl is illustrated

[1] For a summary of the latest discoveries relating to this type of ware see the author's article in the *Burlington Magazine*, lxi, Dec. 1932, p. 281.

here (Fig. 13). It is interesting to compare it with contemporary work in textiles, for instance with the Auxerre stuff (Pl. 44). Decoration in the same impressed technique occurs on the body of a fine aquamanile in the Vignier collection, but the neck is ornamented in the sgraffito method (Pl. 46, *a*). This is one of the few examples of Byzantine pottery of elaborate form that have survived, most of the large number of fragments excavated on various sites belonging to simple bowls, plates, and dishes. Bowls which are ornamented in the same manner as the neck of this vessel also occur, bearing simple inscriptions, floral motives, or drawings of animals.

A group of the tenth to twelfth centuries, best described as 'petal ware', has its prototypes both in second-century Roman art and in Parthian Mesopotamia, though it does not seem to have been very extensively employed in either area. A fine, deep, drum-shaped vessel with green glaze and hatched decoration in the Victoria and Albert Museum and another in the author's possession, which is practically identical, deserve special mention (fig. 8). They are probably to be assigned to the tenth century, and show the survival of Roman or Hellenistic spirit rather than the incoming oriental style.

The very wide group of 'sgraffito' potteries is in general of rather later date. Here the body of the vessel, usually of a fine red ware, is covered over with a white slip. To compose the decoration the slip is removed in places, and the vessel is then glazed. When fired the glaze remains of a light colour above the slip—usually a fine cream or bright yellow—and turns to a red-brown or brown-black where it directly overlies the body. In examples from Constantinople which appear to date between the twelfth and fifteenth centuries, large areas of slip are removed, so that the design is left in reserve. Sometimes even a portion of the body is removed at the same time, so that it stands in relief also, as in a plate bearing a deer in a border of foliage in the Sparta Museum

(Pl. 46, *b*). Geometrical figures, monograms, and birds or animals are the most usual motives, the former being elaborated in a very characteristic Byzantine manner (Fig. 9). A line-drawing technique was apparently more prevalent in Greece proper, though we see it as well on examples which come from Constantinople, and on others from Asia Minor. Fragments of some extremely fine flat plates or dishes come from all these regions, though they are most common at Sparta. They bear carefully drawn floral motives or animals, often of rather oriental character (Fig. 10). A more direct influence of Islamic art is to be seen in the occasional presence of a Kufic script round the border. One of the finest examples of the class, in the Kaiser Friedrich Museum at Berlin, comes from Miletus—it probably belongs to the tenth or eleventh century.

As time goes on the line drawing and the incised techniques tend to combine, and we see as well an elaboration of the design by the addition of coloured glazes, green and brown being most usual, though manganese also occurs. Fine bowls of this style, which are again of very Iranian character, have been found on most Byzantine sites in the Nearer East, and certain forms of vessels or types of decoration were developed in different regions. A rather wide bowl, of fine proportions, on a finely modelled and deeply hollowed base is thus typical of the capital, while in Cyprus a bowl on a high base like an inverted beaker is characteristic. Such bowls bear elaborately drawn flower or figural motives, animals and birds being most usual, though human figures also occur. A fine bowl of the thirteenth or fourteenth century in the author's possession bearing two parrots comes from Salonica; one recently acquired by the Victoria and Albert Museum bearing a human figure is probably Cypriote.

By the fourteenth century the use of two or more glazes for the decoration of vessels has become almost universal, and we see new types appearing where the sgraffito

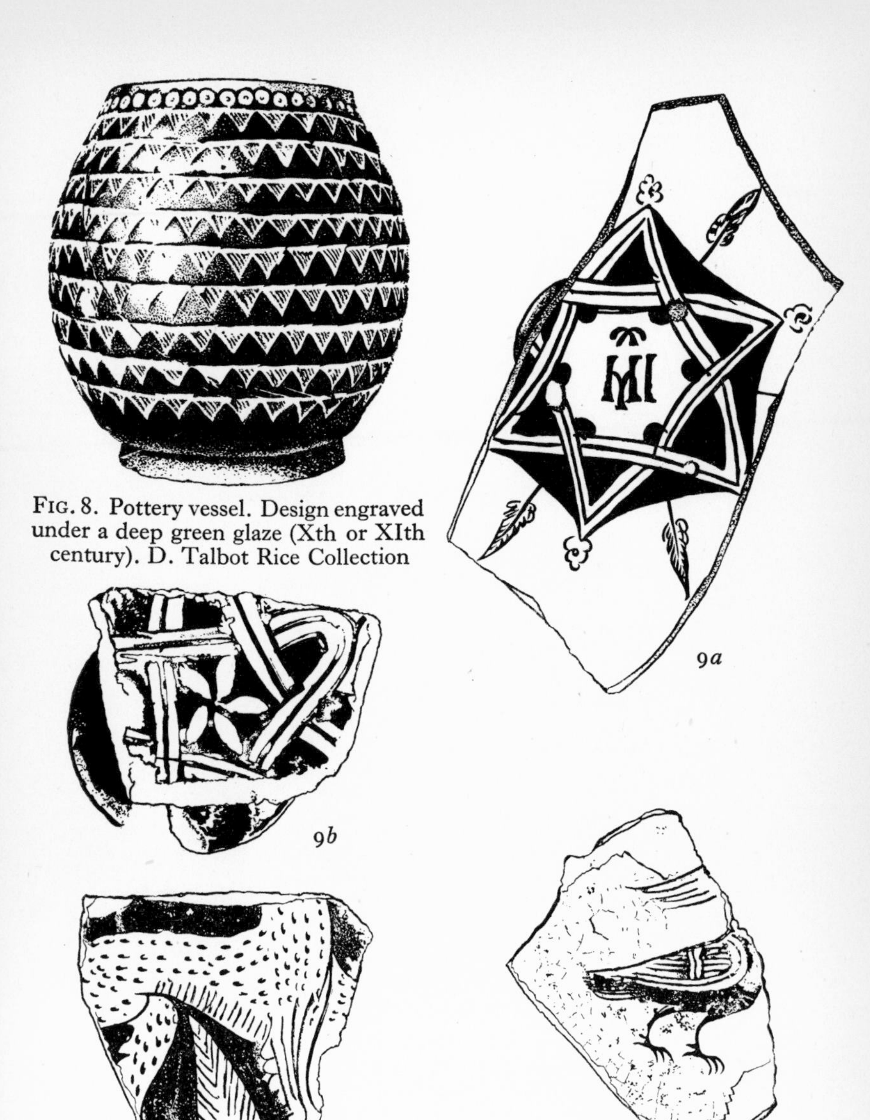

FIG. 8. Pottery vessel. Design engraved under a deep green glaze (Xth or XIth century). D. Talbot Rice Collection

FIG. 9 (*a–d*). Bases of bowls, incised ware. The incised portions brown or black, the rest yellow or cream (XIIIth century). British Academy excavations, Constantinople, 1927

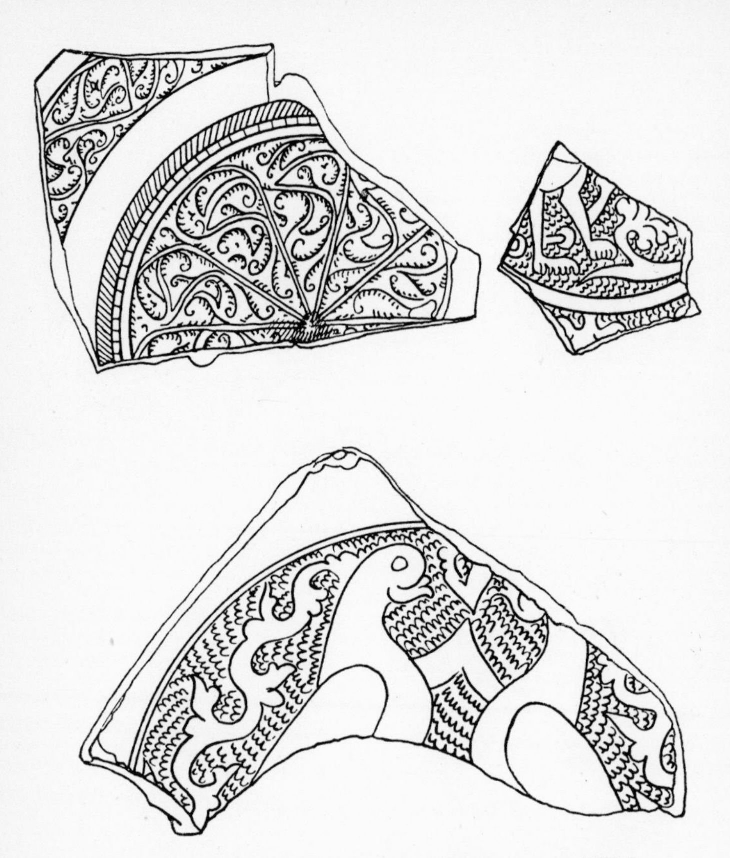

Fig. 10. Fragments of thin sgraffito ware (XIIth or XIIIth century). British Academy excavations, Constantinople, 1927

decoration is omitted. The colouring is composed of thin, runny tin glaze, and it is quite distinct from the thick up-standing vitrifiable colour pigments which we noted on the polychrome group of earlier date. Though the results achieved in these runny colours are often attractive, really fine work is unusual, and the drawing, or rather the painting, is of poor quality. The artists copy and recopy old designs till the original purport has been entirely forgotten. More successful are vessels where the decoration is purely mechanical, such as the marbled wares of late Byzantine and early Turkish times, where the pigments were applied to the vessel, which was then shaken so that they moved and intermingled, though in good work the colours do not 'run'. A group which bears a more carefully drawn and coloured decoration in deep blue and green has been represented in finds at Constantinople, and also in Asia Minor, especially at Miletus. Its origin is probably to be attributed to Seljuk rather than to Byzantine culture, though vessels of the type may well have been made as well as used at Constantinople.[1]

We have already had occasion to note the oriental affinities of Byzantine art from the ninth century onwards, and these affinities are especially obvious in a study of ceramics. But the originality of Byzantine genius is equally apparent, for she not only invented one ware, the polychrome, which is peculiarly her own, and developed the decoration of another in a style which was in every essence Byzantine and not Islamic, but she also transformed the oriental designs which we see on other classes to her own uses. The suggestion which has been brought forward that actual craftsmen came

[1] See article by Sarre, in *Transactions of the Oriental Ceramic Society*, 1920–1, p. 2, where the suggestion of Seljuk character is put forward. A bowl of this class in the collection of Mr. G. Reitlinger, as yet unpublished, bears an inscription in Arabic characters. This is no Byzantine copying of a Moslem model; it is a pure Moslem work and we must hence conclude that the examples found in Byzantine sites are importations.

to Byzantium in large numbers from the East is thus not a likely one, though eastern designs, actual vessels, and occasional workmen doubtless helped in the establishment of workshops. In view of the eastern influence that does exist, however, and in view of the great love which Byzantine culture had for the sumptuous in every art, it is a very surprising fact that no attempts were ever made in Byzantine lands to copy the lustre pottery of Islam, which was so popular in Egypt, Mesopotamia, and Persia; nor, so far as we can tell from the excavations that have up to now been undertaken, was any quantity ever imported from other countries. In the opposite direction it is possible to establish the fact that Byzantine pottery had a considerable influence on the ceramic arts of the West. Certain types of mezza majolica in Italy are thus more closely allied to Byzantine than they are to Islamic wares, while the blue painted ware which Sarre calls Seljuk was also copied in a certain type of Florentine pottery.

BIBLIOGRAPHY

The whole subject is discussed by the author in his *Byzantine Glazed Pottery*, Oxford, 1930. A full bibliography is given there, but the following works which have appeared since or which were there omitted and to which we have not called attention in the footnotes, may be added: Hobson, *A Guide to the Islamic Pottery in the British Museum*, 1932. Ballardini, in *Bolletino d'Arte*, xxv, Serie III, No. xii, 1932, pp. 551, for a discussion of polychrome ware. Philadelpheus, in *Χριστ. 'Αρχ. Δελτίον*, 1923, p. 21, for a description of four large and curious bowls of sgraffito ware from Corinth. Illustrations of three of these Corinth plates, which date from the twelfth century, and which are the most important recent finds as regards ceramics, are given in Volbach, Salles, Duthuit, *Art byzantin*, pls. 68, 69.

B. GLASS

Quite a number of examples of early East Christian glass of one type or another have come down to us, comprising both solid and hollow types. Solid bars for mosaic were manufactured in numerous sites in the Byzantine area, both in Italy and in the East, and by the eighth century, if not before, Constantinople was renowned for this work. The capital probably remained the most important centre until the thirteenth or fourteenth century, when Venice superseded her. Small round weights of glass paste, bearing a monogram on one or both sides, were also made at Constantinople from the sixth century onwards, and little amulets of the same material bearing saints were common until the twelfth century or thereabouts. They were probably made, like the weights, in Syria and in Egypt as well as at the capital.

Of actual vessels the most important in early times were the glasses known as 'fonde d'oro'. The bases of a large number of examples from the fourth to the sixth centuries have survived. The monk Theophilus, writing about 1100, even says that they were still made in his time, though we do not know of any such late examples to-day. Quite elaborate vessels, most of them of bowl form, appear to have been ornamented in this way. Their decoration was composed of a thin layer of gold leaf, delicately cut, and placed between two layers of glass to produce a silhouette effect. Large human figures, elaborately clothed, and akin in style to those which we see on contemporary ivories, usually occur at the bases; smaller figures, orants, or animals, appear in little medallions up the sides of the bowls. Such small medallions have often split away from the rest of the body, so that they are preserved singly. There is a good representative collection of such glasses in the British Museum, and there are four fine specimens at Pusey House at Oxford;[1] but the largest number are preserved in the Vatican, and it was probably in Rome that most of them were made. Alexandria was also important, but no examples can definitely be assigned to Constantinople.

[1] See T. B. L. Webster, 'The Wilshere collection at Pusey House, *Journal of Roman Studies*, xix, pt. 2, 1929, p. 150.

Another fairly common variety of glass in early times is the small bottle for sacred water or for perfume. These bottles often bear a cross in relief on the side or below the base by way of decoration. They were mostly manufactured in Syria or Coptic Egypt, and date from the third to the sixth centuries, though later examples are also known. Considerable numbers of more elaborate vessels were made in Egypt, where all ancient Egyptian and Roman forms appear, and where there is a close link with Mesopotamia and Syria, and it may be that a fine bowl with moulded decoration of the fourth century, recently discovered near Cologne, is to be assigned there. Peirce and Tyler regard it as a herald of Byzantine work.[1] The most typical Coptic vessels have a moulded decoration in relief, but one of the finest examples of this period is a glass in the Stora collection of the fifth century which bears an engraved decoration representing a chariot race (Fig. 11). Though the specimen is probably to be assigned to Egypt, the style is definitely Constantinopolitan, and it is interesting to compare the glass with a sixth-century textile showing the same scene in the Cluny Museum at Paris (Pl. 41, *b*). Though assigned by some authorities to Syria or Egypt, this fabric may well have been made at Constantinople.[2]

Some glass vessels from the region of Kertch in south Russia, most notably a paten of the sixth century bearing the figure and initials of Christ, are importations from Syria, and some glasses of a red colour from the same region, intended for drinking purposes, are probably also Syrian, though later in date. They bear an embossed ornament.[3] In the eighth and ninth centuries Syria was again an important centre of manufacture, fine glasses with a painted or

[1] See their *Art byzantin*, i, pl. 19.

[2] Vollbach, Salles, Duthuit, *Art byzantin*, pl. 82. They give a list of similar textiles.

[3] For an account and for figures of these see Tolstoy and Kondakov, *Russian Antiquities*, St. Petersburg, 1891, vol. iv, p. 32, figs. 24 and 25 (in Russian).

FIG. 11. Glass vessel, bearing quadriga (Vth century). Probably made in Egypt. Stora Collection, New York

FIG. 12. Later glass vessels. A candlestick and a perfume shaker (XIVth century)

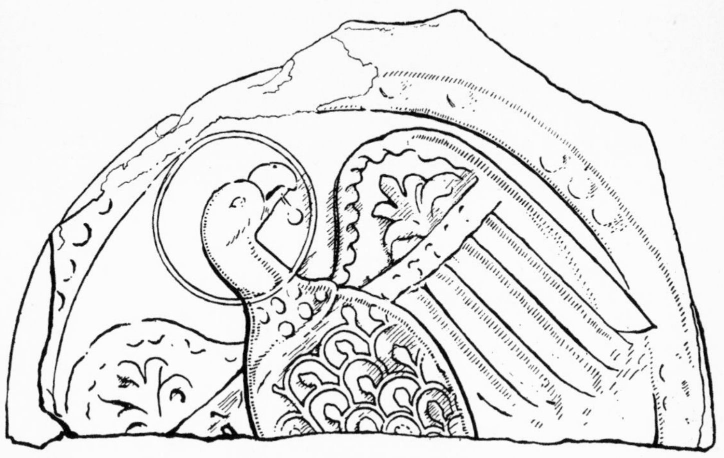

FIG. 13. Base of bowl. Impressed design (XIth century). D. Talbot Rice Collection

enamelled decoration being typical. A beaker of blue glass in the Tyler collection, with a painted decoration of birds in medallions, is doubtless to be assigned to the group.[1] Its affinities are with Moslem rather than with Christian art, though it is highly probable that enamelled glass of this type was made for and by Christians as well as for Islamic patrons.

Of vessels which can be termed Byzantine in the narrower sense of the word, vessels, that is to say, which were made at Constantinople, in Greece, or in Asia Minor, we know practically nothing. There were Jewish glass-workers in Constantinople in the sixth century, and lamps of glass which were perhaps made locally are described as forming a part of the treasure of St. Sophia in 563. They were probably akin to lamps from Jerash or from sites in Egypt, of conical or inverted-bell form, and were used in large numbers in a polycandelon or chandelier.[2]

It is recorded that glass was made at Salonica in the tenth century, but none of it has survived, and material for Constantinople is almost as scarce, though it seems possible to assign lamps of clear or greenish glass in the treasury of St. Mark's to the city on grounds of style. They were certainly brought from there amongst the loot of the crusaders after 1204. They are of fairly elaborate form, being intended for use alone, not merely as oil-containers in a candelabrum, and are usually mounted in gold or silver. They date from the tenth and eleventh centuries, and are characterized by a moulded ornament consisting of a dot surrounded by one or more circles.[3] A Greek inscription on one of them bears out the probability of Byzantine workmanship, though it actually refers to an archbishop of Iberia (Georgia). A fine glass

[1] Vollbach, Salles, Duthuit, op. cit., pl. 42, *b*.

[2] For drawings and a full discussion of such lamps see Grace M. Crowfoot and D. B. Harden, 'Early Byzantine and Later Glass Lamps', in *Journal of Egyptian Archaeology*, xvii, pts. iii and iv, 1931, p. 196.

[3] Illustrations of them appear in Peirce and Tyler, *Byzantine Art*, London, 1926, pls. 60, 61, and 62.

vessel mounted as a reliquary in the Cathedral treasury at Halberstadt bears the same characteristic ornament, and it may well be attributed to Constantinople also.[1] A fine jug, with long wide neck, handle, and lid, in the Grüneisen collection is also of Comnene date, though its provenance is uncertain.[2]

An extremely ornate bowl of red glass which is usually described as tenth- to eleventh-century Byzantine, on account of the antique style of its decoration, is more probably of western manufacture, and may well be later in date.[3] Bowls in the treasury of St. Mark's and elsewhere on which moulded animal motives occur, though they often show similarities with contemporary Byzantine textiles in design, are to be attributed to Moslem rather than to Byzantine art. They are related to the so-called Hedwigs glass of Egypt and to the superb Fatimite rock-crystals. A recently discovered ewer, of typical form and decoration, but of glass and not of crystal, in the collection of the late Mr. W. Buckley, must have been made in the same place as the crystal ewers.

In the twelfth and following centuries it is possible to regard a few shapes as characteristically Byzantine; such are the heavy-based, slim-bodied beaker or candlestick and the tall, thin-necked perfume flask (Fig. 12). But farther than this it is at present impossible to venture, and excavations on Byzantine sites have up to now produced little material that can help us in any way. A number of fragments were unearthed in the region of the great palace during the British Academy Excavations at Constantinople, but none of them

[1] Schmidt, *Das Glas*, Berlin, 1922, p. 39, abb. 19; Lamm, *Mittelalterliche Gläser*, pl. 52, gives figures of most of the St. Mark's lamps. See also Pasini, *Il Tesoro di San Marco*, and Schlumberger, *Épopée byzantine*, i, pp. 697, 700, and 717, and ii, pp. 441 and 513.

[2] See W. de Grüneisen, *Catalogue de la Collection Grüneisen*, Paris, 1930, no. 151, pl. IX. It may be of Constantinopolitan workmanship, but Egypt seems more likely.

[3] Schmidt, op. cit., abb. 18. He favours the Byzantine attribution, whereas Lamm, op. cit., pl. 34, 1, queries it.

was large enough to permit the determination of the form of the vessels to which they had belonged.

BIBLIOGRAPHY

The works of Lamm and Schmidt here alluded to in the footnotes are the most important for the study of Near Eastern glass. Reference to other works need only be made for points of detail.

C. INCRUSTATION

As a result of excavations on Christian sites which have been undertaken since the War, most notably at Constantinople and in Bulgaria, certain new aspects of Byzantine art are being opened up before us. Among the most important of these may be classed the technique of incrustation. The most elaborate example that we know so far is the standing figure of St. Eudoxia of the tenth or eleventh century, now in the Stambul Museum, made up of stones of various colours set in an incised marble slab (Pl. 47, *b*). Numerous fragments of similar technique came from the same site, the church of St. Mary Panachrantos at Constantinople; others of the ninth or tenth century, which are less elaborate, have appeared at Preslav in Bulgaria. A marble slab, similarly cut away, but with the incisions filled with mosaic cubes, showing birds and foliage, is preserved at Monte Cassino, while comparable again, but smaller in scale, is a slab of the eleventh century in the Byzantine Museum at Athens, bearing the figures of three apostles in enamel, on an incised marble ground. A small bread stamp at Halberstadt is akin to the Athens example. The inlay technique is allied to that which we see in the 'opus sectile' floors of the Roman age and is in all probability derived from it; the enamel work is a natural step forward from the incrustation.

As we become more familiar with the less sumptuous aspects of mid-Byzantine art, it seems probable that many more examples, both of enamel inlay and of incrustation proper, will be discovered.

BIBLIOGRAPHY

For the Panachrantos St. Eudoxia see Casson, *Burlington Magazine*, lvii, p. 128, and lix, p. 212; and Vollbach, Salles, Duthuit, *L'Art byzantin*, Pl. 72 (who date it XIth–XIIth cent.). For the Monte Cassino mosaic see Schlumberger, *Épopée*, III, p. 153. For the Halberstadt enamel see *Épopée*, II, p. 517. The origin of the incrustation technique is discussed by D. Talbot Rice in the *Burlington Magazine*, lxii, p. 279, where other references are given.

PART III

Chapter I

BYZANTIUM AND THE EAST

AN entertaining story is recorded by Persian historians that in the time of Shapur the Great (born 309; died 379) a Byzantine artist came to Persia to make a portrait of the Emperor. The portrait was drawn, and the artist took it back with him to Constantinople, where it was reproduced as the subject of decoration of some gold plates in the palace. Some years later Shapur came to the Byzantine capital in disguise; he succeeded in penetrating to the palace during a feast, but one of the guards, remarking his likeness to the portraits on the plates, called attention to the fact. The disguised Shapur was taken before the emperor; he confessed his identity and was thrown into prison, though he soon afterwards contrived to escape. This legend is one of long standing in Persia, and even if it is not strictly true, it serves as an instance of the freedom of communication between Persia and Constantinople, even though the Sasanian and Byzantine states were more or less continually at war.

There are many illustrations of this close relationship, and Byzantine influence is observable in the East as well as Sasanian in the West. Thus Yesdigird became guardian of the young emperor Theodosius, while Shapur I (241–72) gave according to Firdausi long instructions to a Byzantine architect for the building of a superb bridge across the Karun at Shuster. The bridge survives to this day, and it has fulfilled the king's demands, for it was to be like a cord stretched across the river. The immense resources of the treasury were put at the architect's disposal, and the wisdom of all the learned of Rum (Byzantium) was called into play. The castle of Khawarnaq near Hira was again supposed to have been built by a Greek architect; an architect from Constantinople was lent perhaps for the building of Ctesiphon;[1] the Persian chariot, though modelled in the main on the Assyrian, also owed certain modifications to Syria and to Greek lands; Justinian lent artificers to Chosroes I. The Persians frequently employed Byzantine prisoners in the capacity of architects and builders;[2] and there are a great many similarities both in result and in method between the architecture of the two countries.[3]

Contemporary Arab states like the Ghassanids of eastern Syria or the Lakhmids of Hira were in close touch with Constantinople as well as with Persia, and their culture was apparently intermediary between those of the two imperial powers. The Ghassanids were supported continually, and the Lakhmids apparently also at times by the Byzantines, as buffer states between them and Persia. Their kings paid frequent visits to the Byzantine capital; their peoples were in close touch with the Greek outposts.[4]

The counter-influence firstly of Sasanian, and later of Islamic art upon the development of the Byzantine has already been frequently alluded to. It is most clearly to be observed in textiles and ceramics. A few further instances may, however, be noted by way of illustrating the closeness of the contact. Certain sarcophagi from Syria thus show the influence of Parthian art,[5] and it is an influence which reached the Byzantine area by way of such examples. The formal beast ornament which is so popular in Byzantine sculpture from the iconoclast period onwards, though it appears as early as the fifth century, without doubt originated in the East, probably in Mesopotamia, and was developed to a great

[1] See Diehl, *Manuel*, i, p. 185. [2] G. L. Bell, *Ukhaidir*, p. 119.

[3] Huart, *Ancient Persian and Iranian Civilizations*, pt. iii, ch. iv.

[4] See F. Nau, *Les Arabes chrétiens de Mésopotamie et de Syrie du VII au VIII siècle*, Paris, 1933.

[5] S. Ronzevalle, 'A propos de sarcophages émésiens', *Mélanges de la faculté orientale, Beyrouth*, p. 155, vii, 1914–21.

extent by the Sasanians.[1] The peacock's-feather motive which appears so often in Byzantine mosaics and sculpture is, according to Grabar, first found on a Sasanian capital at Taq-i-Bostan.[2] Byzantine costume, insignia, and jewellery show a similar eastern influence. Thus the two small peaks which top the head-dresses on certain early Byzantine coins, for example those of Theodora, are copied from the double wings which appear on Sasanian head-dresses, like that of Chosroes II;[3] the fibula that holds the chlamy on the shoulder is the same on the Theodosius base and the Barberini ivory as on certain Sasanian reliefs;[4] in the thirteenth century the crown which we see on Sasanian coins and reliefs is adopted in the Byzantine region by the Comnenes of Trebizond and by Theodore of Mistra (1383–1407).[5] The royal palace at Constantinople was in the form of a rectangle surrounded by a wall in which were courts, like those in the palace at Mshatta; a certain building within the palace known as the *Περσικὸς δόμος* was of eastern appearance, its inspiration being probably due to Seljuk influence;[6] Bulgarian palaces were laid out on a definitely Sasanian plan.[7] The little clay cylinders with one end glazed which we see inserted into the walls of churches at Tirnovo in Bulgaria are suggestive of the cones with inscribed ends which were used in Baby-

[1] Minns, *Scythians and Greeks*, p. 280, notes that monsters in Siberian and Chinese art are also to be traced to Mesopotamia, and we see a Sasanian influence very akin to that on Byzantine art being exercised in China. See, for example, a winged gryphon in bronze of the Ming period in the Musée Guimet, Paris.

[2] *La Peinture religieuse en Bulgarie*, 1928, p. 139, note i. The date of the Cyprus mosaics, where the motive first appears in Byzantine mosaics, is disputed (see p. 76), but we know the motive in sculpture from the fifth century.

[3] Karabacek, in *Kusejr Amra*, i, p. 221, Ebersolt, *Les Arts somptuaires*, p. 32, fig. 5.

[4] Ebersolt, *Les Arts somptuaires*, pp. 34 and 38. [5] Ibid., p. 125.

[6] Ebersolt, *Le Grand Palais de Constantinople*, pp. 149 and 167.

[7] B. Filov, 'Les Palais vieux-bulgares et les Palais sasanides', in *L'Art byzantin chez les Slaves*, i, p. 80.

lonia and Assyria. A large silver plate of the sixth century from Carthage which was exhibited at the Byzantine exhibition at Paris (No. 388) bore a repoussé ornament at the centre, of marked Sasanian character. Some silver vessels dating between the ninth and the twelfth centuries, which were found in Bulgaria, again show definite Persian influence of the late Sasanian or post-Sasanian period.[1] The cross which is framed below by two acanthus leaves springing up on either side of the stem and which appears so frequently on the sculpture and metal work of the middle period is again a motive, the origin of which is to be attributed to Persia.[2] In an opposite direction the motive of a branch terminating in an animal's head, which we see so often on later Persian textiles and carpets, can be attributed to the Byzantine area, for we see it on sculpture of the eighth century in the Baptistry of Callistus at Cividale, and also on slabs of similar date at Ravenna.[3]

A very similar exchange of motives, of ideas, and of occasional craftsmen is to be observed between Byzantine and Islamic art. At first the Moslems are receivers rather than givers, since for the first century or so of its existence Islam boasted no art of its own. At the time of the rise of Mohammed, that is to say at the middle of the second quarter of the seventh century of the Christian era, the Arabs of Arabia were a wild and rather primitive people, with little religious faith and little religious instinct of a ritual kind. Christianity had passed over the northern part of the region, to be widely accepted in the more cultured parts of Mesopotamia, without

[1] Migeon, 'Orfèvrerie d'argent de style oriental trouvée en Bulgarie', *Syria*, iii, 1922, p. 141.

[2] The author hopes in the near future to discuss the development of this motive in detail.

[3] Rivoira, *Lombardic Architecture*, i, fig. 150. In Persia the motive is especially common on carpets; see, for example, the fifteenth-century fragments in the Musée des arts decoratives which were exhibited in London in 1931, Persian Exhibition, No. 130.

affecting more than a few town-dwellers in Arabia itself. Mazdaism, the State religion of the Persian Empire, had been adopted in the larger towns of central and southern Mesopotamia, as well as by some of the more settled Arab tribes, such as the Ghassanids and Lakhmids. The capital city of the latter, Hira, close to present-day Kufa, was apparently more or less equally divided between Christians and Mazdaeans,[1] and the latter religion had also reached as far as Dura, on the Euphrates. But the real Arabs, the Bedouin, had never been converted, and they still adhered to the old primitive cults of the desert area. In their principal towns, Mecca and Medina, the only developed religion which commanded a large number of followers was the Jewish.

And if there was little religion in the life and thought of the tribes who were first responsible for the spread of Islam, there was still less of anything in the nature of a creative or even of a preservative artistic instinct. Sumptuous foundations were soon to be laid, but existing monuments were thoughtlessly destroyed, and a characteristic of the race seems as apparent at this early date as it does to-day, namely the inability to repair or keep in order any construction whatsoever, whether a building whose appeal was principally religious or aesthetic, or a canal whose importance was mainly utilitarian. If Iraq and parts of Arabia are to-day desert it is not only because of the ruthless destruction of a Tamerlane or a Hulagu, it is not only owing to inevitable climatic pulsations. The listlessness of the Arab race has wrought as much damage as any conquest, however destructive, and has caused as much desiccation as any lack of rainfall. This particular characteristic of the race actually had an even wider effect, for it seems to have influenced practically the whole of Islam, and though the Persians in Achaemenid or Sasanian times appear to have been an energetic people in

[1] D. Talbot Rice, 'The Oxford Excavations at Hira', *Journ. R. Cent. Asian Soc.*, March 1932, and *Antiquity*, Dec. 1932.

whom the preservative instinct was well developed, and whose creative artistic powers can never be disputed, they are to-day as careless of constructions as are the Arabs, and as destructive as were the ravaging Mongol hordes.

At the outset, then, Byzantine, Syrian, or Persian methods, motives, and forms were taken over wholesale, in order to effect the establishment of the individual culture which this new religious state demanded, and its first ruling dynasty, the Omayyad, with its capital at Damascus, adopts a culture which was in essence Syro-Byzantine. The rulers of this dynasty were in fact deliberately attempting to achieve something that was essentially foreign to their old Arab culture when they adopted the settled life of towns, and when they constructed such great religious sanctuaries as the Dome of the Rock at Jerusalem or the Great Mosque at Damascus. The former was frankly designed to draw to it the pilgrim traffic from Mecca and Medina; the latter was originally a Christian basilica, the reconstruction and adornment of which was a magnificent expression of the extravagant ostentation of its patron, the caliph Walid. That the two mosques were successful as religious institutions and that they were so admirable artistically is due to three causes. First of these was the innate curiosity and love of a gay or grand display in the Arab, who would admire such buildings as long as they were bright and fresh. The second was the long and accomplished tradition in Syria and the enterprising spirit of early Christendom which survived there, even among converts to the new faith. And the third was Byzantine culture itself, which was responsible to a great extent both for the conception and for the execution of the actual work. The conception of the plan of the Dome of the Rock would have been impossible, as Creswell has shown, without Byzantine and Christian Syrian prototypes, while the decoration of the Damascus mosque owes its creation to Byzantine culture.

Similar influences are to be traced in the minor arts, as

well as in Omayyad culture as a whole, but they are not always auspicious in the latter case. They were responsible to a great extent for the magnificent artistic manifestations of the Omayyad period, but they were responsible also to a certain degree for the rapid decay of the dynasty. To-day the inhabitants of Egypt are unaffected by the numerous germs which infect the water or the vegetables that they eat, whereas the European at once succumbs. So were the Byzantines and the richer Syrians of the Christian period able to survive the luxurious Byzantine life unharmed, whereas the Arabs, newcomers who were accustomed only to the severe life of the desert or at most the somewhat insecure and harsh life of the towns along the northern coast of the Red Sea, soon became victims of drink and carousal, or fell before the plotting and intricacies of court life. A similar victory was to be achieved by Byzantine luxury at a later date, when the austere Turks conquered the Empire and settled in Constantinople. The gradual decay which then set in continued for almost four centuries; it is only a few years ago that it seems finally to have run its course, a new and more virile régime having arisen. In the Omayyad period we see much the same effect being produced on the early caliphs of Islam, but the results were more rapid, in spite of the fact that it was not Constantinople, but only the chief towns of Syria, Damascus, Aleppo, or Jerusalem which were concerned. And after only about one hundred years of life the Omayyad dynasty crumbled and fell.

When they first appeared in Syria, however, the conquering Arabs were energetic enough, and the defeat of the Byzantine outposts and garrisons was an easy matter. The first Arab victory was apparently that of 629, when the Byzantines were overcome, by guile as much as by force, not far from the Dead Sea. In 634 Byzantine dominion was further shaken by a second great Arab victory which secured for them Damascus, and with it the overlordship of Syria. In 636 the Emperor

Heraclius fled somewhat ingloriously to Constantinople, taking with him the True Cross from Jerusalem. After a brief respite he attempted to regain his losses, but the expedition was a failure, and with Syria assured the Moslems were soon able to overrun Mesopotamia and so to open a secure route to Persia and to further conquest in the heart of Asia. In 641 the conquest of Egypt was completed from Syria. Conquests were also made in the south of Asia Minor, as a result of which the Byzantine emperor was forced to send an ambassador to Syria to sue for peace. A truce was arranged for two years, and there is reason to believe that this respite of hostilities cost the Byzantines a fairly heavy indemnity. In spite of the peace, however, Armenia was lost to Byzantium in the same year owing to a local revolt engineered by the caliph Moawiyah, and soon after Rhodes fell before the Moslem fleet and the famous colossus was sold to a Jewish merchant. Periodic invasions of the frontier of Asia Minor seem to have been continued even during the peace, and they were soon to become an established custom. In 672 a far more ambitious scheme, the invasion of Constantinople itself, was even embarked upon, but it met with complete failure, and the Moslems were forced as a result to submit to a peace which guaranteed a heavy tribute to Byzantium.

Such truces as these were engineered by embassies from one power to the other, and the ambassadors were received in a most friendly manner in spite of hostilities between the two powers. This state of relations is aptly illustrated by a story related by one of the Arab historians. The caliph Moawiyah, it is recorded, had just completed a new palace and had received therein a Byzantine envoy. After the political discussion was finished, the caliph asked the ambassador his opinion of the building in which they had met. He replied: 'The upper part will do for birds and the lower for rats.' No very diplomatic remark, it would seem—but Moawiyah had the building pulled down and rebuilt, which shows his respect for the Byzantine's judgement of architecture and at the same time throws an interesting light on the caliph's character. The tolerance and broadness of mind which would not take offence at such a remark was no common thing at this time, above all in such a society as that to which the caliph belonged.

But in spite of the embassies, hostilities continued, and the increasing power of the Moslem and the onward push from the East are the most striking factors in the history of the period. The Byzantine Empire received a continued series of rude and often dangerous shocks, but the rulers succeeded in resisting them, and the resistance is to be attributed to the quality and innate vigour of Byzantine culture rather than to any special ability on the part of her armies and generals. These made an advance or put up a most gallant defence from time to time; but their most glorious successes were but temporary, and they never exercised as much effect in staying the advancing tide as was produced by the Moslem's respect for Greek and Byzantine culture and art. We see this respect illustrated by much of the life of Omayyad Syria; we see it in Moawiyah's tolerance of the ambassador's scathing remarks about his palace; but most of all we see it in concrete form in the art and architecture favoured by the rulers of Islam during the seventh and eighth centuries.

The space at our disposal does not permit us to trace out in detail the course of relations between the Byzantines and the successors of the Omayyads, the Abbasids. It must suffice to say that with the change of dynasty the whole nature of the Islamic state was altered, and 'the change from the Omayyad to the Abbasid dynasty was', in the words of Arnold, 'the substitution of a Moslem rule for an Arab kingdom'. The new rulers settled down in their eastern city to develop a culture which followed no longer on Syrian or Byzantine lines, but which modelled itself directly on the Persian. The same state of affairs characterizes Egypt.

The Omayyad attempt to capture Constantinople had met with complete failure, and when the dynasty came to an end and the capital was transferred to Baghdad in 748 all ideas of such expansion were forgotten. The Abbasids were from now on fully occupied with the organization of their own portion of the already divided Moslem empire and any danger for Byzantium of an Arab invasion was past. Byzantine influence is from now on rather less vital in the development of Islamic culture, though it is still to be noted in a number of separate instances. The early Abbasid army was thus organized on a Byzantine model, and Mansur even had a corps of fire-throwers who were clothed in a special fire-proof uniform—their fire must have been copied from the dreaded Greek fire of the Byzantine army. Early Abbasid architecture, though mainly under Persian influence, also owed something to immigrant Greeks, and the site of Baghdad was looked upon as especially favourable, for, in the words of one of Mansur's advisers, goods from Byzantine lands could easily be brought down the Tigris.[1] The Byzantine influence apparent in early Islamic book illustration of the Mesopotamian school has already been referred to (p. 93), and Byzantine influence is again apparent in metal-work, especially in the twelfth century. The large class of vessels with inlaid ornament attributed to Mosul often bear Christian subjects, and the fine bowl in the Ferdinands Museum at Innsbruck made for an Ortokid sultan in the twelfth century bears a medallion at the centre of the interior, which shows a seated figure, obviously modelled from a Byzantine coin.

In the opposite direction the influence at this period is obvious and we have already repeatedly called attention to it in the course of this book. The presence of flowered Kufic as a normal decoration on Byzantine pottery, in manuscripts (Fig. 7), or on buildings from the tenth century onwards may be cited here as a typical instance. Islamic stuffs and

[1] Le Strange, *Baghdad*, i, 14.

carpets and an Islamic system of decoration were in great popularity at Constantinople, and, in view of the amount of eastern material that was accumulated there, it is surprising that it did not exercise an even wider effect on Byzantine art. This limitation of eastern influence is in fact a striking proof of Byzantine wisdom and genius. She knew how to adopt when occasion demanded and when opportunity suited; she took what was of service to her, but no more. Never did she copy Moslem models slavishly, owing to a lack of originality or an absence of creative ability on her own part. What we see, both in the Islamic and the Byzantine spheres, is a fruitful traffic in ideas, in culture, and in art motives; it is a traffic which points, when once Islamic art is established, to energy on both sides, never to a weakness or to a placid receptivity on the part of either.

With the arrival of the Turks in western Asia the old aggressive attitude, forgotten during the Abbasid day, was revived, and from the eleventh century onwards the Seljuks began to penetrate Asia Minor. Now the state of affairs which had characterized Omayyad days was to some extent renewed, and we find that the art of the Anatolian Seljuks, more especially their sculpture, was considerably affected by Byzantine influence. Some Seljuk sculptures of the eleventh and twelfth centuries in the Museum at Konia serve as ample proof of this contact, which is to be traced again in the sphere of learning and education. Greek mathematicians and philosophers thus assembled at Konia, while certain of the Seljuk princes were educated at Constantinople.

With the advent of the Ottoman Turks in the thirteenth century the state of more or less friendly relationship, interspersed with periodic hostilities, which prevailed during the Seljuk period, was brought to an end, and a severe and continued struggle began, punctuated by the fall of one Byzantine outpost after another, until the final siege and capture of Constantinople in 1453. Yet even then, in spite of the fact that the Byzantine Empire had disappeared, something of the great heritage of Byzantium was handed on to the new rulers of the Golden Horn, so that in the sixteenth and seventeenth centuries we see the erection at Constantinople of a number of mosques, all of which are adaptations or modifications of the cathedral church of St. Sophia. Without this prototype their construction would have been impossible; without Byzantine imperialism as a forerunner, the Turkish sultanate would never have taken on that peculiar character which made it so famous in European history of the period.

And thus, even after its death, the Byzantine Empire affected the East, just as it influenced it during its life as well as learning from it. A proper appreciation of Byzantine art must thus take account of Islamic and Sasanian culture, as well as of the classical world. In the last chapter we shall show that Europe and the West must also be considered, so that it is in actual fact an age, a whole period of the civilized world's history, that must concern us, and not only that particular aspect of it which was manifested in eastern Europe and western Asia as a result of Christianity.

BIBLIOGRAPHY

For the history of the Omayyad period see the various writings of Père Lammens, the more important of which are collected in *Études sur le siècle des Omayyades*, Beyrouth, 1930. For the Abbasid period see Vasiliev, *Byzantines and Arabs*, St. Petersburg, 1902 (in Russian); a French edition in two volumes is in preparation. A useful bibliography, entitled 'Bollettino byzanto-arabico', by M. Guidi, appears in *Byzantion*, vii, fasc. 2, 1931, p. 396.

Chapter II

BYZANTIUM AND THE SLAVONIC WORLD

THE spread of Byzantine culture in regions beyond her permanent control was very considerable, for the whole of eastern Europe and western Asia was affected, both in north and south. It is impossible to deal with this diffusion in detail, but we shall attempt to give some idea of it in this and in the following chapter. Here we are concerned with Slav countries, where the connexion was a very close one. The nature of the connexion is aptly illustrated by the life on Mount Athos, where representatives of the great Orthodox countries, Russia, Bulgaria, and Serbia, play a part in the monastic life of the peninsula which is closely parallel to that played by the Greeks. Monks of each of these nations live on equality, and it is the monastic life as a whole that counts, not that of any particular nation. And so, in the Orthodox area in the later Middle Ages it was the Byzantine basis that was most important in art and culture, not the variations imposed upon it in particular regions.

We find this Byzantine basis in Bulgaria and Serbia; we find it in Russia and Roumania, and we even find it in other Slav lands which belong to the Catholic and not the Orthodox persuasion, though here it has been to a great extent obscured by later western influences, so that its appearances are usually disconnected. Bulgaria and Serbia have already been alluded to in other chapters. Both these countries were subject to the same fate as the Greek portion of the Byzantine world —they fell under Turkish domination in the middle of the fifteenth century—whereas development in Russia was different. Although part of the land was conquered by the Mongols, a part never came under their domination, and even the conquered area was only subject for a time. Before this subjection Christian art and culture were already firmly

4045 P

established; after it the regions at once became part of a stable Orthodox empire, whose rulers regarded themselves as the direct successors of the Byzantine line after the fall of Constantinople in 1453. In central Russia in fact a homogeneous civilization flourished for some five centuries before the time of Peter the Great, and it was a country where land routes and watercourses afforded a ready communication and made culture essentially universal. The nature of the land and the life led there prevented any possibility of that independent movement in one area or that conservatism in another which often characterizes more mountainous or difficult areas.

In the latter half of the tenth century Vladimir, Prince of Kiev, succeeded in uniting under his rule the greater part of what is to-day southern and central Russia. It was a wild and lawless area, yet Vladimir's ambitions were more than those of a nomad conqueror. He aimed at founding in Russia a great empire with an advanced and distinctive civilization of its own, and he realized that to attempt this without a stable basis of organized religion was impossible. But what religion was he to choose? Islam, to the south and east, was a flourishing and virile faith; Orthodoxy, to the south, was already established to some extent on Russian soil, thanks to Byzantine trade and to Byzantine colonies in the Chersonese; Judaism was a religion hallowed by time; Catholicism in the west had the attraction of youth, and it offered temporal inducements which were extremely alluring—Byzantium would perhaps prove to be an enemy as well as a friend, and in the west powerful alliances could be sought and cemented on the grounds of a common religion. Choice was truly an embarrassment; yet a selection had to be made and the early Slav manuscript known as the chronicle of Nestor tells us that Vladimir sent forth envoys to the centre of each religion with instructions to bring back a report. That of the envoys who visited Constantinople was so much the most impressive and the conditions of acceptance were so much the most favourable, that Vladimir decided to adopt Orthodoxy as the official faith of the new Russia.[1] The tale of the old manuscript is perhaps not strictly true. It was rather the situation of Russia midway between East and West, and the close commercial relations which existed with Constantinople and the Byzantine world of Asia Minor and the Balkans that determined the choice of religion for the new state. But the impression created by Constantinople was also an active factor, which we see illustrated by the way in which the towns of Russia copied the plan and lay-out of the older city; each of the more important of them thus had a St. Sophia, a palace, and a golden gate. The degree to which Byzantine influence penetrated during the next century is striking proof of the appropriateness of the choice made by Vladimir. No other religion would have suited the Russians half so well, and no culture but the Byzantine could have provided such scope for development on national lines. Moreover, the other countries of Slavonic character which were in any way civilized were already of the Orthodox faith, and were closely allied to Byzantium.

In 988 Orthodoxy became the State religion of Russia, and with the priests who went from Constantinople to baptize and preach the new religion there also travelled architects, mosaicists, and painters. A great work awaited them, for during the last few centuries Russian life had been of a nomad character, and there were practically no local buildings or styles of architecture or painting that could be adapted to Christian usage. The centre to which these Byzantines flocked was Kiev, and there the artisans worked to construct a new capital which should be as like the great Constantinople as possible. Kiev too should have its Golden Gate and its palace; but more important, it should have its churches and its cathedral. The church of the Dormition was founded by

[1] For a full account see Schlumberger, *Épopée*, i, p. 707.

Vladimir in 989, the cathedral of St. Sophia by Jaroslav in 1037, and the monastery of the Catacombs by Iziaslav in 1073. All of these were in the main Byzantine buildings, though certain influences which came from the Caucasus independently of Constantinople are to be discerned, as well as those of locality, culled perhaps from the Chersonese. The churches were decorated with Byzantine paintings or mosaics, which show far less deviation from the normal types than do the actual buildings; the mosaics were due in fact entirely to Byzantine workmen and the inscriptions and titles of the scenes which accompanied them were in the Greek language. To-day practically all that survives of the various mosaics of Kiev are the Pantocrator in the dome, and the Communion of the Apostles and the Virgin in the apse of St. Sophia. Interesting paintings showing scenes of the Hippodrome appear on the stairs which connect the church and the palace, and they again are purely Byzantine works.[1] At the same date numerous other churches were built in neighbouring towns. They are again Byzantine monuments in Russia rather than monuments of Russian art. The most important is the cathedral of Tchernigov, built in 1031.

The supremacy of Kiev was not long lived, and in the late eleventh and twelfth centuries we find that it was supplanted as a temporal, cultural, and artistic centre by Novgorod and Vladimir. Novgorod was never the seat of a principality; the patrons of art were rich burghers and merchants, and culture developed along purely Russian lines. Though the first Novgorodian building, the cathedral of St. Sophia (1045–52) was more or less purely Byzantine, the churches that followed it were much more Russian, and we can trace in them the evolution of a new style, founded upon the Byzan-

[1] A fragmentary mosaic of the Communion of the Apostles in the church of St. Michael and paintings in the church of St. Cyril, which were badly restored in 1881, are the other principal monuments of this period in Kiev.

tine, but developed to suit the locality and influenced probably by indigenous wooden architecture. Roofs were thus made more pointed to prevent the snow from settling; bulbous domes replaced the flatter Byzantine ones for the same reason, the height of buildings was increased, since tall structures were prevalent in wood before the introduction of brick or stone construction from outside. Numerous churches were erected in the region; a few of them may be cited as examples. They are: the church of St. George at Novgorod (1119–30); the church at Nereditza (1198); the church of St. Saviour at Kovalevo (1345); and the churches of St. Theodore Stratelates (1360) and the Transfiguration (1374) at Novgorod. Churches at Pskov show a parallel development.

The transformation of architecture in the Vladimir–Suzdal region was of a rather different character. In 1109 Andrew Bogolioubski sacked Kiev and transferred the capital to Vladimir, and a number of important buildings were erected there and in the neighbourhood until about 1238, when culture was arrested by the Mongol invasion.[1] The plans of these churches were due to Byzantine architecture, but they were influenced primarily by way of the Caucasus, not from Constantinople, and certain features which are definitely Armenian rather than Byzantine appear, more especially in the decoration of the exterior with plaques carved in low relief. The finest of these are on the cathedral of the Dormition at Vladimir (1158) and the church at Jurjiev Polski (1230). Other features which are common to central Russia and Armenia alike, such as the single dome, the small size of the buildings, and the stone construction, are also Byzantine, and they cannot therefore be assigned to Armenia alone. An influence which is to be attributed to the Romanesque architecture of the West is also to be observed in the later examples of this group; and had it not been for the Mongol invasion

[1] The Mongols did not penetrate to Novgorod.

an interesting development of the three external trends along local lines might well have taken place. As it was, when the Mongols were finally expelled in the fifteenth century, Moscow, the new centre and capital of Russia, looked to Novgorod for its culture and art rather than to the Vladimir–Suzdal region.

We have already seen that a new and essentially Russian architecture was developing at Novgorod, strongly influenced by locality. In painting the change was less marked, for although the monumental style of the middle Byzantine period, which had been responsible for the Kiev mosaics, was only active in the twelfth century, the Byzantine revival made itself felt in the fourteenth century in Russia just as much as in the Balkans, so that Byzantine inspiration was continuous in both areas. Novgorodian paintings are to be divided into three groups. In the first (XIIth and XIIIth cents.) the style was still related to the monumental Byzantine tradition, and some of the painters were Byzantines; others were Slavs who had learnt in the Greek schools. The most important monuments are: St. Sophia, at Novgorod (paintings 1144); the monastery church of Spaso Mijorski near Pskov (1156); St. George at Staraya Ladoga (end of XIIth cent.); the church of St. Saviour at Nereditza, near Novgorod (1199).

At the beginning of the second period (XIVth and XVth cents.) a number of painters came to Russia from Byzantium, most famous of whom was Theophanes the Greek. They established local schools and taught the new manner of the revival. But their Slav pupils soon equalled, even excelled them, and Rublev, who worked in the late fourteenth and early fifteenth centuries, was a greater artist than his master Theophanes. The most important wall-paintings are in the church of the Dormition at Volotovo (1363); in St. Theodore Stratelates (*c.* 1370), and the church of the Transfiguration (1378) at Novgorod; the church of the Transfiguration at

Kovalevo (1380); in the church of the Nativity in the cemetery of Novgorod (*c.* 1390), and in the cathedral of the Dormition at Vladimir (1408). In many of these, however, the work is either fragmentary or over-restored.

The third period is illustrated by paintings signed by the painter Denys and dated to 1500 in the Theraponte monastery, not far from Moscow. They are in a minute icon painting style, akin to the Cretan school of Byzantine art. But they are distinguished from the Byzantine by a definitely Russian manner which is to be seen here in embryo, but which was to influence the work of the following centuries and to make of Russian religious painting something as akin to but as distinct from the Byzantine as English Gothic was akin to yet distinct from the Gothic of France.

Closely related to wall-paintings, and often by the same masters, were icons. Here, however, no school of Kiev is to be distinguished, for it seems that at this period panel paintings were usually imported from Constantinople or were executed by Byzantine emigrants. A few already show the birth of Russian art in pre-Mongol times.[1] Finer and far more numerous are the icons of the fourteenth and fifteenth centuries, which are to be assigned to Novgorod. They show Russian painting at its best, and later schools, more especially that of Moscow and that known as the Stroganov, were directly derived from that of Novgorod. Such later work is often accomplished and interesting, but it is seldom of the very first class. We can do no more than mention it here.

Various explanations have been offered to account for the superb quality of Novgorod painting. The original explanation, put forward by Kondakov and Likhachev, thus explains them by the widespread introduction of Italian models into Russia. But recent discoveries, to which we have called attention in the chapter on painting, show that the Byzantine

[1] For the importance of 'pre-Mongol' painting in Russia see I. Grabar, *Problems of Restoration*, I, pp. 7 ff., Moscow, 1926 (in Russian).

revival of Palaeologue times took place entirely independently of such influence, and began in fact as early as the latter half of the twelfth century. The Byzantine character of Novgorodian painting is not to be disputed and, in view of these discoveries, the Italian thesis is no longer tenable. Similarities which exist between Byzantine and Italian painting are rather to be accounted for by the influence of the former upon the latter, and similarities between Russia and Italy are to be accounted for by the Byzantine elements at the base of both. The line of development of Russian work is only to be understood when the history of the Byzantine revival is taken into account.

To trace the history of Russian art after the foundation of Moscow is beyond the scope of this chapter. It was an art fundamentally Byzantine though now it had become thoroughly Russianized. Architecture had been changed even more by locality, and it was in addition at an early date influenced to quite a considerable degree from the West. With the fuller westernization of Russia in the seventeenth and eighteenth centuries western architects became more popular than Russian ones, and European painting similarly became the vogue in secular art. The old Byzantine manner was, however, retained for religious usage, though decline had set in and most of the work was of a purely artisan character. An attempt to revitalize it in recent years is, however, something more than a purely revivalist movement, for the old forms have been resorted to and re-employed for new ends, and work which is thoroughly vital and suitable to the demands of the present day has been produced, much of which is of a very high quality.[1]

So long, so flourishing, or so independent a history can

[1] Work of this character has been made popular in the West, in the scene designs of the Russian ballet and opera, more especially in those of Gontcharova. Soviet paintings which follow the icon tradition, but depict scenes of agriculture or modern life, are again not without merit.

hardly be traced in the art of other Slav lands, and throughout the text of this book we have considered the monuments of Bulgaria and Serbia along with and beside those of Greek Byzantine art. A brief résumé of the history of the two countries may, however, be conveniently given here, for the character both of Bulgarian and Serbian art is closely linked up with historical events.

The Bulgars came to the Balkans from the region to the north of the Caspian and established themselves as an independent power in 679. An analysis of their culture at this time shows that it is possible to distinguish two distinct branches, the Slav and the proto-Bulgar or eastern. The earliest monuments of art in the land are closely linked with the latter. Palaces at the first capital, Aboba Pliska, are thus related to Sasanian palaces in plan; rock reliefs at Madara are again Sasanian, while metal work and ornaments of the seventh century follow eastern prototypes. The famous treasure of the ninth century found at Nagy Szent Miklos in Hungary, in which the Sasanian elements are striking, is probably to be associated with proto-Bulgar culture.[1] As time went on the influence of locality began to exercise an effect, and Hellenistic elements established in the region at an earlier date penetrated art. By the mid-ninth century Eastern and Hellenistic elements were more or less equally balanced. The development of art followed in fact much the same lines as those we regard as characteristic of Constantinople, though in central Bulgaria the main basis was eastern and the influence Hellenistic, whereas in Constantinople the basis was Hellenistic and the influence eastern. In the south of Bulgaria, however, Hellenistic elements were always uppermost, and Byzantine influence penetrated from the earliest times by way of Salonica, which was the most characteristic and the most important city of the Byzantine world after Constantinople.

[1] See Filow, *Geschichte der altbulgarischen Kunst*, pp. 17–25.

In 864 Bulgaria officially accepted Christianity, and from that time on Byzantine influence penetrated the whole area. The country was controlled by a number of competent rulers, most important of whom were Boris (853–88) and Simeon (893–927), and a number of cities and religious edifices were founded. Recent research has shown that Preslav, the capital, was a flourishing city, and churches there and in the region are closely linked with contemporary ones in Constantinople, especially in their decoration. In 1018 Bulgaria became a Byzantine province, and for the next century Constantinopolitan influence penetrated even more fully.

From 1186 to 1393 Bulgaria was again an independent power, with capital at Tirnovo. A number of churches were built which are architecturally more definitely Byzantine than those of the first Empire. The paintings within them are again closely related, and some of them are due to Greek masters. That Greek painters of the first rank worked in the Balkans at this period is in no way surprising if we remember that just at this time, when Bulgaria was a strong and fairly stable power, Constantinople was suffering the Latin domination. The work of such Greeks was in general probably confined to the larger churches in the most prosperous regions of the country, and it was just these churches that were destroyed during the period of Turkish rule. Small buildings in the mountains have in general survived and in many of them there are excellent paintings, most of which are the work of Bulgarian artists. These have already been mentioned in the chapter on painting; paintings at Tirnovo and in St. George at Sofia and the very remarkable and more purely Bulgarian work at Boiana (1259) may be noted here by way of example. Bulgarian minor arts were equally closely related to the Byzantine, and it is hard to tell products of the land from those of Greek artisans on grounds of style alone until well after the Turkish conquest.

The history of Serbia is in a way akin to that of Bulgaria, though it does not go back nearly as far. In early times in fact we know little of the region and it was apparently something in the nature of a wild outpost. The country was Christianized in the ninth century owing to the labours of two Greek monks of Salonica, Constantine and Methodius. In the tenth century part of the land was for a time subject to Bulgaria; in the eleventh it was under Byzantine control. Only in the twelfth century was independence achieved, under the leadership of Stephen Nemanja. The religion of the independent Empire was Orthodox Christianity, the culture Byzantine, and the closeness of relationship is illustrated by the fact that Nemanja retired in 1198 to Mount Athos, to live as a monk in the Serbian monastery of Chilandari which was on terms of equality and friendliness with the Greek foundations there. Nemanja was joined with the Byzantine emperor as patron of more than one Greek monastery on the peninsula.

The growth of Serbia as an independent power in the following century was assisted by the troubles with the Crusaders which were harassing Byzantium, and we see a number of powerful rulers such as Stephen II (1219–27) and Milutin (1257–1320) widening the bounds of the empire considerably. Dushan, who came to the throne in 1331, even dreamed of founding a Graeco-Slav empire with himself at its head, but he died at Adrianople in 1355 before his ability to carry out his ambitious scheme of capturing Constantinople could be put to the test. These rulers were great builders, and in the thirteenth and fourteenth centuries a large number of churches sprang up. Their architecture, though fundamentally Byzantine, was much altered by local and western traits, and Millet notes in addition certain eastern influences.[1] Their paintings were more faithful to the old Byzantine heritage, and many of them were the work of

[1] *L'ancien Art serbe; Les Églises*, pp. 44 ff.

Greek artists. It is in fact in Serbia more than anywhere else, with the exception of Mistra and Athos, that we can study the finest manifestation of Byzantine painting in the revival manner. In 1389 the independence of Serbia was ended by the Turkish victory at Kossovo, but the country enjoyed comparative independence for another seventy years; it then became a Turkish pashalik or province, but retained its Christian religion and way of life. The eastern and central region constituted one of the most important of the heritors of Byzantium in the Balkans under Moslem rule; the western region was, however, to a great extent catholicized, though the culture remained more Byzantine than Italian.

One further heritor of Byzantium may be mentioned here, namely Roumania. She was essentially an heritor, for few of the more important churches of the land were built during Byzantine times. She was, however, the most successful of all the Balkan countries in resisting the Turks, and she remained from the sixteenth century a stronghold of Orthodoxy. Numerous monasteries and churches were erected and decorated, and their architecture, their paintings, and their treasures are definitely of the Byzantine family, though much altered by western influence. The art was, however, more energetic and flourishing and much less retrospective than that of countries which constituted Christian minorities within the Turkish Empire, and it therefore forms an interesting subject of study, though it can hardly rank with the great arts of the world. And that Byzantine art of the best periods can so rank is, we hope, now a generally accepted fact.

BIBLIOGRAPHY

For Russia see L. Reau, *L'Art russe*, vol. i, Paris, 1921, where an excellent general outline and full bibliographies are given. M. Alpatov and N. Brunov, *Geschichte der altrussischen Kunst*, Augsburg, 1932, is a fuller and more recent work. Bulgaria is even better served by Filow's *Geschichte der altbulgarischen Kunst*, Berlin and Leipzig, 1933. No general outline exists for Serbia—the small volume, *Serbia*, published in the series 'L'Art et les artistes' during the War is perhaps the most convenient. See also Millet, *L'ancien Art serbe; Les Églises*, Paris, 1919. For Roumania see the volume *Roumania* in the series 'L'Art et les artistes', and also Iorga and Balz, *L'Art roumain*, Paris, 1922. R. W. Seton-Watson's *History of the Roumanians* gives an excellent account of events.

Chapter III

BYZANTIUM AND THE WEST

THE actual division between the Byzantine and the western world varies considerably at different periods. Thus in early times the whole of Italy must definitely be included in the former; by the seventh century most of that country can no longer be classed as Byzantine, though it is still closely related; in the eleventh century we find that parts of Italy, most notably Venice and Sicily, are essentially Byzantine in culture, whereas the rest of the land has become definitely and finally a part of the West. In her Byzantine character Italy does not concern us, for to trace out relationships between the central Byzantine sphere and the cultures directly derived from it or from which it was derived, such as those of the Balkans or Syria, is not the purpose of this chapter. Our aim is rather to call attention to the legacy of Byzantium with regard to the art of other civilizations, and hence, when we speak of the West or more narrowly of Italy, we refer only to the areas of western, not to those of Byzantine culture.

In the period that concerns us principally, from the seventh to the twelfth centuries, the West is more or less synonymous with the Carolingian and the Ottonian empires, that is to say a part of Italy, France, and Germany. England must also be considered, and so must the north of Europe, for it has been suggested that there is some link between Byzantine art and that of Scandinavia. Little of this can be regarded as due to a direct Byzantine influence, though church plans both in Norway and Sweden show distinct Byzantine affinities.[1] Similarities in ornament are to be accounted for rather by the fact that both the Byzantine area and northern Europe owed something to the region to the east—the Altai-Iran of

[1] For a summary account of these similarities see L. Reau, *L'Art russe*, i, p. 86.

Strzygowski—and because we see elements culled from a common source being developed in both. Ireland, on the other hand, though primarily linked with Scandinavia or the La Tène culture of Europe, was also affected by Latin culture from south and east, and to some extent also by the Byzantine. There seems to be a definite link between Irish art and that of northern England in the eighth and ninth centuries.

In the eastward direction our field must also be defined, for we are concerned with Byzantine influence in the West, and that of other cultures—Sasanian Persian, Moslem Syrian, or Moslem Egyptian—only concerns us in so far as their influences travelled by way of the central Byzantine area.

In discussing the relationship between Byzantium and the West, a further distinction must be made, this time with regard to the nature of the relationship. Two main types of connexion can be observed. The one may be termed a diplomatic connexion: various objects are interchanged as presents; a number of specimens of Byzantine art of one kind or another reach the West in this manner and are preserved there. Sometimes they are copied, but the copy is a direct one; the artist remains a copyist, not a creator; the effect is superficial, and the result can be observed at first glance. The other type of connexion is brought about by interpenetration, and it implies a change of outlook. The Byzantine object is not merely copied; its whole spirit is assimilated and, though the presence of such an influence is often harder to distinguish, its effect goes much deeper and is of a far more permanent character. We see a connexion of this type most marked at two periods, in the eighth century and again in the fourteenth, and we can trace it in three ways: in iconography; in style, colouring, or technique; and in content or the feeling which underlies the work. The relationship may be very subtle and not clearly to be discerned; it may be clearly evident, though individual objects show little actual similarity, or it may be all embracing, influencing feeling, material, and appearance simultaneously. Such influence will be noted when it arises, but it seems in general most satisfactory to consider the problem chronologically and to note briefly the evidence for connexion between Byzantium and the West century by century.

Of the fourth and fifth centuries we know little, but there seem to have been a number of Jews settled in the West, especially at Arles, who maintained definite contact with Palestine and who undoubtedly imported from their homeland certain works of art, more especially glass and textiles. Ivories were also doubtless brought back from Palestine by Christian pilgrims; the importance of religious pilgrimage even at this early date is clearly shown by the large number of flasks to contain holy water, which are found at such a shrine as that of St. Maenas in Egypt. Textiles of linen or wool may well have come to the West from Egypt or Syria, but silk was a monopoly held by Constantinople until the eighth century. It was much exported after the end of the sixth century; before this the knowledge of its cultivation was not known to the Byzantines and all the material had to come by way of Persia: it is because of this that we see so much Persian influence in Byzantine silks. But before the knowledge of its cultivation was sold to Justinian the price of the material must have been prohibitive.

In the sixth century relationships between the West and Palestine were just as important on account of pilgrimage; with Constantinople they became somewhat closer, and certain travellers from the West passed that way in order to reach the holy cities. Thus Réoval, a doctor of Poitiers, went to Constantinople to discourse with the doctors there, and in the reign of Justin II (565–78) Radegonde visited the Byzantine capital and took back wood of the True Cross and other relics, including a finely bound copy of the Gospels.

Shortly after this visit Justin sent a reliquary to Radegonde, which is probably that now in St. Croix at Poitiers, and a large cross was sent to Rome.[1] Tiberius II (578–82) sent similar presents to Chilperic. Towards the end of the century Gregory of Tours visited Constantinople, where by now most of the more important relics had been assembled; he apparently brought some back on more than one occasion, for he was very familiar with all the Byzantine lands and seems to have travelled much in the East.

In the opposite direction we find that Greeks visited the West at this period and there was a whole colony of them established at Narbonne. A painting of the crucified Christ there was quite possibly a Byzantine work.[2] The further extent of Greek trading colonies in the West is shown by the large number of Byzantine coins, dating from about A.D. 300 to 641, which are found in France. They were in circulation there for a time and later served as models for Frankish dies. There can be little doubt that Byzantine ivories served in a similar way as models for Frankish sculpture, both on a large and on a small scale. Byzantine saints too were popular in the West at this time, and we see a church at Chartres being dedicated to SS. Sergius and Bacchus, though later the patron became St. Nicholas.

Relations between East and West in the seventh century must have been of a similar character, but Constantinople was now as important as Palestine for the pilgrim traffic, not only because it was the seat of temporal power, but also because it became in this century the home of the True Cross. Jerusalem, moreover, fell to the Persians in 614 and though recaptured by Heraclius in 629—he came to be regarded almost as a saint in the West because of this—it finally

[1] For figures of these see Ebersolt, *Les Arts somptuaires de Byzance*, figs. 3 and 4.

[2] See Ebersolt, *Orient et Occident*, i, p. 22, for a very entertaining legend about this.

fell to the Moslems in 637. Pilgrims still continued to visit the Holy Land, though it can have been no easy journey, and one, St. Bercaire, abbot of Montier en Der, Haute Marne, brought back ivory plaques from Palestine, which must be counted as more or less Byzantine works. But it seems that most of the pilgrims visited Constantinople as well, and one of the most famous, Arculf of Gaul, wrote a guide which served for some time as a pilgrims' 'Baedeker'. Colonies of Greeks and Syrians still existed in the West, for instance at Orleans, where it is recorded that St. Columbanus met a Syrian family with whom he lodged for some time. It was in this manner that Byzantine influence of a more personal character penetrated to Ireland and England. We have a considerable amount of evidence of trade communication, notably in the discovery of eastern objects in the West. Byzantine coins are common the world over, and in Ireland Chinese seals have been unearthed to attest the distance which such small objects would travel.[1]

In the eighth and ninth centuries the relationship assumed a much more intimate character, for the Carolingian rulers, however powerful themselves, did not cease to look to Byzantium as the centre of culture and civilization. Numerous embassies and presents were interchanged between the emperors, and many of those which came from Constantinople still survive in the West as concrete proof of the intercourse. Thus Constantine V Copronymus sent envoys to Pepin le Bref in 758. Charlemagne received others at Aix in 812, whilst in 814 an embassy was again sent from Constantinopie to Louis at Aix-la-Chapelle. Another followed in 824 to Rouen, another in 833 to Compiègne; another in 839 to Ingelheim. Costly gifts were sent on every mission, and we see the court of Charlemagne clothed in silks, many of which were of Byzantine manufacture. A textile from the emperor's

[1] See R. A. S. Macalister, *Archaeology of Ireland*, 1928, p. 344, and E. Getty, *Notices of Chinese Seals found in Ireland*, Belfast, 1850.

tomb at Aix is of Constantinopolitan workmanship, though it was probably introduced there at a rather later date. Both Charlemagne and Louis the Pious were familiar with the Greek language, and we find a knowledge of Greek in certain western monasteries, most notably at Corbie, where it is recorded that the Greek language and Gospels were much admired. Louis received from Michael II (820–9) silks and a copy of the works of Denis the Areopagite; there is record of a lengthy correspondence between Basil the Macedonian (866–86) and Louis II; Charles the Bald appeared in Byzantine dress at the assembly of Ponthieu in 876; numerous Byzantine objects were brought to the West as relics and were preserved in the various monasteries.[1] Many are to be seen in them to this day.

With so much actual Byzantine material in the West, an influence which reaches fairly deep is to be expected, and we can trace this to a far more marked degree than many authorities on the early arts of western Europe are prone to admit. And the relationship goes deeper than mere admiration of Byzantine objects in the West, deeper than a mere pose of copying the Constantinopolitan court, for there can be little doubt that with the iconoclast persecution artists and artisans came to the West in considerable numbers, there to practise their art unhindered. They themselves worked for western patrons and established workshops where the local craftsmen were taught, and it is to these immigrants that we are indebted to a great extent for the birth of Carolingian art. Whatever may be said to the contrary, Italy was

[1] For example, Fortunatus, patriarch of Grado, who had been several times to Constantinople, brought to France in 803 'two doors of ivory, magnificently carved'. In the abbey of St. Wandrille there was a fine Byzantine text. At St. Denis there were textiles with animals, birds, and gryphons as their decoration. At the abbey of St. Riquier in Ponthieu were numerous relics of saints, most of which had come from Constantinople, probably with their mounts or caskets. There were others at Chartres, Sens, Paris, &c. See Ebersolt, *Orient et Occident*, vol. i, for full list.

but in a sorry state at this time, while Germany and France had a fine primitive, but no developed, art. It seems therefore far more natural to attribute the sudden revival which occurs in these lands to skilful masters who were immigrants, rather than to the illiterate and ignorant native artisans who would have been quite incapable of producing unaided the superb works which we now attribute to them. We read, moreover, that a great interest was taken in the West in the iconoclast movement, and special councils were held to discuss it, at Gentilly in 767, at Frankfurt in 794, and at Paris in 825. In the ninth century the penetration of Byzantine influence continued, owing to the immense vitality of the new period which we know as the second Golden Age or the Macedonian Renaissance. The artistic energy of the Byzantine world was at this time so great that it made itself felt far afield, and we see, interestingly enough, a similar renewal of Byzantine influence in the West of a rather different character some four centuries later, when the Byzantine world again sees a revival which constitutes, as far as it is concerned, a third Golden Age.

We do not wish to overstress the importance of the Byzantine element in the West, however, for though we consider that the art of the period was to a great extent of Byzantine origin, it was, of course, essentially a western art in its development, just as Byzantine art of the period was Byzantine and not Hellenistic or Syrian or Persian art. The individuality and at the same time the similarities are perhaps most clearly to be seen in architecture, where we see that the first Romanesque style owes its niche and arcaded ornament to the East, yet develops it in its own characteristic manner. Strzygowski thought that this ornament came by way of the Black Sea coast, the tradition being carried by the Goths,[1] but Puigh i Cadafalch has recently shown most ably that the arcades which we first see in ancient Babylonia are developed in

[1] *Kleinasien, ein Neuland*, p. 206; *Amida*, p. 274.

Sasanian architecture, and that from there they come to Constantinople, and thence to the West, to be developed in an individual manner in each area; the West therefore owes its debt to Byzantine culture and not directly to the East. In the light of this evidence Rivoira's theory of Italian origin can no longer be accepted. A similar manifestation is to be observed in the Mudéjar architecture of the twelfth and thirteenth centuries in Spain, where the eastern element arrived by way of Moslem north Africa, not by way of Romanesque Europe.[1]

In the realm of sculpture a similar development is to be observed in England in the seventh and following centuries, due to the close contact between England and the East Christian world. Benedict Biscop thus visited Rome and brought back treasures; St. Theodore, who was responsible for the most important Christian work in England in the seventh century, was a Greek of Tarsus; his contemporary, Adrian, also came from a Byzantine province. Along with them there came a number of artisans; it is thus recorded that when Wilfrith decorated St. Andrew's at Hexham between 672 and 674, foreign craftsmen assisted in the work.[2] These masters executed certain works themselves—the slab with scrolls and human figures at Hexham is thus perhaps due to a foreigner—but they also founded schools locally, and the individual character of much of the carving proves it to be due to the hands of these pupils. But the closeness with which they followed Byzantine models is aptly shown by the south face of the Ruthwell cross, where Christ appears as an essentially eastern figure (Pl. 48, *c*). Strzygowski's suggestion

[1] 'Decorative Forms of the First Romanesque style; their diffusion by Moslem Art', *Art Studies*, 6, 1928, p. 15. Also *Le premier Art romain*, Paris, 1928.

[2] G. F. Browne, *The Ancient Cross Shafts at Bewcastle and at Ruthwell*, pp. 19 and 24. For an account of relations between England and the East Christian world at this time see Clapham, *English Romanesque Architecture*, vol i, 1930, pp. 58 ff.

that this eastern character is due to Armenia is not supported by the facts, for we have no records of a connexion with that country, whereas there was a definite link with Italy and the Byzantine world, and the earliest example of stone carving in Armenia, the church of Achthamar on Lake Van (915–21), is an isolated monument, which is dated at least two centuries later than are the English crosses.[1] Irish carvings on crosses, which are far more numerous, and again on slabs, are mostly rather later. The majority are allied to the interlacing art of England or La Tène, rather than to the figural style of England, but a definite Byzantine influence is present in some of them. A stele at Fahan in Donegal of the latter half of the seventh century thus bears an inscription in Greek, while certain scenes, more especially the miracle of the multiplication of the fishes on a cross at Castledermot, are copied from East Christian models.[2]

A similar influence due to imported Byzantine ivories is also to be seen in England at a later date. In the tenth century the Romsey rood shows unquestionable Byzantine traits, as do the carved slabs at Bradford on Avon; the relief in the church of St. Dunstan at Stepney of the tenth–eleventh century is an obvious and fairly direct copy of a Byzantine portable ivory (Pl. 48, *b*). The Byzantine affinities of the York Madonna, again to be dated to the eleventh century (Pl. 48, *a*), cannot be doubted,[3] and a relief of Christ, full-

[1] Rivoira's suggestion of twelfth-century dating for the crosses is definitely disproved. Collingwood assigns them to the mid-eighth century, but the latter part of the seventh century seems more likely. See Clapham, op. cit., p. 56.

[2] In this particular case the iconography is Syrian rather than Constantinopolitan, and the model copied in Ireland must have been very similar to that which served the painter of Tokale Kilisse in Cappadocia. For a detailed discussion of the influences to be observed in these Irish carvings see Henry, *La Sculpture irlandaise*, Paris, 1933, pp. 15, 145, 163, 173, 175, 180 *et passim*.

[3] See S. Casson, 'Byzantium and Anglo-Saxon Sculpture', *Burlington Magazine*, lxi, Dec. 1932, pp. 265 and lxiii, Jan. 1933, p. 26.

length, at Lincoln, of slightly later date, has the same eastern character. Equally striking are the two panels in Chichester Cathedral. In the realm of miniature paintings the same affinities are to be traced. Professor G. F. Browne remarks:[1] 'the art of these beautiful books, which we in England and the Scots in Hibernia carried to a higher pitch of excellence than other races did, came to us from or through Byzantium, as did the actual book presented to Vitalian by the Byzantine Emperor when he became Pope in 657'.

These conclusions, arrived at on stylistic and iconographical grounds, are borne out to some extent by the chemical researches of Professor A. P. Laurie, who states that in Ireland the Purpura shell-fish was used for pigment as in Byzantine and Carolingian work, though it is not known elsewhere.[2] Carolingian miniature painting often shows a strongly marked Byzantine character, as for instance in the portraits of the Evangelists in a ninth-century manuscript in the John Rylands Library at Manchester (show case 2, No. 7) which was probably painted at St. Gall, or in a psalter of the first half of the eleventh century from Germany, formerly in the Chester Beatty collection.[3] An influence of ivories upon sculpture akin to that which we have noted in England, exemplified by a sudden change and improvement in style, is to be traced in Germany, more especially in the tympanum of the church of St. Godehard at Hildersheim. We read that there were Greek monks in the monastery there, as there were also at St. Gall and at Reichenau, and there were colonies of Greeks in Lorraine. As there were Irish here also, it is probable that the relationships which we have already noted between Ireland and Byzantium are due to some extent to a connexion of this kind, which had been first

[1] Op. cit., p. 19, note.

[2] *The Pigments and Mediums of the Old Masters*, London, 1919, p. 78.

[3] Millar, *Descriptive Catalogue of the Library of A. Chester Beatty*, vol i. Oxford, 1927, no. 39.

established abroad. We can even trace concrete examples of such a connexion, for some of the figure work in the book of Kells of the eighth century seems to owe something to the influence of Byzantine enamels. We see here a curious style which appears to be due to copying an enamel or a drawing of an enamel, without thoroughly understanding the conventions which the use of the gold cloisons or partitions entailed. The mouths of some of the figures are thus shown twice, the artist having copied, not the actual mouth of the enamel, but the two gold cloisons which separate the pink pigment of the lips from the surrounding dark tint of the beard.[1]

In Eastern Europe Byzantine influence was of an even stronger character during the tenth century, being imposed intentionally from above, as well as penetrating below owing to the power and automatic expansion of the Byzantine elements. Otto II, Emperor of the Holy Roman Empire from 973 to 983, thus married a Byzantine princess, Theophano, who brought with her to the West not only all the traditions of the Byzantine court, but also a number of craftsmen. The pronounced Byzantine character of German sculpture for the next two centuries is due to the workshops that they founded, and to the favour in which Byzantine culture was held. Otto III (983–1002) thus attempted to make Rome into a second Constantinople.[2] The thoroughly Byzantine character of art and culture in Venice in the middle ages had, moreover, a far-reaching effect in Italy,

[1] I am indebted to Mr. Casson for this suggestion. The portraits of SS. Matthew, Luke, and John are the more striking in this respect, though similar influence is also to be seen in the drawing of the angel and eagle which top the Eusebian canons of folio 5r. The body of the eagle would seem to be copied wellnigh directly from a Byzantine original.

[2] An ivory in the Cluny Museum shows Christ blessing Otto and Theophano and is in a purely Byzantine style, as is the repoussé frame of an ivory book-cover at Gotha which bears Otto III and Theophano his mother. See Schlumberger, *Épopée*, i, p. 440, for discussion of the question.

parts of the country taking on a renewed Byzantine apparel almost as pure as that which they had worn in the old days of Justinian and the exarchate of Ravenna.[1] Outside the frontier of Italy itself we can trace this superposed influence in France, as for instance in the twelfth-century cathedral of St. Front at Perigueux, which reproduces in Western style and technique the Byzantine plan of the sixth-century church of the Holy Apostles at Constantinople, followed also in St. Mark's at Venice.[2] The eleventh-century paintings in the Cathedral at Puy and the church at Berzé la Ville (Saône et Loire)[3] again show marked Byzantine influence. In the former we see a St. Michael who not only wears Byzantine costume, but who is also in a pure Cappadocian style; in the latter a whole series of paintings suggest Cappadocian affinities, though their style is individual. French manuscripts too, such as the Godesalc Gospels, reproduce Byzantine forms and ornaments.

In Spanish churches of the eleventh century in the Léon and Valladolid regions we see paintings which are in the Byzantine tradition, though the inscriptions are often in Arabic; similar affinities are to be observed throughout the work of the important Catalan school, in paintings which date from the middle of the twelfth century onwards. Here, however, the Byzantine influence came partly by way of Moslem art and partly via Italy.[4] A Byzantine influence in Spanish Romanesque architecture has already been alluded to (see p. 229).

Actual communication between Byzantium and the West was increased considerably after the eleventh century; the

[1] For Byzantine work done for Italy at this time see Diez and Demus, *Byzantine Mosaics in Greece*, p. 21.

[2] The same influence is to be seen in numerous other churches in the Dordogne. See Diehl, *Manuel*, ii, p. 719.

[3] For illustrations see Ebersolt, *Orient et Occident*, i, pls. XVII–XX.

[4] See L. Kuhn, *Romanesque Mural Paintings of Catalonia*, Harvard, 1930.

Byzantine Empire and the West united to restore the Holy Sepulchre to Christendom and in 1099 the first crusade reached Jerusalem. The majority of the troops, both on this occasion and later until the third crusade, went by way of Constantinople, and with them travelled a number of ecclesiastics. They all attended services in the churches of Constantinople; a special and more than usually impressive service was held in St. Sophia for the members of the first crusade. Other pilgrims and travellers followed in the steps of the crusaders and some fifty years later Louis VII, the leader of the second crusade, was received by Manuel I (1143–80) at the Blachernae palace and was shown the churches and treasures of Constantinople. Louis took back a number of silks, which were now apparently the most usual official present. Numerous western princes and nobles had Greek wives, and in 1176 relationships were more closely cemented by the marriage of the Byzantine prince imperial, Alexis, with Louis's daughter, Agnes. She came to the throne as his wife, but survived him and married the next emperor Andronicos I, whom she again survived, to marry a Byzantine nobleman, Theodore Branas. The crusaders who visited Constantinople brought back numerous treasures, and their travels seem to have affected minor arts also, for the close similarity which is to be observed between Byzantine 'sgraffito' pottery and that of the West, more especially in France and England, is perhaps to be accounted for in this manner. A great deal of the influence which is attributed to the East in general or to Moslem Palestine in particular was in actual fact due to the Byzantine world, and was brought to Europe owing to the links established in cultural and in civil life by the crusaders. In painting a considerable Byzantine influence is to be seen in Pisan and Genoese work of the twelfth and thirteenth centuries, as for instance in that of Giunte Pisano.[1]

With the thirteenth century a new era opens, for in 1204

[1] See Muratov, *La Peinture byzantine*, p. 134.

the fourth crusade, instead of routing the infidel, turned its energies to the sack and looting of Constantinople. The vastness of the treasure that was destroyed at this time is inconceivable; it was far greater than the very large amount which was stolen and transported to the West, some of which we can see to-day in various cathedral treasuries, more especially in St. Mark's at Venice.[1] But the day of fabricating such treasures was over, both in East and West, and the Byzantine loot was prized and revered, but it was not copied, as were ivories, illuminations, or works in metal in Carolingian times. And though in 1470 Louis XI sent for Greek and Italian workmen to manufacture silk, the Moslem area from now on takes the place of the Byzantine to a great extent as a furnisher of sumptuous materials.

The role of Byzantium was not yet at an end; it was now in fact perhaps even more important than ever before, for not only were manuscripts of the Greek philosophical writers brought to the West to serve as the basis of a new philosophy,[2] but also a new age was opening in the sphere of art, that of painting, and a new and subtler form of interrelation commenced. The art is no longer so rich as regards material, but it is less didactic, less a servant of imperialism, and hence far more universal in character.

Relations are again to be traced in three primary ways: in iconography; in style, technique, and colouring; and in kindred feeling, though the last of these may also result from similar conditions in the two areas and be in no way due to relationship. The former is a sure guide, however, and Millet

[1] See Riant, *Des dépouilles religieuses enlevées à Constantinople au treizième siècle*, Paris, 1865, Mém. de la Soc. des Antiquaires de la France, 4me série, tome 6.

[2] The influence of Greek philosophy in the West is beyond the scope of this book, but it may here be noted that it was owing to the copying by Dominican friars that the correct text of Aristotle first became known in the West at this time. Hitherto knowledge of such writers had come indirectly through the Arabs. See Sandys, *A History of Classical Scholarship*, 3rd edn., Cambridge, 1921, vol. i, p. 561.

has examined in minutest detail all links between East and West from the thirteenth century onward in his book *L'Iconographie de l'Évangile.* There is now little that can be called Byzantine in the west and north of Europe; it is Italy with which we are primarily concerned and with painters like Cimabue (1276–1337), Duccio (after *c.* 1282), Giotto (1276–1337), and Cavallini (*c.* 1259–1344), whose works show the very strongest Byzantine affinities. Some frescoes by Rainaldictus which were until the War in a secularized religious library near Spoleto and which are now in the Worcester Art Museum, Mass., U.S.A., must also be considered as examples of this later Byzantine influence and not merely as survivals of an earlier Byzantinized art in Italy.[1] The debt that these painters owe to Byzantium cannot be discussed in detail here. The student who wishes to pursue the subject may turn to *The Birth of Western Painting*, where numerous reproductions of Byzantine and early Italian paintings are placed side by side to serve as tangible proof.[2] It may here be noted, however, that Byzantine influence is not only to be traced in the work of the primitive; even accomplished Renaissance artists such as Mantegna show it often to a marked degree.

There were from this time onwards a large number of Greek painters living and working in Italy, who produced more or less pure Byzantine work themselves until the seventeenth century. They were responsible by teaching pupils for the survival of the Byzantine manner in certain places when it had long been forgotten by the less conserva-

[1] Rowland, in *Art in America*, xix, Oct. 1931, p. 89.

[2] See also an interesting article by P. Schweinfurth, 'Die Bedeutung der byzantinischen Kunst für die Stilbildung der Renaissance', in *Die Antike*, ix, 1933, pt. 2. He thinks that the early Italians are directly modelled upon the Byzantines, and the later Renaissance artists on the early Italians. There is thus much that is Byzantine at the back of the Renaissance, though all the intermediary links of the chain must be seen before we can realize its continuity and the importance of the part it played.

tive Renaissance artists of larger and more progressive cities.[1] The most important colony of these artists was at Venice, though there was another distinct one in the south at Otranto. Their pictures are to be found in the Vatican, the Uffizi, and most other Italian galleries.

Far more important than these for the study of Byzantium and the West is Domenicos Theotokopoulos, the Cretan, the greatest Greek painter of all time, who is better known as El Greco. He was in all probability brought up as a Byzantine painter in his native Island of Crete,[2] and though his manner changed much, the Byzantine character of his conception and colouring and also of many of his figures remained to the very end. Other characteristics were imposed above it, however, first in Italy and then in Spain, so that at times it was almost completely obscured.

Such was, we believe, the Byzantine legacy. We find the Byzantine tradition at the basis of Carolingian, of Ottonian, and of Northumbrian art; we can trace its influence throughout medieval Europe and even in Spain, though not always to a very marked degree; we can trace it in Ireland; it was perhaps vital in the history of Saxon art in England; it was of great importance in Germany in the tenth and eleventh centuries, and we see its influence as a fundamental element in the work of the greatest early painters of Italy; it appears again in paintings of the Renaissance. It was Byzantium that made later European culture possible; it is to Byzantium that our art now turns for support, for prototypes and for justification, and it is in Byzantine art, more especially in that of the fourteenth-century revival, that the most satisfactory

[1] See Lazarev, 'Über eine neue Gruppe byzantinisch-venezianischer Trecento-Bilder', *Art Studies*, 8, pt. ii, p. 30.

[2] See Achilles A. Kyros, *Domenicos Theotokopoulos, the Cretan*, Athens, 1932 (in modern Greek), and an appreciation of this work by F. Rutter in the *Burlington Magazine*, lx, June 1932, p. 274.

and most natural comparison is found to explain the strivings and abstract ideals of much of what is being done to-day. A knowledge of Byzantine art and civilization is thus not only an important study, an entertainment and a delight in itself; not only an essential for the full understanding of European culture and history; it is also something which enables us to sympathize with the efforts of the modern movement, and helps us, perhaps, to comprehend to some extent the demands and ideas of this troubled age through which we are passing.

BIBLIOGRAPHY

For the earlier periods see Ebersolt, *Orient et Occident*, vols. i and ii, Paris, 1928 and 1929, where full references are given. Much interesting matter is also contained in Dawson's *The Making of Europe*, London, 1932. Various articles deal with different aspects of the subject. Such are Halpen, 'La Cour d'Otton III à Rome', *École française de Rome, Mélanges d'archéologie*, xxvi, 1905; J. Gay, 'L'abbaye de Cluny et Byzance au début du XIIme siècle', *Échos d'Orient*, xxx, 1931, No. 161; Gasquet, *L'Empire byzantin et la monarchie franque*, Paris, 1888.

The first to appreciate the immensity of the debt to Byzantium was Lethaby, in *Mediaeval Art*, London, 1904.

For the connexion with early European painting see R. Byron and D. Talbot Rice, *The Birth of Western Painting*, London, 1930, and P. Schweinfurth, 'Die Bedeutung der byzantinischen Kunst für die Stilbildung der Renaissance', in *Die Antike*, ix, pt. 2, 1933, p. 105.

IMPORTANT DATES

THE EAST

Seleucid and kindred dynasties	330 B.C.–200 B.C.
Parthian period	200 B.C.–A.D. 222
Sasanian period	222–650
Arab conquest of Persia, Mesopotamia, Syria, and Egypt	638–642
The Omayyad dynasty (capital at Damascus)	661–750
The Abbasid dynasty (capital at Baghdad)	750–1258
Arab conquest of Spain	710–712
The Seljuks. In Persia	1037–1194
The Seljuks. In Asia Minor (Seljuks of Rum)	1077–1327
The Ottomans. In Asia Minor	1300–1453
The Ottomans. At Constantinople	1453–1924

THE CENTRAL AREA

The First Bulgarian Empire	679–1018
Byzantine domination of Bulgaria	1018–1186
Second Bulgarian Empire	1186–1393
Stephen Nemanja	1169–1196
Stephen Dushan	1331–1355
Conquest of Serbia by Turks at Kossovo	1389
Conquest of Sicily by Arabs of Tunis	827–878
Byzantine domination of Sicily	878–909
Domination of Sicily by Fatamids of Egypt and Syria	909–1071
Norman conquest of Sicily	1071
The Iconoclast period	726–843

THE BYZANTINE EMPERORS

Dynasty of Constantine.

Constantine I, the Great	died 337
Constantius	337–361. Sole Emperor after 351
Julian the Apostate	361–363. Sole Emperor

Jovian	363–364. Sole Emperor
Valens	364–378

Theodosian Dynasty.

Theodosius I, the Great	379–395. Sole Emperor after 392
Arcadius	395–408
Theodosius II.	408–450. Anthemius regent 408–414
Marcian	450–457

Leonine Dynasty.

Leo I	457–474
Leo II.	474
Zeno	474–491
Anastasius I.	491–518

Justinian Dynasty.

Justin I.	518–527
Justinian I	527–565
Justin II	565–578
Tiberius II	578–582
Maurice	582–602
Theodosius co-Emperor	590–602
Phocas	602–610

Heraclian Dynasty.

Heraclius I	610–641
Constantine II	641
Heracleonas	641
Constantine III (Constans II)	641–668
Constantine IV, Poganatus.	668–685
Justinian II, Rhinotmetus	685–695
Leontius	695–698
Tiberius III, Apsimar	698–705
Justinian II. (Second reign)	705–711
Philippicus, Bardanes	711–713
Anastasius II, Artemius	713–715
Theodosius III	715–717

Isaurian Dynasty

Leo III, the Isaurian	717–740
Constantine V, Copronymus	740–775
Leo IV, the Chazar	775–780
Constantine VI	780–797
Irene	797–802
Nicephoras I	802–811
Stauracius	811
Michael I, Rhangabe	811–813
Leo V, the Armenian	813–820

Amorian Dynasty.

Michael II, the Amorian	820–829
Theophilus	829–842
Michael III, the Drunkard	842–867

Macedonian Dynasty.

Basil I	867–886
Leo VI, the Wise	886–912
Alexander	912–913
Constantine VII, Porphyrogenitus	913–959
Romanus I, Lecapenus (Co-Emperor)	919–944
Stephen and Constantine	944–945
Romanus II	959–963
Nicephoras II, Phocas	963–969
John I, Tzimisces	969–976
Basil II, Bulgaroctonos	976–1025
Constantine VIII	1025–1028
Romanus III, Argyrus	1028–1034
Michael IV, the Paphlagonian	1034–1041
Michael V, the Calfat	1041–1042
Theodora and Zoe	1042
Constantine IX, Monomachus	1042–1055
Theodora	1055–1056
Michael VI, Stratioticus	1056–1057
Isaac I, Comnenus	1057–1059

Ducas Dynasty.

Constantine X, Ducas	1059–1067
Romanus IV, Diogenes	1067–1071
Michael VII, Parapinaces	1071–1078
Nicephoras III, Botiniates	1078–1081

Comnenian Dynasty.	
Alexius I, Comnenus	1081–1118
John II, Calojohannes	1118–1143
Manuel I, Comnenus	1143–1180
Alexius II	1180–1183
Andronicus I	1183–1185
Angelus Dynasty	
Isaac II, Angelus	1185–1195
Alexius III	1195–1203
Isaac II and Alexius IV	1203–1204
Alexis V, Murtzuphlus	1204
Lascarid Dynasty. Nicaean Empire 1204–1261	
Theodore I, Lascaris	1204–1222
John III, Ducas Vatatzes	1222–1254
Theodore II, Lascaris Vatatzes	1254–1258
John IV, Ducas Vatatzes	1258
Palaeologue Dynasty.	
Michael VIII, Palaeologos	1258–1282
Andronicos II	1282–1328
Andronicos III	1328–1341
John V	1341–1347
John VI, Cantacuzenus	1347–1355
Andronicos IV	1376–1379
John VII	1390
Manuel II	1391–1425
John VIII	1425–1448
Constantine XI	1449–1453

BIBLIOGRAPHY OF GENERAL WORKS

SHORTER WORKS

BRÉHIER, L. *L'Art byzantin.* Paris, 1924.
L'Art chrétien. Paris, 1928.

DALTON, O. M. *Guide to the Early Christian and Byzantine Antiquities in the British Museum.* London, 1921.

DIEHL, C. *L'Art chrétien primitif et l'art byzantin.* Paris, 1928.

GLÜCK, H. *Die christliche Kunst des Ostens.* Berlin, 1923.

GRABAR, A. *La Décoration byzantine.* Paris and Brussels, 1928.

MILLET, G. 'L'Art byzantin', in André Michel's *Histoire de l'art,* vols. i and iii. Paris, 1905 and 1908.

PEIRCE, H., and TYLER, R. *Byzantine Art.* London, 1926.

LONGER WORKS

DALTON, O. M. *Byzantine Art and Archaeology.* Oxford, 1911.
East Christian Art. Oxford, 1925.

DIEHL, C. *Manuel de l'art byzantin,* 2ième édn. Paris, 1925–6.

KAUFFMANN, K. M. *Handbuch der christlichen Archäologie,* 3rd edn. Paderborn, 1922.

PEIRCE, H., and TYLER, R. *L'Art byzantin,* vol. i. Paris, 1932. Vol. ii. Paris, 1934. Three further volumes will appear.

WULFF, O. *Altchristliche und byzantinische Kunst.* Berlin, 1914–18, 2 vols.

INDEX

PRINTED IN
GREAT BRITAIN
AT THE
UNIVERSITY PRESS
OXFORD
BY
JOHN JOHNSON
PRINTER
TO THE
UNIVERSITY

a

b

Constantinople, S. Sophia (523–537). (*a*) Exterior; (*b*) Interior

PLATE 2

(*a*) Salonica, the church of the Holy Apostles (1312)

(*b*) The church at Kurt Boghan, near Trebizond (XVth or XVIth century)

(*a*) Rome, Sta. Constanza. Vault mosaic (326–337)

(*b*) Ravenna, S. Vitale. Mosaic. The Empress Theodora and her court (526–547)

(*a*) Rome, Sta. Maria Maggiore. Mosaic. Right side of the Triumphal arch (432–440)

(*b*) Rome, SS. Cosmo and Damian. Apse mosaic (526–530)

Salonica, S. Demetrius. Mosiac (VIIth century)

(*a*) Salonica, Hosios David. Apse mosaic (Early Vth century)

(*b*) Damascus. Mosaics in the Great Mosque (715)

(*a*) Daphni. Dome mosaic. The Pantocrator (late XIth century)

(*b*) Constantinople, Fetiyeh Djami. Dome Mosaic. The Pantocrator and the twelve Apostles (XIVth century)

PLATE 8

(*a*) Sicily, Cefalù. Apse mosaic. Christ, Angels, and Saints (1148)

(*b*) Nicaea. Apse mosaic. The Virgin (*c*. 800)

(*a*) Torcello. Apse mosaic. Virgin and Child (XIIth century). Apostles (XIth century)

(*b*) Palermo, the Martorana. Mosaic. The Admiral George of Antioch at the feet of the Virgin (*c.*1143)

Constantinople, Kahrieh Djami. Mosaic. The Dormition of the Virgin (1310–1320)

a

b

Constantinople, Kahrieh Djami. Mosaics (1310–1320). (*a*) The Nativity; (*b*) The founder offers the church to our Lord

a

b

Miniature mosaics. (*a*) The Transfiguration (XIIIth or XIVth century). Louvre. (*b*) The Crucifixion (XIVth century). Kaiser Friedrich Museum, Berlin

Cappadocia, Tokale Kilisse. Paintings in the old church. The scenes are: 1st register; Annunciation; Visitation; Proof of water; Journey to Bethlehem; Nativity. 2nd register; Pursuit of Elizabeth; Angel appears to the Baptist; Baptist preaching; Baptist meets Jesus; Baptism; Feast of Cana. 3rd register; Entry into Jerusalem; Last Supper; Betrayal; Jesus before Pilate (Xth century)

(*a*) Cappadocia, Qeledjlar Kilisse. Painting. The proof of water; Zacharias and the Virgin (Xth century)

(*b*) Macedonia, Nerez. Painting. The Deposition (1164)

(*a*) Bulgaria, Boiana. Painting. Head of Christ (1259)

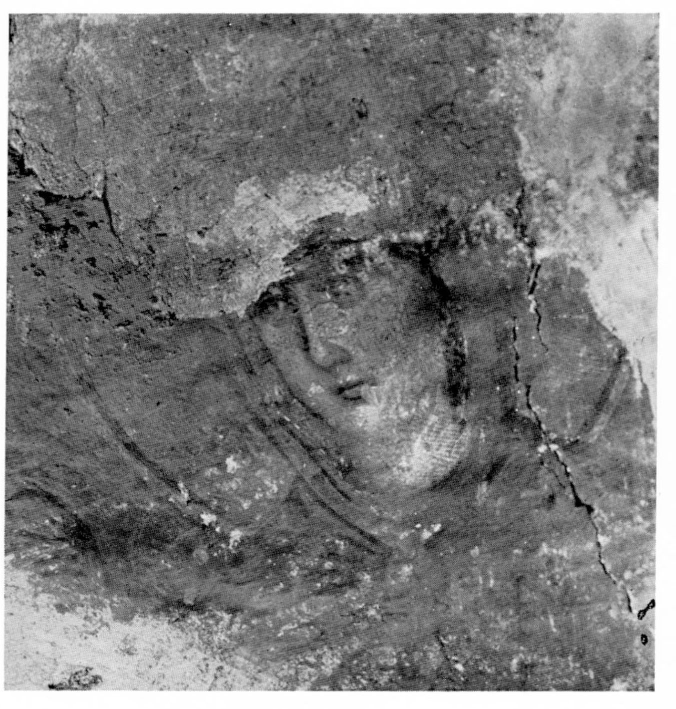

(*b*) Mount Athos, Karyes, the Protaton. Painting. Head of the Virgin (probably XIVth century)

PLATE 16

Mistra, the Pantanassa. Painting. The Raising of Lazarus (1428)

(*a*) Mistra, the Pantanassa. Painting. Head of a Bishop (*c*. 1428)

(*b*) Mistra, the Peribleptos. Painting. Head of a Saint (late XIVth century)

(*a*) Mount Athos, Monastery of Xenophontos. Painting. The Nativity (1544). Cretan School, by Anthony

(*b*) Serbia, Sopoćani. Painting. Left portion of Crucifixion (*c*. 1250)

(*a*) Macedonia, Vodoca. Painting. The Forty Martyrs (XIIIth century)

(*b*) Sofia, S. George. Painting. The Twenty-two Prophets (XIVth century)

(*a*) Trieste, Cathedral of S. Just. Painting on silk. St. Just (XIth or XIIth century)

(*b*) Athens, Benaki Museum (formerly in the Church of S. Saviour, Galata, Constantinople). Panel Painting. The Transfiguration (XIIIth century)

(*a*) The Joshua Rotulus. Miniature. Joshua and the Angel (Vth or VIth century, restored in IXth century). Vatican

(*b*) Manuscript of Cosmas Indicopleustes. Miniature. Movement of the Heavens round the Earth (XIth century). Sinai

(*a*) Miniature: from a psalter (V. Palat. Gr. 381). David between Wisdom and Prophecy (Xth or XIth century). Vatican

(*b*) Miniature. The Emperor Nicephoras III between St. John Chrysostom and the Archangel Michael (1078–1081). Paris, Bibl. Nat., Coislin, 79

Miniature from a manuscript of John Cantacuzenus. The Transfiguration (1347–1355). Paris, Bibl. Nat., Gr. 1242

(*a*) Marble sarcophagus from Synnada, Asia Minor. Sidamarra or Lydian type (IVth century). Angora Museum

(*b*) Portion of an ambon from Salonica (VIth century) Constantinople Museum

(*a*) Side of an ambon from Aidin, Asia Minor (VIth century). Constantinople Museum

(*b*) The entry into Jerusalem (Vth century). Constantinople Museum (from S. John Studion)

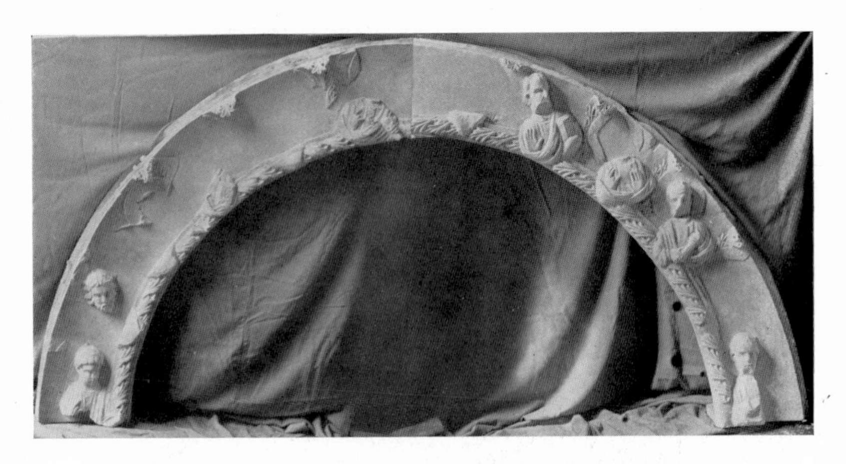

(*a*) Ciborium arch (VIth or XIth century). Constantinople Museum (from S. Mary Panachrantos)

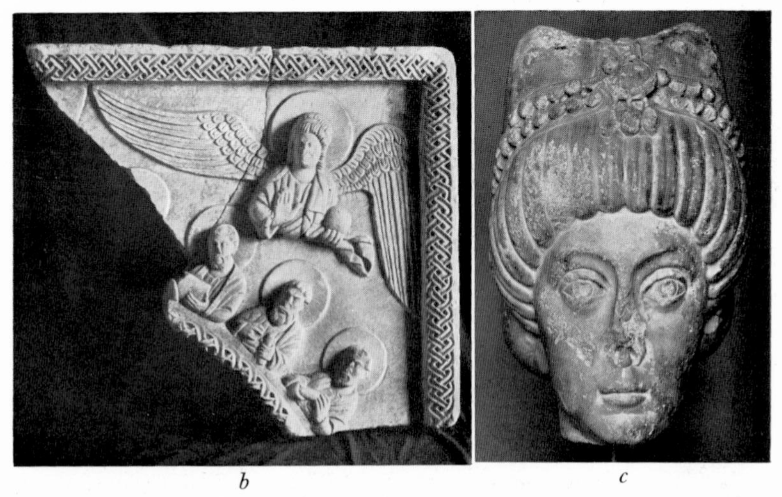

b *c*

(*b*) Portion of Ciborium arch (VIth or XIth century). Constantinople Museum
(*c*) Head, perhaps Theodora (VIth century). Milan, Castello

Capitals. (*a*) Theodosian (IVth century); (*b*) With winged horses (VIth century); (*c*) Ravenna, S. Apollinare in Classe. Wind-blown acanthus (Vth or VIth century); (*d*) Ravenna, S. Vitale (VIth century)

Fragmentary relief. The Virgin (XIth century)
Constantinople Museum

a

b

(*a*) Diptych of the Symmachi (IVth–Vth century). Victoria and Albert Museum. (*b*) Leaf of diptych, the Archangel Michael (Vth or VIth century). British Museum

a

b

(*a*) Pyxis. The Sacrifice of Abraham (IVth century). Berlin, Kaiser Friedrich Museum. (*b*) Panel. The Adoration of the Magi. Syrian work (VIth century). British Museum

(*a*) Top of the Veroli casket (*c.* Xth century). Victoria and Albert Museum

(*b*) Front of casket (Xth or XIth century). Troyes

(*c*) Side of casket (XIIth century). Florence, National Museum

a

b

(*a*) Ivory Panel. Christ (IXth century). Victoria and Albert Museum. (*b*) Ivory Panel. Virgin and Child (XIth century) Utrecht

(*a*) Plaque. St. John the Baptist and Saints Philip, Stephen, Andrew, and Thomas (XIth century). Victoria and Albert Museum

(*b*) Plaque. The Coronation of Romanos and Eudoxia by Christ (Xth or XIth century). Paris, Bibl. Nat.

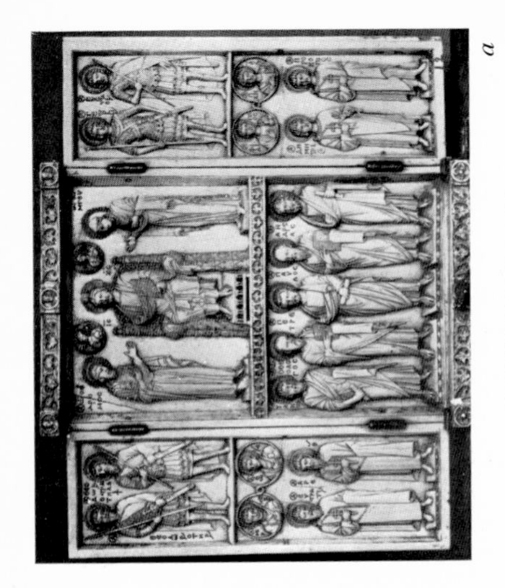

a

c

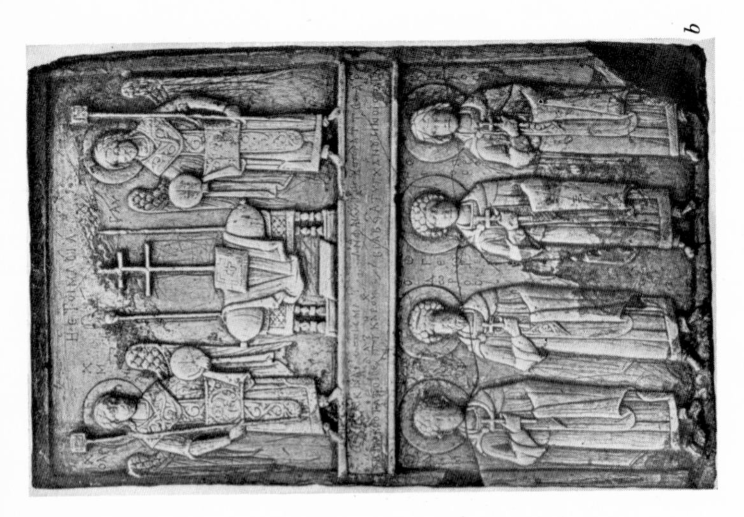

b

(*a*) The Harbaville triptych (XIth century). Paris, Louvre. (*b*) Steatite plaque. (Above) The Throne of the Hetoimasia; (below) SS. Demetrius, Theodore Stratelates, George, and Procopios (XIth century). (*c*) Steatite. Head of an Emperor (Xth or XIth century). Berlin Béhague Collection.

(*a*) Paten, from Riha on the Orontes. The Communion of the Apostles (VIth or VIIth century). Washington, Bliss Collection

(*b*) Silver dish from Kyrenia, Cyprus (VIth century). J. Pierpont Morgan Collection

PLATE 36

(*a*) Chalice (Xth or XIth century). Venice, Treasury of St. Mark's

(*b*) Paten (Xth or XIth century). Venice, Treasury of St. Mark's

(*a*) Triptych, cast bronze (XIth or XIIth century). Victoria and Albert Museum

(*b*) Bible cover, probably of Nicephoras Phocas (963–969). Mount Athos, the Lavra

(*a*) Book cover. The centre Byzantine repoussé work (XIth century), the sides Western. Manchester, John Rylands Library

(*b*) Reliquary in repoussé work (XIth century). Urbino

(*a*) The Beresford Hope cross (VIth or VIIth century). Victoria and Albert Museum

(*b*) Cross. Georgian workmanship, with three Byzantine enamels attached (XIth century). Formerly in the Monastery of Nicorzminda, Georgia

(*a*) Enamel book cover (XIth or XIIth century). Venice, Treasury of St. Mark's

(*b*) Reliquary (XIth or XIIth century, outer border XIIIth or XIVth century). Cathedral of Estergom, Hungary

(*a*) Woven stuff. A military saint (VIIth or VIIIth century). Rockefeller Collection

(*b*) Silk. Quadriga (VIth century). Paris, Cluny Museum

(*a*) Silk. The Annunciation and Nativity (VIth century) Vatican

(*b*) Silk. The shroud of St. Victor (VIIIth century). Sens

(*a*) Silk from the tomb of Charlemagne at Aix-la-Chapelle (Xth century)

(*b*) Silk damask. The shroud of St. Siviard (Xth or XIth century). Sens

Silk. The shroud of St. Germain l'Auxerrois (Xth or XIth century).
Auxerre

(*a*) Silk. The mantle of Charlemagne (XIIth century). Metz

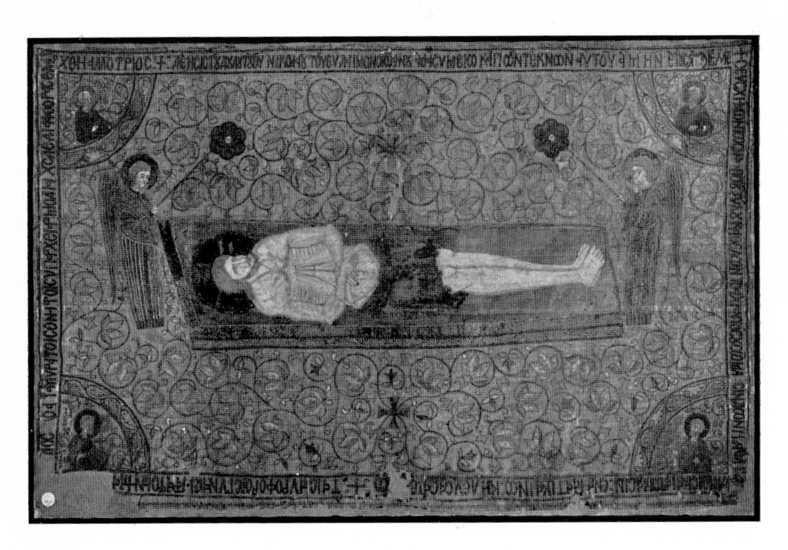

(*b*) Embroidered silk epitaphios, dated 1407. Victoria and Albert Museum

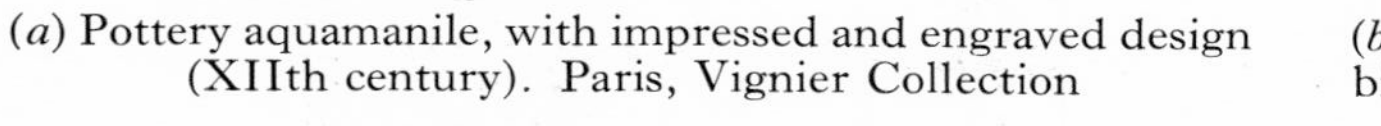
(*a*) Pottery aquamanile, with impressed and engraved design (XIIth century). Paris, Vignier Collection

(*b*) Dish, sgraffito ware. A deer in a border of foliage, birds, and animals (XIVth century). Greece, Sparta Museum

(*a*) Ceramic icon. St. Theodore (IXth or Xth century). From Patleina, Bulgaria

(*b*) Incrustation work. Plaque: St. Eudoxia (Xth or XIth century). Constantinople Museum (from S. Mary Panachrantos)

a

b

c

(*a*) York Minster. Limestone relief. English (XIth century). (*b*) St. Dunstan's Church, Stepney. Limestone relief. English (XIth or XIIth century). (*c*) The Ruthwell Cross, S. face (VIIth or VIIIth century)

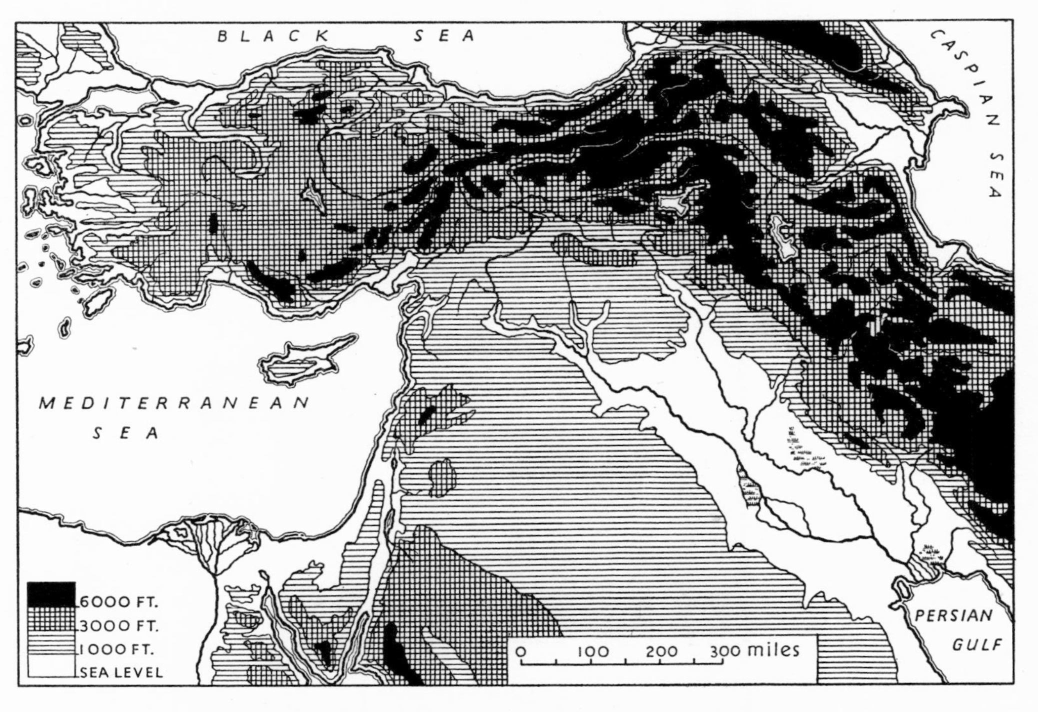

PHYSICAL FORMATION OF THE NEARER EAST

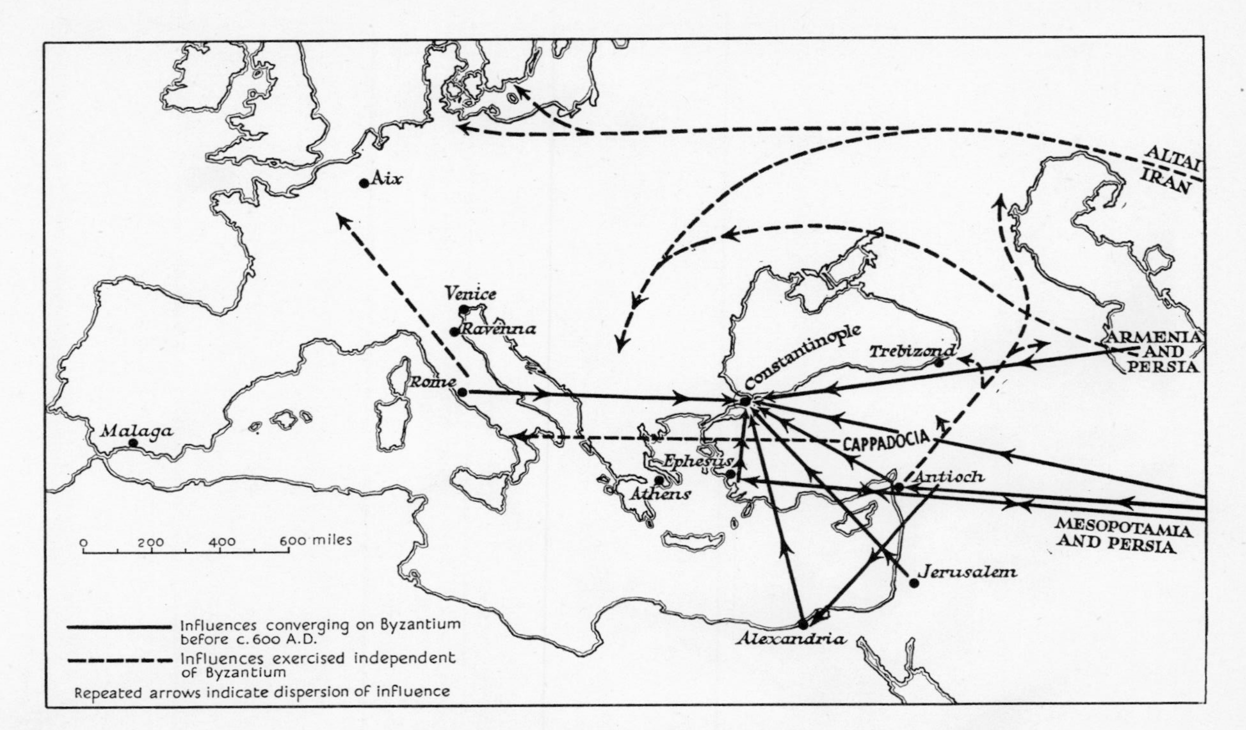

ART INFLUENCES IN THE NEARER EAST

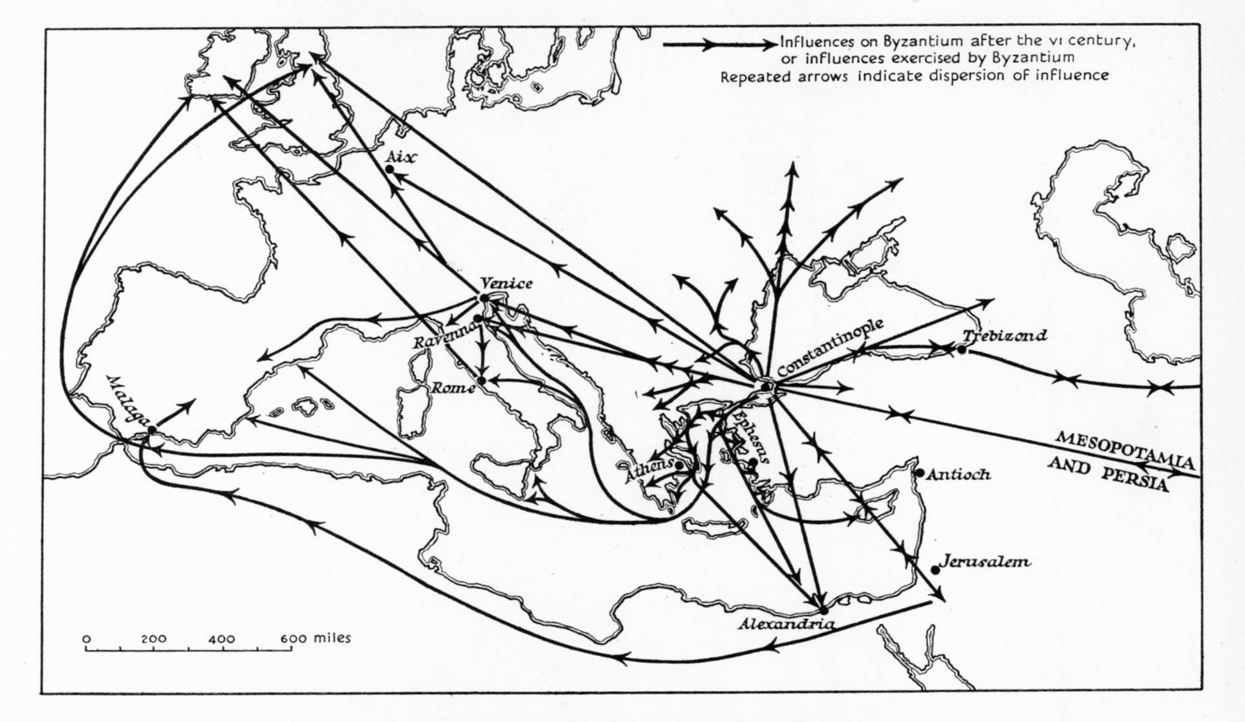

ART INFLUENCES IN THE NEARER EAST

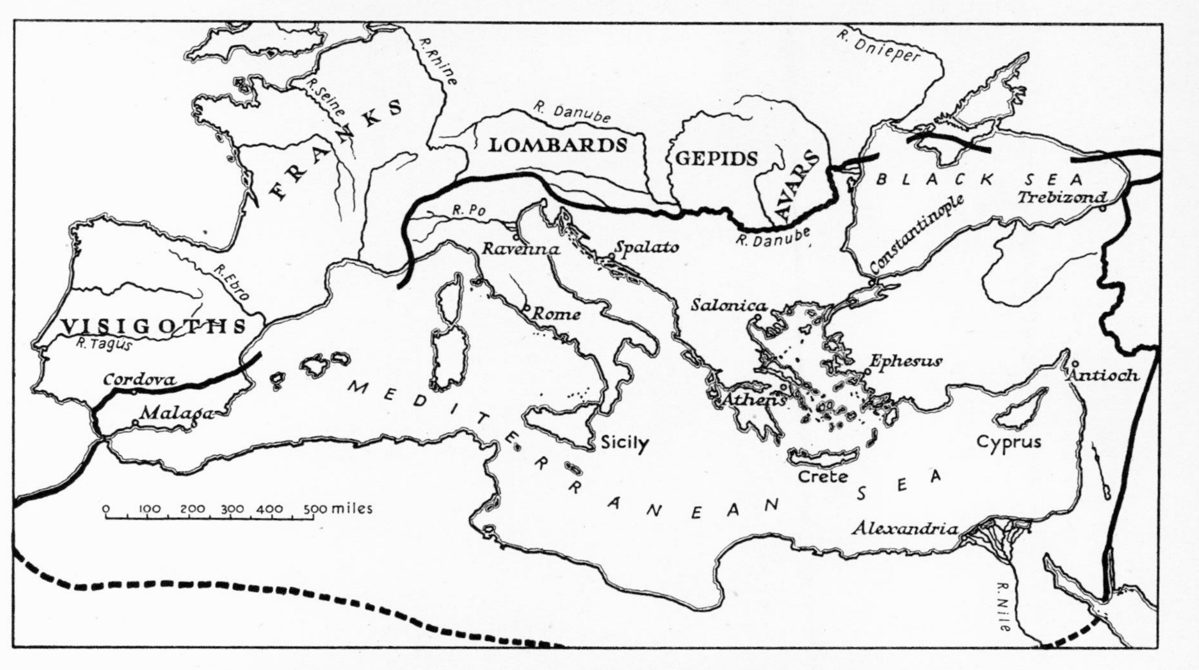

THE EMPIRE OF JUSTINIAN AT ITS GREATEST EXTENT, *c.* 565 A.D.

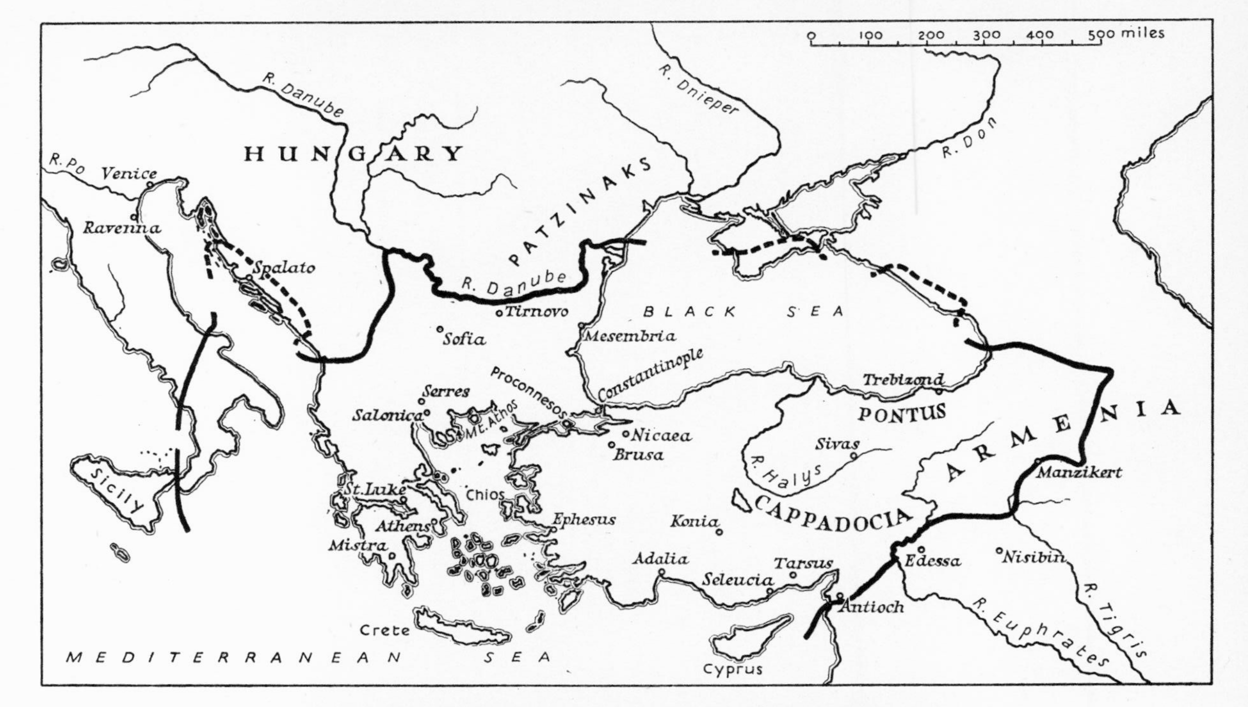

THE BYZANTINE EMPIRE IN MACEDONIAN TIMES